DYNAMIC CAPABILITY-BASED

APPROACH

TO VALUE APPROPRIATION

Marta Najda-Janoszka

DYNAMIC CAPABILITY-BASED

APPROACH

TO VALUE APPROPRIATION

Jagiellonian University Press

The book has been financed from the funds of National Science Center
(DEC-2013/11/D/HS4/039650)

REVIEWER
Prof. dr hab. Wojciech Czakon

COVER DESIGN
Marta Jaszczuk

ISBN 978-83-233-4107-9
ISBN 978-83-233-9439-6 (e-book)

www.wuj.pl

Jagiellonian University Press
Editorial Offices: Michałowskiego St. 9/2, 31-126 Cracow
Phone: +48 12 663 23 82, Fax: +48 12 663 23 83
Distribution: Phone: +48 12 631 01 97, Fax: +48 12 631 01 98
Cell Phone: +48 506 006 674, e-mail: sprzedaz@wuj.pl
Bank: PEKAO SA, IBAN PL 80 1240 4722 1111 0000 4856 3325

ACKNOWLEDGEMENTS

I would like to express a special recognition to Professor Małgorzata Bednar-czyk for a cordial invitation and introduction to the world of science, shared knowledge and endless support through the years. Exceptional thanks I direct to Professor Wojciech Czakon for insightful, critical reflections, which enhanced greatly the content of this work. I am grateful to managers of investigated firms for openness and kindness while sharing a great body of practical knowledge.

Since much of the burden of the preparation of this book has fallen on those at home, a special thanks and appreciation go to my dearest husband Łukasz, and sons Szymon and Michał.

CONTENTS

1 INTRODUCTION

1.1 BACKGROUND OF THE STUDY

In the field of strategic management the main enduring question concerns how firms generate and sustain a competitive advantage. The extant literature provides a wide array of diverse propositions, reflecting a heated debate on the relation between value creation and value appropriation (Hansen, 2008). Nevertheless, this on-going discussion is strongly affected by difficulties in reaching a conceptual consensus on the understanding of the generic concept of value (Bowman & Ambrosini, 2000; Pitelis, 2009; Lepak et al., 2007; Mazur, 2011). Consequently, for some scholars value creation is a more important perspective for investigating long term performance of an organization than the one of value appropriation, as the former represents a key driver of discovery, continuous innovation, economic development and adaptive efficiency (Moran & Ghoshal, 1997). In contrast, other research works point at capture as a more pertinent concept for exploring competitive advantage of firms, since value appropriation[1] makes a direct impact on the profitability of an organization (Coff, 1999; Makadok & Coff, 2002). However, between those radical stances there is also a recently developed, balanced perspective that emphasizes the interrelationship and possible trade-offs between value creation and value capture, and the fact that both refer to necessary but insufficient conditions for an effective long term performance of a firm (Mizik & Jacobson, 2003; Ellegaard et al., 2009). By stressing interdependency and continuity, this balanced view is the most promising direction for investigating dynamics of both processes. There is a growing number of studies focused on exploration of the interplay between forces of competition and cooperation that affects value creation and

---

[1] In this work terms "value appropriation" and "value capture" are used interchangeably. Justification of the stand point is presented in section 2.1.5.

appropriation processes (e.g. Zakrzewska-Bielawska, 2013; Czakon, 2012; Czakon & Rogalski, 2012; Cygler, 2009; Stańczyk-Hugiet, 2011; Jankowska, 2012). However, although extant research provides useful insights concerning dyadic coopetitive relations, the impact of redundancy of resources on the balance of competitive and cooperative forces, the impact of structural context on the dynamics of performed cross-organizational activities, the majority of published studies are in fact focused on value co-creation. Thus, a review of extant management literature confirms that developed frameworks and concepts provide a quite comprehensive picture of the dynamic nature of value creation, whereas value appropriation has received much less scholarly attention. "In recent history [management science] privileged problem of creating value at the expense of its mirror reflection, which is distribution of the created of value" (Czakon 2012, p. 92). Meanwhile, the rationale for distinguishing and exploring value capture on the strategic management ground refers to the fact that the logic of value distribution may or may not follow the rules governing the value creation process. Hence, organizations can extract and appropriate less, equal or even more value that have actually created (Brandenburger & Nalebuff, 1996). Nevertheless, the number of research works devoted to the complex issues of value receiving, protecting and retaining is at the moment relatively modest, concerning both theoretical and empirical dimension. There is a paucity of coherent theoretical frameworks providing insights into the dynamic nature of value appropriation (Coff, 2010). In case of empirical studies, the majority is focused on analyzing the use and effectiveness of selected, individual value protection instruments without taking into account the existing tension between other available mechanisms, and ignoring potential discontinuities in effectiveness of implemented action patterns (Fischer, 2011). In result, there is no coherent framework for analyzing value appropriation beyond the mere point of transaction.

A thorough review of research advances in the field of strategic management that pertain to the dynamic perspective of scientific inquiry, resulted in defining a second, complementary area of exploration, the dynamic capabilities perspective. The dynamic capabilities perspective reflects a change in the scientific discourse on strategy development, from the problem of sustainability of competitive advantages toward the capacity building for the management of innovation and change (Brown & Eisenhardt, 1997; Teece, 2007). At the same time, it is also chronologically the youngest concept explaining the process of achieving a competitive advantage, and consequently it is still at the stage of development (Barreto, 2010).The concept of dynamic capabilities has been developed on a quite diverse theoretical foundation, with leading contributions coming from the resource based view of the firm (Wernerfelt, 1984; Barney, 1991; Peteraf, 1993) evolutionary economics (Nelson & Winter, 1982), behavioral theory of the firm (Cyert & March, 1963), organizational learning (Argyris & Schon, 1978), schumpeterian concept of innovation based competition (Schumpeter, 1934, 1942). Development of the dynamic capabilities perspective has provided conceptual tools to overcome the limits of the static perspective of the resource based view, and to explain organizational behavior in terms of adaptive mechanisms (Nelson, Winter, 1982). The field has been generating a significant and systematic growth of scholarly attention. Outcomes of that research effort confirm a substantial step forward on a developmental path of dynamic capabilities from a vague and obscure concept toward a cohesive paradigm. However, although it is commonly agreed that the logic of dynamic capabilities lies in the intentional change in the organizational action patterns, extant research works present divergent perspectives with regard to the content of dynamic capabilities (Zollo & Winter, 2002; Teece, 2007; Eisenhardt & Martin, 2000; Wang & Ahmed, 2007; Verona & Ravasi, 2003; Zott, 2003), the underlying processes (Eisenhardt & Martin, 2000; Helfat & Peteraf, 2003; Verona & Ravasi, 2003), the impact on firm's performance (Teece et al., 1997; Eisenhardt & Martin, 2000; Ambrosini, Bowman & Collier, 2009). Thus, despite that remarkable flow of research, the framework still retains some unsolved issues and inconsistencies regarding its core elements.

Nevertheless, regardless of the difficulties in the conceptualization and operationalization of dynamic capabilities, the concept has exhibited a great potential for enhancing explanation of the dynamic nature of value capture. Exploration of theoretical links suggested and roughly outlined by Coff (2010), enabled building an integrated conceptual ground for developing a cohesive and valuable answer to the existing knowledge gap in the field of strategic management. Thus, the research effort was directed toward development of a comprehensive dynamic capability-based framework enabling exploration of complex patterns of value appropriation activities and mechanisms used for branching those patterns in response to changing context. It complies explicitly with the aim of theory building and development. Since undertaken research was focused on identifying changes in the environment, their relations to changes in organizations within the process of value appropriation, studying the sequence and content of alternated compositions of isolating mechanisms, the value of obtained research results refer to the evolutionary perspective of the dynamic approach in management sciences (Czakon, 2010a; Cyfert et al., 2014).

1.2   RESEARCH OBJECTIVES

The aim of this study was to enhance the understanding of a complex and context-bound process of value appropriation by deploying the dynamic capabilities perspective. The rationale underlying the choice of the area of study relates to the identified knowledge gap in the field of strategic management. The extant literature in that field has tend to provide a rather static view of value appropriation. Despite the fact, that scholars have discussed the problem of protecting and retaining value streams, there is a lack of a coherent framework for approaching the dynamics of that process. Recent advancements in the field concerning development of the dynamic capabilities perspective shed more light on the core problem and this study draws on those advancements by approaching value appropriation with the dynamic capability-based framework.

The author's interest in the value capture process emerged along an extensive study of the literature and research work conducted in previous research projects in the years 2004–2013 under the leadership of professor M. Bednarczyk.[2] Obtained results suggested existence of certain inefficiencies in organizational patterns during studied processes of virtualization and innovation (Bednarczyk, 2006; Najda-Janoszka, 2010; Bednarczyk, 2011; Najda-Janoszka & Bednarczyk, 2014). Confrontation of collected evidence with with the model of innovation value chain for regional tourism developed by Bednarczyk (2014, pp. 56–57) enabled location of the problem within the value appropriation practices. Further research work guided by the logic of competitive gaps (Bednarczyk, 2006, 2011; Najda-Janoszka, 2011) and focused on a broad issue of protection of value generated from innovations (Bednarczyk & Najda-Janoszka, 2014) helped to define the research area of interest. Resulting publications and conference papers of the author clearly confirm the evolvement of the research concept for this study. The initial problem definition was iteratively reviewed in accordance with the feedback received from reviewers, conference participants, research project partners, as well as business practitioners participating in projects. Confrontation with recent advancements in the strategic management field during conferences enhanced not only the conceptual framework of the research but also the methodological basis of the study. In result of that broad spectrum of valuable inspiration, the initially defined problem of value capturing was approached with the dynamic capabilities perspective, and become a part of a broader project conducted by the author and financed by the Polish National Science Centre (Narodowe Centrum Nauki) (2013/11/D/HS4/03965).

Given that the logic of value appropriation introduced by management scholarship has been based on both value receiving (point of transaction) and value retaining (longer time span) the main assumption of this study

---

2   Projects financed by the Polish Ministry of Science and Higher Education, and focused on strategic management issues of management system virtualization in small and medium--sized enterprises (1 H02D 065 26), entrepreneurship and competitiveness in the tourism economy based on knowledge (N N115 3730 33), management of regional tourism innovative value chain (N N115 321339).

is that value is not captured instantaneously as it takes time to capture extracted value streams. According to the logic of the dynamic perspective, the efficiency of value appropriation process is determined by firm's ability to build and use specific compositions of isolating mechanisms, and equally by firm's ability to reconfigure those compositions in response to changes occurring in organizational and environmental contexts. Thus, it is argued that value capture should involve both types of organizational capabilities: those focused on ensuring productivity of existing processes and replication of effective practices, and those driven by organizational learning processes and enabling branching of existing practices. Acknowledging that the identified knowledge gap extends over theoretical and empirical dimensions, the main purpose of the study was defined in terms of two integral modules:

- *the conceptual objective* – conceptualization and operationalization of organizational capabilities that enable shaping configurations of value appropriation mechanisms, and
- *the research objective* – providing a rich qualitative evidence of routine-based approach to replication of effective value appropriation practices and alternation of existing action patterns in response to perceived threats and opportunities.

Thus, in order to achieve those objectives the research effort was directed toward:

- a thorough analysis and cohesive synthesis of insights gathered from extant literature into a cohesive picture of strategic management approach to value appropriation (Chapter 2),
- an explanatory systematization of the current state of art of the dynamic capabilities perspective (Chapter 3),
- development of a dynamic capability-based framework of value appropriation (Chapter 4),
- development of a research procedure compliant with methodical rigor of multiple case design (Chapter 5),
- collection and analysis of data according to the replication logic of multiple case design and criteria set for a high quality research (Chapter 6),
- identification of the contribution to the theory and practice of strategic management field and limitations of conducted study (Chapter 7).

The main contribution of this study to the management theory, the dynamic capability-based framework of value appropriation, was formulated on the basis of a cumulative knowledge generated from a wide range of theoretical and empirical studies on value capture and dynamic capabilities, and further was verified and improved during an empirical investigation. In order to provide useful and information rich evidence for reliable verification of the framework, three related research questions were formulated:

1. How does the perception of a selection factor affect the way a firm introduces changes into existing practices of value appropriation?
2. Does the pattern branching response to identified opportunities or threats tend to be structured along activity clusters of dynamic capabilities?
3. How do contextual conditions affect the content and implementation of a response?

Since to best of author's knowledge, no studies have yet explored value appropriation practices with reference to dynamic capabilities perspective, providing answer to those questions implicated elaboration of theoretical links, that have not yet received a scholarly attention. Hence, the problem was addressed with a qualitative approach and a study case method, as it is argued that case study research provides fine-grained views from different standpoints, and thus enables gathering rich and versatile data necessary for gaining new knowledge about specific phenomena (Yin, 2014; Eisenhardt & Graebner, 2007; Czakon, 2013). In order to provide a sound and compelling ground for theory building, the research strategy was built on a multiple case design and followed a developed formal procedure compliant with methodical rigor of a chosen research method.

Provided theoretical and empirical evidence that value appropriation is an on-going process and that configurations of isolation mechanisms are continuously developed and changed, should enable a shift in scientific discourse from the problem of providing an immutable value protection built on an individual effectiveness of selected protection tools, towards analyzing complex compositions of value capture mechanisms and a firm's ability to manage change in their configuration. The significance of this reorientation underlines the fact that developing strategies for value appropriation is not a simple extrapolation of activities performed within the value creation process, because value appropriation requires a completely different kinds of knowledge and capabilities (Pitelis, 2009). Thus, revised accents should provide a strong support for explaining why some enterprises are more successful in creating value whereas other in its capturing.

1.3 OUTLINE OF THE STUDY

This study begins with a discussion of the extant literature, continues with methodological considerations and empirical findings, and ends with contributions. Accordingly Chapter 1 introduces the background of the study as well as presents its main research objectives.

Chapter 2 presents a strategic management approach to value appropriation. Chapter begins with a brief discussion on the notion of value in the management science. Next, Chapter defines two intertwined processes of value creation and value appropriation. Following that theoretical introduction Chapter highlights most relevant features of a broad collection of ideas developed mainly in the field of management but also in economics. A thorough review provides useful insights into subtle points pertinent to the problem of value capture, hence presents a persuasive illustration of interconnected theoretical contributions that build current understanding of value appropriation at an organizational level.

Chapter 3 is devoted to the dynamic capabilities perspective. Thus, the content of the chapter begins with a recognition of the importance of multi-source flows of theoretical contributions. Drawing on those theoretical foundations Chapter provides clarification on the concepts and terms used in the dynamic capabilities perspective by discussing key terminological issues. Further, based on a review of seminal approaches presented in the literature a cohesive interpretation is attributed to relations between the overall construct and its components. Finally, the chapter presents a discussion on the important issue concerning relation between dynamic capabilities and firm's performance.

Chapter 4 presents the dynamic capability-based framework of value appropriation, which was initially formulated on the basis of a cumulative knowledge generated from a wide range of theoretical and empirical studies on value appropriation and dynamic capabilities, and further was verified and improved during an empirical investigation. Thus, Chapter provides the final, empirically reviewed version of the framework by presenting a detailed picture of main elements of the framework, i.e. concept of path dependency, activity clusters of sensing, seizing and reconfiguring.

Chapter 5 provides insights into the research methodology of the study. Thus, it begins with philosophical underpinnings and further describes in detail research design and developed research procedure, case-selection process, as well as data-collection and data-analysis methods.

The findings of the study are presented in detail in Chapter 6. Given that the research was guided by the replication logic the structure of the Chapter reflects the line of reasoning and consists of two integrated parts: within-case analysis and cross-case analysis. In order to provide most readable picture of investigated action patterns the narratives in the first part were broken down to more theory oriented descriptions. In order to enhance the analysis structured descriptions included also tabular displays and graphical illustrations of gathered data.

The final Chapter 7 elaborates on the contribution of the study to the theory and practice of the strategic management field. In addition, Chapter also addresses the limitations of the study, and highlights further research opportunities.

2 STRATEGIC MANAGEMENT APPROACH TO VALUE APPROPRIATION

As value stands for a central purpose of economic activity and a cornerstone of economic thought (depicted as utility) it became a key term underpinning contemporary business studies by replacing product as the object of production and exchange. Firm performance is shaped by value creation and its appropriation (Mizik & Jacobson, 2003; Ellegaard et al., 2009; Czakon, 2012). Those intertwined processes have received an immense scholarly attention, yet the extant body of knowledge on management does not provide a comprehensive picture of value appropriation that captures its dynamic nature (Ellegaard et al., 2009; Czakon, 2012). Thus, the aim of this chapter is to disentangle value appropriation as an object of theoretical inquiry and empirical analysis. Hence, presented discussion concerns the notion of value in the strategic management field, starting with a generic definition of the term and then shifting the focus toward the interrelation and a non-linear occurrence of processes of value creation and value appropriation. Drawing on the assumption that both processes are separable at conceptual and analytical level, following two sections introduce the concept of value creation according to a contingent perspective. Acknowledging contingency conditions the next section explores the nature and the underlying logic of the concept of value appropriation in the strategic management field. That introduction to the contemporary understanding of the concept is followed by a detailed picture of the state of art on the subject, which is discussed in the next four sections. Presented reflections are based on a thorough review of seminal contributions referring to the industrial organization perspective, game theory conceptualizations, the resource based view of the firm and the profiting from innovations perspective. Thus, provided insights pertain not only to the field of management but also economics. In order to map those broad intellectual roots in a comprehensive and appealing way, conclusions formulated in the final section of this chapter are enhanced by a scheme illustrating interconnections between discussed theoretical contributions.

2.1 THE CONCEPT OF VALUE IN STRATEGIC MANAGEMENT

This section provides the foundations for understanding the concepts of value creation and value appropriation. Therefore, discussion begins with valuable insights to the the notion of value in the strategic management field. This generic concept is then conceptually dissagregated into value creation and value appropriation processes.

2.1.1 GENERIC DEFINITION OF VALUE

Although value is a fundamental term in management, the literature provides a wide spectrum of distinct use of the term depending on a particular context and the locus of its creation (Bowman & Ambrosini, 2000; Makadok & Coff, 2002; Pitelis, 2009; Vargo & Lusch, 2004). Reflecting the tension on the philosophical ground concerning axiological dilemma of objectivity and subjectivity of values (Hartman, 1967), their intrinsic and extrinsic notions (Miles, 1961), approaches to be found in the extant management literature tend to either make a distinction between value and evaluation or integrate them into one complex concept (Kahle & Valette-Florence, 2015, pp. 13–15). Moreover, a multidisciplinary nature of the field of management has generated different perspectives to investigate value that emphasize financial performance (e.g. Miles, 1961; Park, 1999), market competitiveness (e.g. Porter, 1985) or social context (e.g. Vargo & Lusch, 2004).

Nevertheless, it is quite characteristic that in most works authors make a reference to "value" as to a generic concept, yet do not provide any comprehensive definition of the term (Pitelis, 2009; Makadok & Coff, 2002; Bowman & Ambrosini, 2000; Lepak et al., 2007). Given the overlapping content in contributions concerning value added, value creation, value capture, exchange value (Miles, 1961; Priem & Butler, 2001; Makadok & Coff, 2002; Helfat et al., 2007; Lepak et al., 2007), it appears that in the strategy field value remains as a rather elusive and latent variable in terms of analysis (Pitelis, 2009). Moreover, in the strategic management literature many authors refer to the term rent as an indicator of value or performance (Lewin & Phelan, 2002), yet the usage of the rent concept remains in large extent imprecise. Although there is an emerging consensus on understanding rent as a price of the service of a productive input, scholars tend to use rent interchangeably with profit (e.g. Rumelt, 1987; Peteraf, 1993) or confound different types of rents, i.e. Ricardian rent, Marshallian rent, Paretian rent, quasi-rent (e.g. Rumelt, 1987; Peteraf, 1993; Mahoney & Pandian, 1992). Thus, due to the complexity of the rent concept and the lack of a clear and cohesive view on the subject in the strategic management field, this study does not discuss the concept in more detail other than to recognize that rents are conceived as the prices of services yielded by resources (Lewin & Phelan, 2002).

Difficulties in reaching a conceptual consensus on understanding value concern primarily a significant variance in the parties for whom value is created (Lepak et al., 2007; Di Gregorio, 2013), potential sources of value (Pitelis, 2009) and the locus of its creation (Porter, 1985; Makadok & Coff, 2002; Vargo & Lusch, 2004). Depending on the focus of the study value is defined with respect to customers (Bowman & Ambrosini, 2000; Vargo & Lusch, 2004; Priem, 2007), internal and external stakeholders (Coff, 1999; Lavie, 2007; Bowman & Ambrosini, 2010), in terms of shareholders returns (Porter, 1985; Simon, Hitt & Ireland, 2007) or even society (Lepak et al., 2007). Given the variety of potential beneficiaries the generic definition of value should embrace all value-creating cases even those that are not subjects to direct market pricing (Makadok & Coff, 2002). Therefore, this study is build on a proposal of Pitelis (2009), that addresses the challenge by defining value as "perceived worthiness of a subject matter to a socio-economic agent that is exposed to and /or can make use of the subject matter in question" (Pitelis, 2009, p. 1118). This definition provides a suitable basis for analyzing notions of value equally at an individual, organizational and industry level. For purposes of this work, investigation is focused on value engendered by organizations and perceived as worthy by internal and external stakeholders.

In the literature organizational value is further disaggregated into potential and realized utility (Ramirez, 1999; Moran & Ghoshal, 1997; Bowman & Ambrosini, 2000; Pitelis, 2009; Di Gregorio, 2013). This disaggregation builds a legitimate basis for investigating value creation and value appropriation (Bowman & Ambrosini, 2000; Lepak et al., 2007; Hansen, 2008; Fischer, 2011). Accordingly, in their seminal article Bowman and Ambrosini (2000) introduced a concept of use value and exchange value build on the classical economic thought. According to their proposal "use value refers to specific qualities of the product perceived by customers in relation to their needs" (Bowman & Ambrosini, 2000, p. 2). Thus, in contrast to Miles (1961) and his widely recognized definition of use value and esteem value, this approach embraces qualities deriving from both the performance of the product and its aesthetic features. Moreover, the concept of use value presented by Ambrosini and Bowman (2000) applies to various types of purchases made by different economic-agents besides final customers (Bowman & Ambrosini, 2000; Lepak et al., 2007; Di Gregorio, 2013). Therefore, while considering purchases made by managers of an organization, it becomes legitimate to conceive inputs analogously to use value (Sojer, 2011), hence there is no need for introducing an additional concept of cost value (Miles, 1961).

Nevertheless, since use value is a notion of a highly individual and subjective judgment (Amabile, 1996), it raises the challenge of conducting a feasible, quantifiable and reliable assessment of performed evaluation of a particular offering (Di Gregorio, 2013), even when attempting to translate perception into monetary terms (Brandendburger & Stuart, 1996). Apart from personal bias, in case of resource acquisition by managers of an organization, use value perception becomes more obscure due to the difficulties with identification of usually complex causal linkages between the qualities of the resource and the need of profit making (Bowman & Ambrosini, 2000). Lack of visible streams of revenues makes potential value highly abstract and challenging for a thorough investigation (Di Gregorio, 2013).

A visible notion of value is recognized as an exchange value, and refers to the monetary amount realized at the point of transaction between customer/ user and the seller of a particular task, good, service or product (Bowman & Ambrosini, 2000; Lepak et al., 2007). According to the developed logic at this focal point use and exchange value of an offering coincide. While exchange value adds to the earnings of the seller, it adds to the costs of the buyer, yet the buyer in fact incorporates use value of the purchased subject matter (Bowman & Ambrosini, 2000). Hence, use value transferred into the production process of the buyer generally does not reflect the actual exchange value of purchased resources (Fischer, 2011). The difference is recognized as customer surplus, the difference between perceived value and the price paid (Bowman & Ambrosini, 2000). Nevertheless, obtained use value reflects no more than a potential that can be quantified and realized only at another point of sale (Pitelis, 2009).

Therefore, it brings the discussion back to the main issue and premise of this study, that creating a potential value is a necessary but insufficient condition for building a competitive advantage. New potential value needs to be exploited in order to add wealth to society (Moran & Goshal, 1997). The required complementary process that impacts the bottom line is value appropriation, as emphasized by Bowman and Ambrosini (2000, p. 4) "organizations create perceived use value and they capture exchange value." Thus, given the variety of contributions and resulting mixed picture of value creation and value appropriation in the management literature, it becomes more clear that the differences between presented approaches revolve around the underlying definition of value.

2.1.2 INTERTWINNED PROCESSES OF VALUE CREATION AND VALUE APPROPRIATION

According to the approach to understanding value presented in the previous chapter an organization is involved in intertwinned processes of potential value creation and realized value appropriation. A study of management literature reveals a heated debate on the causality dilemma between value creation and value capture, ergo on the prevailing perspective in the strategy field. This inspiring discussion represents a more recent development in the strategic management knowledge (Hansen, 2008). The extant contributions can be divided into value creation oriented (Moran & Ghoshal, 1997; Kaplan & Norton, 2001), value appropriation oriented (Coff, 1999; Makadok & Coff, 2002), and those that present a rather balanced view (Mizik & Jacobson, 2003; Narayandas & Rangan, 2004; Lepak et al., 2007; Ambrosini & Bowman, 2010; Czakon, 2012) or define value appropriation as a part of value creation (Ellegaard et al., 2009).

Scholars representing the first of above mentioned approaches argue that value creation is a more important perspective for investigating long term performance of an organization than the one of value capture, as value creation lies at the heart of organizational strategy. Creating a superior value for customers is perceived as a basis for building firm's competitive advantage (Anderson, 1995; Woodruff, 1997). Further, according to this perspective value creation represents a key driver of discovery, continuous innovation, economic development and adaptive efficiency (Moran & Ghoshal, 1997). On the contrary, the second stream of research views value capture as more pertinent concept for exploring competitive advantage of firms, since value appropriation makes a direct impact on the profitability of an organization (Coff, 1999). It is assumed that customer use value is just one among many different determinants of value captured by the firm, and as such is indirectly relevant to firm profitability and to the main focus of the strategy field (Makadok & Coff, 2002). Nevertheless, it is quite interesting that scholars contributing to either of those contrasting approaches claim substantial imbalance in the management literature that favors the opponent while leaving the focal process poorly understood and underexplored (Moran & Ghoshal, 1996, p. 41; Di Gregorio, 2013).

Departing from those radical perspectives, a third group of contributors emphasize the interrelationship and possible trade-offs between value creation and value appropriation, and the fact that both refer to necessary but insufficient conditions for an effective long term performance of a firm (Mizik & Jacobson, 2003; Ellegaard et al., 2009). This view is built on the general theoretical construct of exploration and exploitation (March, 1991), therefore it assumes that firm performance is influenced simultaneously by both complementary processes. Thus, the key strategic task for an organization is to "balance sufficient support for value creation efforts with adequate investments in capabilities that facilitate the appropriation of value" (Mizik & Jacobson, 2003, p. 65).

Given the main objectives of this study the line of reasoning of the balance-oriented perspective provides the most suitable and sound ground for analyzing value capture within the framework of dynamic capabilities. Nevertheless, this moderate "balance-oriented approach" is not homogeneous. There are two standpoints with regard to the nature and logic of interrelation between value creation and value appropriation. Some scholars argue that value creation and value capture should be viewed as distinct, separate processes that evolve in subsequent stages (Bowman & Ambrosini, 2000; Mizik & Jacobson, 2003; Enders et al., 2009; Lepak et al., 2007). Hence, it is assumed that value creation precedes value appropriation, yet it does not necessarily imply subordination of the latter. Conversely, other contributors focused on the dynamics of value creation and value capture argue that both processes are continuous, interwoven and as such hardly separable (Ellegaard et al., 2009). Thus, presented discussions combine both processes to the extent that value appropriation is conceptualized as a part of value creation (Ellegaard et al., 2009) or in other works value appropriation mechanisms embrace value maximization (Czakon, 2010b, 2012). Further, by introducing a time-span dimension authors call for a shift of the scope of analysis from "points in time" toward "periods of time." It is assumed that analyzing both processes over a substantial time span would reveal their nonlinear occurrence, hence that value capture can follow, precede or occur simultaneously with value creation (Ellegaard et al., 2009).

Confrontation of the content of those perspectives with the approach to understanding value introduced in the previous chapter and the aims of this work has revealed a strong conceptual connection with the view claiming distinctive nature of value creation and value appropriation. The main premise of this work is that value appropriation can be conceptualized within the dynamic capability-based framework. The underlying logic is built on a disaggregation of organizational value into potential and realized one, and an assumption that delivering either of those values requires different resources and capabilities, which can be identified and evaluated. Thus, both processes are viewed as interrelated and intertwined, yet separable at a conceptual and analytical level. It provides consistent and uniform terminology throughout the work and prevents overlapping and misleading interpretation of used terms and formulated conclusions. Moreover, given the focus on dynamic capabilities, which are expected to provide evidence of repeated performance (Nelson & Winter, 1982; Eisenhardt & Martin, 2000), and are inherently associated with change, presented discussion and analysis include a time span dimension by drawing on the concept of a nonlinear occurrence of the value creation and value appropriation. Thus, the resulting final approach of this work follows the logic of integration, yet not conceptual eclecticism.

2.1.3 DEFINING VALUE CREATION

Strategic management scholars use different interpretative lenses to characterize value creation, hence in the extant literature value creation refers to both the content – what constitutes value for a user, and the process – underlying activities that generate new value (Lepak et al., 2007; Nogalski & Bors, 2000). This conceptual duality is reflected in a vast array of imprecise definitions, which subsume similar but distinctive concepts (i.e. value, use value and customer surplus) under the heading of value creation (Porter, 1985; Helfat et al., 2007). Given the formulated assumption of this work concerning the intertwined yet distinctive nature of value creation and value appropriation, it is important to disentangle and clarify all key conceptual ideas referring to either of those processes.

Building on the conceptual ground discussed in the previous chapters value creation process consists of three key components recognized as potential use value, created value and cost incurred in providing an offering (Bowman & Ambrosini, 2000; Enders et al., 2009), as presented on Figure 2.1. Value is created through complex organizational processes that transform sets of resources. In line with Schumpeter new resource combinations are recognized as the source of new potential value to be created (Moran & Ghoshal, 1997). Although those new combinations may be allocatively inefficient in the short run (Moran & Ghoshal, 1997), over time they enhance adaptive efficiency by enabling discovery of new uses for resources (Di Gregorio, 2013). In other words value creation involves a given set of resources and a given set of preferences in a given time. Therefore, created value becomes a function of the way in which resources are managed (Marr & Roos, 2005). This line of reasoning emphasizes the role of management in the value creation process, hence is consistent with the resource-based theory and the dynamic capabilities perspective, which provide a conceptual ground for further discussion and analysis in this work. It is assumed that value is not created by resources, but rather by processes by which resources are deployed, combined, acquired, renewed and released (Penrose, 1959; Eisenhardt & Martin, 2000).

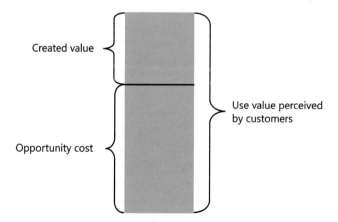

Figure 2.1 Value creation
Source: Author's own work.

In the terminology followed in this work value created[1] is defined as the difference between customer/user perceived use value from a given product and opportunity cost associated with all inputs necessary for providing that product (Enders et al., 2009), including cost for inputs from suppliers, cost stemming from combining inputs with organizational processes, labor costs, capital costs etc (Figure 2.1). However, in order to maintain symmetry between both sides of transaction, which is important for further discussion on value appropriation, opportunity cost does not reflect actual prices paid for particular inputs. It is conceived analogously to use value, though in reverse manner (Brandenburger & Stuart, 1996; Sojer, 2010, p. 11). Decision on particular combination of resources is determined by the perceived value of alternative deployments, i.e. value of the next best alternative use of a resource. Opportunity cost considerations referring to resource deployment form a base line for further discussion on the choice between alternative organizational responses to a given stimuli.[2] Nevertheless, following Brandeburger and Stuart (1996), opportunity cost can be defined as the amount of money that makes supplier indifferent between status quo of having the resource and a new situation of having the money but less the resource. In order to create value opportunity cost, needs to be less than the use value from a given product as perceived by its customer (Brandenburger & Stuart 1996; Besanko et al., 2000). Thus, firms can enhance value creation by managing to either increase use value by deploying resources with superior features or reduce costs by using resources more cost-effectively. Those two generic determinants for value creation form a fundamental point of reference for various proposals of leverages for value creation presented in the literature (Amit & Zott, 2001; Lepak et al., 2007; Pitelis, 2009). The influence of leverages such as innovation (Amit & Zott, 2001; Pitelis, 2009; Lepak et al., 2007), entrepreneurship (Lepak et al., 2007), strategic networks (Amit & Zott, 2001), human resources (Lepak et al., 2007; Pitelis, 2009) on value creation can be direct or indirect through complex multilateral interactions. Thus, the leverages may impact value creation simultaneously within the frames of both generic determinants of value creation, by enhancing perceived use value and concurrently by reducing cost of creating the product.

Undoubtedly the approach presented above highlights the importance of the customer in value creation. However, some scholars, building on the concept of use value, prioritize the role of the customer to the extent that firms are viewed only as facilitators of value creation (Grönroos & Voima, 2011; Vargo & Lusch 2004; Hansen, 2008). According to this perspective value creation essentially occurs in the context of interaction between the

---

1   It is important to emphasize that the use value would be defined differently for investors than for the customer.

2   See more in Chapter 3.

user and the offering (Hansen, 2008; Grönroos & Voima, 2011). Despite the meaningful implications of a service-dominant logic and its concept of customer's creation of value in use (Grönroos & Voima, 2011), it contributes largely to the marketing field of study, which reaches beyond the scope of this investigation. Introducing into the discussion on value creation a strategic management perspective consistent with the RBV and the dynamic capabilities approach, provides a sound ground for directing attention toward the provider sphere of activities (Makadok & Coff, 2002). Nonetheless, the underlying logic of conceptual ground for this work allows for recognizing the relevance of customers' utility functions for explaining firm performance, yet only as one among different organizational and environmental determinants.

2.1.4 VALUE CREATION AT DIFFERENT LEVELS OF ANALYSIS

According to the contingent perspective presented by Lepak et al. (2007), value creation can by analyzed at the individual, organizational and societal level depending on the source and targets of value creation. At the first of mentioned levels the analysis is centered around individual attributes that underpin creative acts exhibited by given individuals and targeted toward the employer. Such acts refer to various contributions perceived to be of greater utility or lower cost for the target user (employer) over the closest alternative (Felin & Hesterly, 2007). Therefore, the emphasis is on the initial conditions of individuals that influence their creativity and job performance.

Moving to the organizational level shifts the focus of the analysis to a collective activity embraced in organizational routines and processes (i.e. management, new product development, organizational knowledge creation) that provide value for the customer. A particular configuration of those organizational processes is widely conceived as a value chain (Porter, 1985), which is built on three main components: value creation processes, their interconnections and coordinating system (Porter, 1985). It has been argued that developing a distinct activity system provides a basis for building a competitive advantage (Porter, 1985). Although subscribing to the same basic model of an activity system, firms tend to implement it using individual approaches (Porter, 1985). In other words implemented activity systems reflect certain commonalities in key features of the basic model typical in a particular industry, yet reveal idiosyncrasy in configuration details (Eisenhardt & Martin, 2000, p. 1108). There is an ongoing discussion in the strategic management literature concerning notions of uniqueness within organizational activity systems that could be defined as a source of competitive advantage of firms (Barney, 1991; Eisenhardt & Martin, 2000; Teece et al., 1997). A dynamic capabilities approach represents a focal concept in that debate, and as such is thoroughly described in the following sections of the Chapter 3.

Finally, analysis of value creation at the societal level concerns macroeconomic conditions in the external environment that generate incentives for entrepreneurship and innovation, hence create value for the society (Lepak et al., 2007). Studies referring to this level explore wide spectrum of governmental policies as sources of value creation for a given society (Porter, 1990).

Nevertheless, the study of the management literature on business relationships reveals existence of an additional level of analysis while considering value creation (Lavie, 2007; Ford et al., 2011; Czakon, 2012; Niemczyk et al., 2012). Scholars argue that a widespread phenomenon of creating value within interorganizational collaborative structures, shifts the focus of an investigation toward multiple interdependencies among involved business entities, social actors, activities and resources (Hakansson & Snehota, 2005; Ford et al., 2011). The analysis of those interdependencies reaches beyond the scope of the organizational level, yet does not involve issues considered at the societal level. Therefore, extant contributions introduce the interorganizational level of analysis, which complements the contingent perspective of value creation proposed by Lepak et al. (2007).

From the strategic management perspective organizations can create value in an "exclusive" manner by combining own internally developed resources and capabilities or "collectively" with the use of external resources and capabilities accessed through inter-organizational relationships (Lavie, 2007; Ellegaard et al., 2009). Due to a growing dynamics of the environment, pace of global competition, technological change on the one hand and resource constraints of organizations on the other, firms are rarely able to perform all their activities in-house (Lechtenhaler, 2009; Farag, 2009; Collis & Montgomery, 1995). According to the literature, creating value in inter-organizational structures enables a considerable extension of the range of performed value chain activities (Lavie, 2007; Niemczyk et al., 2012). Such enrichment generally exceeds the limited capacity of a single organization (Dyer & Singh, 1998).

In the management scholarship strategic bundling of internally and externally available resources is conceptualized as an inter-organizational networking, cooperation or collaboration. Hence, concepts are commonly conceived as equivalent and authors tend to refer to those concepts in an interchangeable manner (Camarinha-Matos & Afsarmanesh, 2006). However, Camarinha--Matos and Afsarmanesh (2006) argue that in the context of value creation those concepts convey quite distinct content with respect to the level of commitment of engaged parties, common goal-oriented risk taking, range of resources invested into a joint endeavor. According to Camarinha-Matos and Afsarmanesh (2006), concepts of interorganizational relationships should be conceived on a continuum of collaborative structures, where each subsequent concept extends the former one by an additional feature of integration. In result, the inter-organizational networking placed at the starting point of that continuum, involves mutual communication and information exchange without structuring individual contributions around any common goal. Thus, networking does not imply a common generation of value. The subsequent concept of coordination involves extending the inter-organizational networking by aligning activities performed by engaged entities. Introducing work synchronization enables efficiency enhancement, however value creation process maintains on the individual organization level. Moving to the interorganizational cooperation implies tightening of integration by involving "sharing resources for achieving compatible goals" (Camarinha-Matos & Afsarmanesh, 2006, p. 3). Nevertheless, it is feasible to identify and evaluate individual contributions, since value created in such a cooperative structure is an aggregation of components generated quasi-independently by involved organizations. The ultimate concept of interorganizational collaboration, which subsume all other concepts, adds a joint creation facet. Mutual engagement of involved organizations refers to joint planning, implementing, and evaluating for achieving a common goal. Such a high level of integration may generate an image of a joint identity for outside observers, and make it difficult to determine individual contributions (Camarinha-Matos & Afsarmanesh, 2006, pp. 3–4). Thus, it can be concluded that moving along the continuum of interorganizational relationship arrangements reveals a growing integrity between actors, activities and resources of engaged organizations (Ford et al., 2011). Only higher levels of integrity enable a common generation of value instead of a rough aggregation of individual contributions.

The extant literature provides a relatively wide spectrum of drivers for entering collaborative inter-organizational structures (Czakon, 2007; Cygler, 2009). Among those of a special concern are expectations of additional opportunities for value creation that derive from sharing resources and integrating activities (Ritala, 2012). By engaging in joint endeavors firms gain an opportunity to access extended set of resources and capabilities owned/controlled by partners, thus it can be concluded that an interorganizational dimension introduces additional mechanisms for leveraging deployable resources. Complementary resources provided by cooperating partners may directly contribute to firm performance through enrichment (Lavie, 2007). This mechanism extends the range of strategic opportunities available for a focal firm by a rough and immediate supplementation of the existing resource base of a firm with resources otherwise unavailable or difficult to develop internally (Mowery et al., 1996). The second mechanism for leveraging resources involves achieving positive synergy effects through strategic bundling of internally and externally accessible resources (Dyer & Singh, 1998; Lavie, 2007). This combination strategy generally implicates a deeper commitment of certain resources to the relationship together with a more concerted effort over longer time periods for synergies to emerge (Larsson & Finkelstein, 1999). Finally, organization may implement an absorption mechanism that is focused on development of the internal resource base by internalizing external resources through imitation, learning or acquisition (Lavie, 2007). Nevertheless, participating in collaborative endeavor can generate synergies not only at the level of the resource base of collaborating parties but also across their activity systems (Ford et al., 2011). Organizations can integrate performed activities through upstream and/or downstream linking and by bringing together those of similar nature in order to gain economies of scale. Given that value created is conceived as a function of the way resources are managed (Marr & Roos, 2005), interorganizational relationships may generate additional opportunities for value creation by leveraging resources and integrating activities in a simultaneous manner.

However, it needs to be emphasized that new opportunities for value creation imply both potential additional benefits and potential additional costs for parties involved in interorganizational relationships (Najda-Janoszka, 2010). It is a quite challenging task to accurately assess costs incurred by collaborating parties in subsequent transactions over the life of a given relationship. The difficulty raises as a collaboration reaches higher levels of integrity (common goals, resource sharing, integration across activity systems), since such assessment embraces quantifiable aspects of costs as well as those that are subject to judgments and interpretations according to collaborators' priorities and perspectives on future development of a given relationship (Ford et al., 2011). Moreover, as pointed by Hakansson and Snehota (2005), each interorganizational relationship should be evaluated in the context of other relationships of an organization due to existing explicit and implicit interdependencies affecting the final assessment. Ford et al. (2011) identify two types of costs specific to a particular relationship that are not considered as a part of the general overheads of the company. First type is labeled as initial costs of a relationship. Those costs stem from information searching, communicating, negotiating and adapting to particular offering / input and relationship arrangements. Hence initial costs are incurred before any transaction between collaborating parties have taken place. Conversely, recurrent costs of relationship are incurred regularly as a relationship evolves trough time, since those costs refer to development, management and maintenance issues. Many of those costs cannot be associated directly with a single transaction between organizations at a particular point in time, as they are the outcome of multiple factors that occur over varied timeframes. Thus, given that costs and benefits generated within interorganizational relationships evolve according to their own logic, there is a necessity for a time-based analysis of the content of value creation process across such arrangements (Ford et al., 2011). It brings back the idea of intertwined processes of value creation and value appropriation, as a comprehensive answer to the underlying questions requires exact insight into both concepts.

In case of this study formulated research objectives are concerned with collective activities defined under the terms of dynamic capabilities and value appropriation. Given that dynamic capabilities are embedded in organizational processes, which in turn form the activity system of an organization, it is assumed that an organization represents the party that produces the value and is intended to benefit from it, hence is expected to capture the value that it has created. The definition of value creation introduced earlier in this chapter that links the process directly with effective and efficient management of resources is also consistent with the organizational level of analysis. Nevertheless, it is assumed that organizations are not operating in isolation rather function as entities embedded within complex interorganizational relations (Hakansson & Snehota, 2006). Thus, organizations are intended to create an individual and common value within collaborative structures and to appropriate its certain proportion. Therefore, including an interorganizational level of analysis as an accompanying approach in exploring dynamic capabilities for managing value appropriation appears as a legitimate procedure.

2.1.5 DEFINING VALUE APPROPRIATION

According to the insights presented in the previous chapter a new potential value is created through new combinations of resources. However, necessary conditions for any purposive deployment of value creating resource combinations embrace not only existence of a particular opportunity and motivation, but equally include an expectation for capturing some value from that deployment (Moran & Ghoshal, 1997). Thus, the logic of wealth creation places value appropriation at the forefront of decision making on the resource deployment. As emphasized in the literature, economic development requires potential value to be realized, i.e. "value must be generated, appropriated and eventually handed-on" (Moran & Ghoshal, 1997, p. 6). Therefore, the following sections present the definition of and dominating approaches to the concept of value appropriation, supported by the discussion on research advances on the subject.

In the management literature authors use different terms to address the problem of created value distribution such as value capture, value appropriation, value distribution, value allocation, value realization. Nevertheless, a thorough study of seminal works leads to a conclusion that there are two main categories aspiring to become a dominant label in the management literature, namely value capture (e.g. Bowman & Ambrosini, 2000; Lepak et al., 2007; Priem, 2007; Lavie, 2007; Fischer, 2011) and value appropriation (e.g. Mizik & Jacobson, 2003; MacDonald & Ryall, 2004; Czakon, 2012; Mazur & Kulczyk, 2013; Di Gregorio, 2013). In order to investigate existing tendencies in terminology used a bibliometric method was applied. For the literature review three main databases holding comprehensive citation lists for management field were chosen – ABI/INFORM (Proquest), Academic Search Complete and Business Source Complete (EBSCO), Social Sciences Citation Index (ISI Web of Knowledge). Selected databases were searched for key terms of "value capture" and "value appropriation" located in the whole body of text and abstract of scientific papers (scholarly journals, books, dissertations[3]) published between 1996 and 2015, and related to the management field. Since the SSCI database does not capture all the relevant research (books, dissertations) and some seminal articles are not indexed (e.g. Bowman & Ambrosini, 2000), for further investigation the ABI/INFORM, ASC and BSC databases were used. Moreover, in order to identify most influential management journals Thomson Reuters Journal Citation Report of 2013 was also reviewed.

Table 2.1 Terminology used for describing created value distribution

	Proquest ABI/INFORM		EBSCO ASC + BSC	
	Text	Abstract	Text	Abstract
Value capture				
Overall scientific articles, dissertations, books	663	114	780	137
Classification Code: Management	208	35	214	86
Top 20 Management Journals JCR 2013	18			
Value appropriation				
Overall scientific articles, dissertations, books	495	72	489	67
Classification Code: Management	169	22	116	62
Top 20 Management Journals JCR 2013	11			
Value capture + value appropriation				
Classification Code: Management	89	3	67	4

(as for 12th of May 2015)

Source: Author's own work.

The usage of either of those terms in scientific works on management has been comparable in absolute numbers, with a slight predominance of "value capture" (Table 2.1). This predominance is more visible when considering a time frame of publications (1996–2015). Until 2009 the usage of both terms was at a quite similar level. The next decade has begun with an evident turn toward "value capture." Following years 2010–2015 indicate a growing tendency to use that term over value appropriation. However, since the content of both terms is in its deep sense the same, many authors have also begun to use those labels interchangeably emphasizing their synonymous character (Pitelis, 2013; Mazur & Kulczyk, 2013; Duhamel et al., 2014). Nevertheless, terminology

---

3   Books reviews, editorials, newspapers and duplicate papers were excluded from the search.

usage should follow the principles of precision and utility. Acknowledging, that the term appropriation encompasess the issue of property and conveys the notion of value as a bundle of contracts serving allocation of property rights, value appropriation is used as the main category throughout this work, while other labels including value capture serve as supportive, synonymous expressions for text enhancement.

For many authors contributing to the management field a common starting point for discussing the problem of created value distribution is the neoclassical economic view of the firm (Bowman & Ambrosini, 2000; O'Hara, 2001; Lieberman & Balasubramanian, 2007). Conceptualizations are build on the assumption that potential value becomes realized at the point of transaction (Bowman & Ambrosini, 2000; Lieberman & Balasubramanian, 2007). The focal producer is expected to capture the difference between the price charged for a product (exchange value) and incurred costs in the form of a profit, while a customer is intended to appropriate customer surplus defined as the difference between perceived use value and exchange value (O'Hara, 2001). The concepts of customer surplus and producer surplus are commonly illustrated by means of a supply curve and market demand curve for a given product. As companies operate mostly in non-monopolistic environments the actual exchange value is affected by the amount of consumer surplus provided by competitors. Exchange value usually declines as the number of competitors offering similar product increase, even though use value may become substantially enhanced (Lepak et al., 2007). Nevertheless, given the assumption about perfectly competitive factor markets, suppliers are not ascribed with the power to extract any shares of the value generated by the firm. In that case the task of value distribution is transferred to resource markets (Argadoña, 2011). Thus, the neoclassical economic view envisage in fact only two types of agents that can capture value created at the exact point of transaction: the firm itself (producer) and its customers (Lieberman & Balasubramanian, 2007). On the firm level the underlying, basic assumptions of the neoclassical theory (i.e. absence of externalities, perfect competition in all markets, firm-specific investments, free entry and exit from all markets, sufficient information to make optimal decisions) allowed to consider only owners of equity shares as legitimate claimants of the firm's residual income (Argadoña, 2011; Klein et al., 2012). Thus, according to this line of reasoning, streams of payments directed toward managers and other employees can be conceived solely as costs and not shares of value created (Klein et al., 2012).

Given that overly narrow conceptualization of the neoclassical view cannot be upheld in practice, further exploration in the economic and management field has challenged the perspective by extending the analysis beyond the point of transaction and by emphasizing that created value may also flow to various trading partners of the focal organization, e.g. labor, suppliers, customers

(Bowman & Ambrosini, 2000; Coff, 1999; Castanias & Helfat, 1991; Lippman & Rumelt, 2003; Mazur, 2011). Repealing simplifying assumptions of the neo-classical theory by the advances of transaction cost economics (Williamson, 1985), modern property rights perspective of incomplete contracting (Grossman & Hart, 1986; Mahoney, 2012), market-process perspective (Foss, 1994; Jacobson, 1992), and strategic management (Freeman, 1984) enabled a more nuanced understanding of the value streaming through value creation and appropriation. New proposals have been built on the idea that inter-temporal relationships between the firm and its trading partners usually involve co-specialized investments of resources controlled by each party. Under new approach ownership is no more equated with residual rights to income but defined as residual control rights in the deployment of a particular resource (Grossman & Hart, 1986; Mahoney, 2012). Since value is co-created by mutual deployment of property owned/controlled by trading partners and the focal firm, all engaged parties may have the claim to that co-created value. The decision upon resource deployment is determined by the reasonable expectation of a return on investment, i.e. a residual interest (Klein et al., 2012). Thus, in order to evaluate entire economic value creation and distribution the analysis should embrace also transactional partners in terms of benefits generated beyond their opportunity costs (Mahoney, 2012). Breaking the shareholder primacy has broadened the analysis of value apportioning by introducing additional equally legitimate claimants commonly labeled as stakeholders. However, the literature provides various approaches to define stakeholders. Most broad ones embrace not only agents contributing to the wealth-creating potential of the firm but also parties involuntarily exposed to the risks induced by actions undertaken by the focal firm (Freeman, 1984; Mahoney, 2012). Such definitions result in too large sets of potential stakeholders for any reliable analysis. An empirical investigation requires a more narrowed and operational view. Hence, this study follows the property rights approach built on the assumption that "returns to co-specialized investments take priority over other investments that are affected by the firm's actions" (Klein et al., 2012, p. 311). Thus, the key distinction for defining stakeholders concerns the issue of reasonable expectations of returns.

Introduction of a stakeholder concept into the strategic management scholarship has triggered the research effort toward searching a comprehensive explanation to the key question of how value created by the original source can be split between other receiving agents (Pitelis, 2009; MacDonald & Ryall, 2004; Lepak et al., 2007). The rationale for distinguishing and exploring value appropriation on the strategic management ground refers to the fact that the logic of value distribution may or may not follow the rules governing the value creation process. Hence, organizations can extract and appropriate less, equal or even more value that have actually created (Brandenburger & Nalebuff, 1996). In the attempt to enhance the understanding of that disparity many authors use a very appealing metaphor by explaining that value created establishes the size of a pie and value capture represents the share of that pie received by respective agents (Brandenburger & Stuart, 1996; Jap, 2001; Gulati & Wang, 2003; Blyer & Coff, 2003). As created value contains a mixture of original contributions it is quite difficult to divide it into shares matching the quantity and importance of original inputs. For one part, it is due to the level of complexity of a particular value creation process. For the other part, difficulties arise from multiple strategic interdependencies among variety of economic actors involved directly and indirectly in that value creation process (Brandenburger & Nalebuff, 1996). Given that relationship--specific investments and returns can arise according to distinct developmental paths (e.g. may occur after a particular transaction is completed), management scholars argued for extending the analysis over time periods to enhance under-standing how a wide range of internal and external stakeholders may be able to capture some of the value created attributable to the resources they control (Di Gregorio, 2013; Ellegaard et al., 2009). Figure 2.2 illustrates the concept of value appropriation used as a reference point for the discussion in this study.

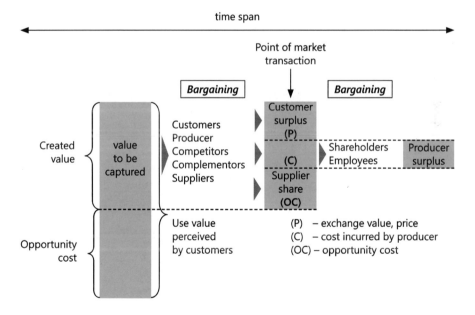

Figure 2.2 Concept of value appropriation

Source: Author's own work.

Drawing on the advances in the strategic management field the logic of value appropriation introduced in the framework presented on Figure 2.2 has been based on both value receiving (point of transaction) and value retaining (longer time span). Due to the fact that resources exhibit stickiness and time dependency in terms of their accumulation and deployment (Dierickx & Cool, 1989), the process of extracting value from those resources is also affected by time-compression diseconomies (Cool et al., 2012). In line with that argument, value is not captured instantaneously as it takes time to appropriate extracted value streams. Guided by the concepts of industrial organization (IO) and resource based view (RBV) the understanding of the appropriation issue has been extended from pure value extraction to simultaneous use of modes for restricting competitive forces (Jennewein, 2005; Teece, 2001; Rumelt, 2003; Fischer, 2011). Since competition is conceived as the core construct underlying value appropriation, the introduced framework is centered around processes concerned with establishing and defending power and position of transactional partners that expect returns on their mutual investments. Thus, it is worth noting that some authors conceive value capture and value protection as distinct concepts (Foss, 2003; Mol et al., 2005) and align them with different stages of value systems. According to this proposition horizontal axis, formed by organizations occupying the same stage in the value system (competitors), does not concern actual transactions, hence involves value protection to prevent competitive imitation. Since profits are generated along vertical axis, due to transactions between upstream and downstream entities, within this dimension profits can be realized as value captured (Mol et al., 2005). Despite valuable insights explaining new entry and vertical integration strategies, such approach derives from a narrow perspective considering value appropriation as an instantaneous act occurring at the exact point of transaction. Hence, it does not stand for a point of reference for the presented framework, which assumes that bargaining for appropriation streams occurs between broad spectrum of external as well as internal stakeholders.

Competition on product and factor markets determines "the slice of the pie one gets to keep" (Afuah, 2014, p. 156). It affects the level of opportunity costs, and further the actual prices paid for products and resources (Figure 2.2). Thus, the prices of products and resources reflect the outcome of barganing and previous calculation of alternatives (Brandenburger & Stuart, 1996). Most studies elaborate on inequalities of bargaining power between given entities (Hamel, 1991), positions held within particular organizational and social structure (Burt, 1992) and isolating mechanisms influencing that power and positions (Figure 2.3).Those isolating mechanisms embrace tangible and/or intangible barriers preventing replication of a particular behavior of a given firm (Rumelt, 1984).[4] Nevertheless, it is important to emphasize that value appropriation involves a wider spectrum of activities besides those concerned

---

4   A more detailed discussion on the nature of isolating mechanisms is presented in section 2.2.3.

with structure, positioning and bargaining power. There is also an important category of ad-hoc, opportunistic actions as emphasized by game theory conceptualizations (Brandenburger & Nalebuff, 1996). Although it is widely acknowledged that acting upon opportunity in an entrepreneurial manner may refer not only to value creation but equally to value appropriation, in case of the latter the literature has emphasized almost exclusively negative connotations (Williamson, 1996). Thus, value capture actions of a given firm are discussed rather in terms of avoiding opportunism (behavior of a trading partner) than embracing opportunities (behavior of a focal firm). Meanwhile, observable business practice confirms the key role of alertness and quick response in effective value appropriation. A distinctive character of an opportunistic action refers to the fact that it does not have to be based on any particular level of bargaining power or position in a given structure. Thus, even though such entrepreneurial actions alone usually do not bring durable first-mover advantages (Di Gregorio, 2013), they should be conceived and explored as an integral part of value capture activity (see Figure 2.3).

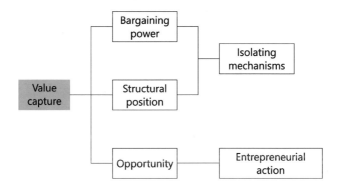

Figure 2.3 Key elements of value capturing activity

Source: Author's own work.

The extant management literature confirms that the notions of those key elements of value capturing activity illustrated on Figure 2.2 may vary depending on the level of analysis. Accordingly presented framework distinguishes intra-organizational and inter-organizational dimension of value appropriation (Lepak et al., 2007; Di Gregorio, 2013; Mazur, 2011). At the intra-organizational level the spectrum of investigated claimants embraces individuals, i.e. shareholders, managers, executives, other employees, who expect to capture value created in a form of a higher salary and/or other quantifiable personal benefits (Coff, 1999; Bowman & Ambrosini, 2000; Mazur, 2011). Hence, the analysis is centered around personal attributes that allow individuals to enhance their position in a social network of a given organization, to hinder imitation of performed processes and in result to increase bargaining power over their employer (Chacar &Hesterly, 2008).

When considering inter-organizational (or organizational according to typology presented in Lepak et al., 2007) value appropriation the investigation involves distribution of value created among external stakeholders, i.e. competitors, complementors, suppliers, customers. The focus is shifted from personal attributes toward organizational features, tasks, procedures, processes, market and industry structures. The review of the management literature reveals that this dimension has been studied through different theoretical perspectives – industrial economics (e.g. Porter, 1985), resource-based view (e.g. Barney, 1991; Dierickx & Cool, 1989; Peteraf, 1993), dynamic capabilities (Teece et al., 1997; Eisenhardt & Martin, 2000), profiting from innovations (Teece, 2001), and in diverse contexts – buyer-supplier relations (Bowman & Ambrosini, 2000), strategic alliances (Lavie, 2007), joint-ventures (Inkpen & Beamish, 1997), dyadic co-specialization (Teece, 1986), interorganizational networks (Ellegaard et al., 2009; Czakon, 2012). Given that the very nature of inter--organizational arrangements implies coexistence of competition, cooperation and control relations and that the extant literature confirms a growing trend of using various interorganizational structures to implement business ventures (Niemczyk et al., 2012; Czakon, 2012), considering value appropriation in such context appears to be a current and important area of inquiry. As pointed by Håkansson and Snehota (1989), no business is an island, hence the embeddedness of a firm in a network of business relations has considerable implications for its performance, i.e. value capture (Dyer & Singh, 1998).

It is worth mentioning that some authors identify an additional level of the analysis for exploring value appropriation. Lepak et al. (2007) contribute to discussion by calling for cohesiveness in studies on value creation and value appropriation, thus emphasize necessity to extend the analysis of value capture with additional societal level, where the legitimate claimants include societies, states, communities. Building on the Porter's diamond framework (Porter, 1990) a particular society can restrict competitive forces by developing and maintaining unique resource advantages, strong demand conditions, related and supporting industry infrastructure and competitive markets (Lepak et al., 2007). Those factors can be conceived in terms of isolating mechanisms for given societies. Nevertheless, given that the presented value appropriation framework follows the narrow definition of stakeholders (entities with reasonable expectations of returns), the societal level extends beyond the research area of this study. The following section presents a review of seminal contributions to the interorganizational dimension of value appropriation.

2.2 MANAGEMENT APPROACHES TO VALUE APPROPRIATION

Given that capturing and retaining value is a necessary condition for firm's survival and growth, the extant management literature provides a variety of perspectives and concepts that have evolved over the years forming a combined body of knowledge, yet not free from inconsistencies and blind spots. This section highlights some general, yet most important features of this collection of theoretical frameworks and empirical investigations. Discussion starts with the industrial organization perspective, followed by game theory conceptualizations, the resource based view of the firm, and ends with interesting insights provided by studies focused on profiting from technological innovations. Conclusions concerning the most important contributions to the value appropriation theory are summed up and presented on a scheme in the last section of the chapter.

2.2.1 INDUSTRIAL ORGANIZATION PERSPECTIVE

Value appropriation is a prominent domain of external-focused approaches built on the concepts of industrial organization economics (IO). Studies deriving from structure-conduct-performance paradigm are focused on investigating industry structure as a key source of profit differentials across stages within a given value system, along its horizontal and vertical axis (Porter, 1985). Hence, developed theoretical concepts share the same key assumption that strategic position in product and factor markets is the key determinant of value capture. Contributions drawing on that assumption have provided valuable insights concerned with barriers to the entry into a market (Bain, 1956) or more generally mobility barriers (Caves & Porter, 1977) that hamper access to particular industry or value system for new entrants while enable incumbents to continue performance (Geroski et al., 2001). Given the premises of the main paradigm of IO that industry structure determines the behavior of firms, which in turn determines various aspects of market performance, for many authors one of the major conceptual challenges has concerned the extent to which barriers to capital mobility result from actions undertaken by incumbent firms aiming at breaking symmetries induced by fundamental structural conditions (Geroski et al., 2001).

According to the first definition formulated by Bain (1956, p. 3) a barrier to entry embraces anything that allows incumbent firms to use competitive pricing without attracting new firms to enter a given industry. Such logic induced correlation between entry barriers and profits, hence allowed for identification of cost advantage, capital requirements and scale economies as entry barriers. On the contrary, Stigler (1968) departed from revenue-dependent sources of entry barriers and defined entry barrier as an additional cost incurred by entrants while not by incumbents. Thus, according to this contrasting line of reasoning cost disadvantages incurred by entrants in a form of penalties from suboptimal levels of production are not entry barriers, because those costs result from demand conditions in the market, which are equal for entrants as well as incumbents. In the same vein capital requirements do not represent a barrier to entry unless incumbents never paid them (Stigler, 1968, p. 67). Further research advances confirm clearly that from the original proposal formulated by Bain (1956) only absolute cost advantages have gained undisputable acceptance, while capital differentiation and scale economies have been subjects of a heated and continuous discourse not only among economists but also antitrust lawyers (Geroski et al., 2001; McAfee et al., 2004). Over the years the concept of entry barriers has been developed according to different approaches ranging from antitrust legislative concepts, normative perspective addressing welfare consequences of entry (Fisher, 1979; von Weizsacker, 1980) to contributions introducing time dimension and stressing the importance of time required for effective entry to a particular industry (Carlton & Perloff, 1994). Despite the advances in research the extant literature has not provided a broad consensus over the very nature of barriers to entry.

All subsequently developed perspectives embraced investigation of incumbency value, structural characteristic and economic consequences of entry, however early and subsequent conceptualizations differ substantially with respect to the level of analysis. Early literature derived from Bain's concept (1956) of structural barriers to entry of new capital into a market was focused exclusively on the level of an industry. Economies of scale, cost advantages of incumbents and product differentiation were conceived as industry sources of barriers to entry (Lewin et al., 2004). Recognizing inter-firm strategic differences within an industry, which might even excess those between industries, enabled conceptualizing mobility barriers as impediments to the movement of resources not only in and out of an industry but also within its borders (Caves & Porter, 1977). It changed the notion of potential competition and provided a sound ground for exploring competitive advantage and value appropriation equally at the industry, strategic-group and generic-firm levels (Porter, 1980).

By synthesizing practical implications of IO Porter (1985) introduced a firm-level analysis of value capture focused on strategic positioning of the firm within its industry and on shielding against five competitive forces: competition within the industry, the potential competition, the bargaining power of customers, the bargaining power of suppliers, the threat of substitutes. It has been argued that facing highly intensive competition, low entrance barriers and readily available substitutes firms may experience high competitive discount

on created value that significantly reduces monetary streams ultimately captured by the firm. Thus, exploration has been directed toward considering
structural and behavioral factors including creation of mobility barriers and
usage of means for harnessing market forces to establish unequal dependence,
i.e. market-based bargaining power over trading partners (Foss & Foss, 2002).
Such uneven dependence is established when one party maintains an option
to cost-efficiently replace a transaction partner while the latter is unable to
do the same recourse as it faces considerable replacement costs (lock-in). An
organization having a bargaining power over its trading partner may use it
in a form of direct or implicit threat in order to maintain or enlarge the share
of captured value (Hamel, 1991). Such considerations are in line with studies
centered around the problem of co-specialization[5] needed for an effective use
of innovation, yet leading to bargaining dilemmas due to bilateral dependence
(Teece, 1986). Provided insights have triggered further discussion on value
appropriation and subsequent studies have contributed to development of
a comprehensive body of knowledge on profiting from innovations, which is
discussed in Chapter 3.2.4 (Teece, 2001; Jacobides et al., 2006).

Industry structure results from partly designed and partly emergent rules
governing arrangement and interdependence between economic actors. Acknowledging that "the ways in which roles [in a given industry] are distributed among a set of interacting firms" are shaped simultaneously by technical
(technology driven), behavioral (activity of firms) and regulatory (legislative
nature) determinants (Jacobides et al., 2006, p. 1204), enabled refocusing from
isolated dyadic relations between the focal firm and its individual trading
partners to industry-wide architectures. Due to a relative stability in the way
existing industry-wide templates describe the distribution of activities and
produced value (e.g. publishing, chemical industry), scholars have begun to
explore the emergence of such structures in the first place (Jacobides, 2005;
Morris & Ferguson, 1993). Investigations conducted in various industries have
lead to a conclusion that not only a birth of a new sector, but any substantial
technological, institutional or demand discontinuity allows for reorganization
of the system of interfaces between economic agents – i.e. emergence of the
industry-wide template (Jacobides et al., 2006). Hence, provided insights have
inspired further studies on the role of interorganizational arrangements (strategic alliances, networks, pressure groups, industry associations) in the process of
establishing new quality standards or dominant technological design within or
across industries (Gomes-Casseres, 1994; Teece, 2001; Baldwin & Clark, 2006),
and introduced the concept of architectural advantage into the discussion on
profiting from technological innovation (Jacobides et al., 2006; Teece, 2001).

---

5   Co-specialization – a concept developer earlier and to a large extend independently from
    capabilities theory (see: Teece, 1986).

Thus studies drawing from IO concepts have brought awareness of industry embedded power circumstances to discussions focused on explaining the key dilemma, why companies creating high levels of value (either through low cost or high perceived use value) may end up capturing only disproportional fraction of this value (Teece, 1986). Nevertheless, further exploration questioned the dominance of the structure-conduct-performance paradigm due to its limitations in providing comprehensible insights to the problem of value dissipation. Subsequent empirical investigations reported persistence of variations in firms' performance even though firms operated in similar external contexts (Wernerfelt & Montgomery, 1988; Rumelt, 1991). The management literature proliferated with research works confirming negligible (from 9 up to 20 percent) impact of external factors. It challenged the external perspective and encouraged studies focused on internal firm-specific factors. New conceptual streams introduced a groundbreaking assumption that firms operating in the same industry can make discretionary choices over different sets of alternatives. Thus, it has triggered a departure from the "black box" approach and provided a fertile ground for developing one of the most prominent theories in strategic management, the resource based view of the firm (thoroughly discussed in the following chapter).

However, a thorough review of the extant studies on the performance variability, raised a broad set of questions regarding interpretations and methodological issues: sample composition, industry definition, variable adjustments in statistical methods employed (Bowman & Helfat, 2001). Differential methodological approaches, contradictory results and interpretations confirmed a high complexity of a problem of estimating industry, corporate and business segment effects. McGahan and Porter (1997) addressed the issue by emphasizing the necessity for distinguishing the degree of impact of a particular factor on the direct performance from the degree of impact of the same factor on the persistence of performance of a given firm. Moreover a significant proportion (ranging from 60 to 80 percent) of performance variations observed in seminal studies (Schmalensee, 1985; Rumelt, 1991; Powell, 1996) were due to unexplained factors. This substantial grey area "has provided strategy researchers with a significant and challenging field of inquiry" (Powell, 1996, p. 331) as it has consisted of a mixture of both industry- and firm-specific factors. It can be concluded that despite losing a dominant position in an ongoing discussion, the argument of importance of industry structure and firm positioning in explaining the tension between value creation and value appropriation, has maintained its validity. The concept needed more clear ramifications of interaction between value capture actions of positioning and restricting competitive forces. Thus scholars have reached for a different conceptual lens provided by game theory frameworks (e.g. Brandendburger & Stuart, 1996; Brandenburger & Nalebuff, 1996).

2.2.2 GAME THEORY CONCEPTUALIZATIONS

Given that game theory is an extension of the classical decision theory (Morgenstern, 1963), it has been applied to business problems to analyze decision-making situations involving two or more players with conflicting preferences with regard to available set of alternatives. Hence, it addresses bargaining situations between companies, customers, suppliers, business units, employees (Drechsel, 2010). Game theory provides two approaches to explore those decision-making situations: non-cooperative and cooperative (Harsanyi, 1966). According to the first approach players are unable to make any binding agreements and theory specifies all possible, yet only individual actions for every involved decision maker in search for the best strategy for each one (Harsanyi, 1966). Hence, in non-cooperative games players are not allowed to negotiate, they play the game for their own sake. Prisoner's dilemma is one of the most well-known models of a non-cooperative game. The way of modeling and analyzing situations provided by a non-cooperative game theory was very appealing to concepts developed in the field of IO, thus the extant literature provides a broad range of its diverse applications (see more: Fudenberg & Tirole, 1991). On the contrary, under a cooperative approach correlated mixed strategies are allowed and the analysis is focused on patterns of coalition formation. Hence, this approach more clearly captures the notion of unanimous exchange (Chatain & Zemsky, 2001). In cooperative games interests of players are partially cooperative – binding and enforceable agreements for value creation, and partially conflicting – distribution of payoffs. As argued by Stuart (2001), when contrasting a cooperative and non-cooperative game theory, the first one can be considered a structural and the latter a procedural theory. Cooperative game theory allows for specification of the particular business context for a firm (in terms of power distribution), while non-cooperative game models are designed for describing a whole set of strategic moves a firm can undertake. It has been argued that due to a sparse formalism allowing for modeling free-form interactions between players, a cooperative game theory to a much greater extent corresponds with unstructured real-life situations and the actual processes of value creation and appropriation (Brandenburger & Stuart, 1996). Hence, with the seminal work of Brandenburger and Stuart (1996), which introduced added value approach to strategy, a cooperative game theory has gained a growing attention in the management scholarship (Brandenburger & Stuart, 1996; MacDonald & Ryall, 2004; Adner & Zemsky, 2006; Ryall, 2013; Henkel & Hoffman, 2014). In the cooperative game theory it is assumed that through unrestricted bargaining all players can pursue any favorable deals available (Myerson, 1991), since the price-setting power can only emerge from the structure of the game. The cooperative game theory specifies just the structure of the game consisting of a player set and a characteristic function specifying the amount of value that can be created and captured by any group of those players, i.e. the worth of each coalition (without cooperation with outside players) (Brandenburger & Stuart,1996). Given that the game is defined by its structure, any modification of a player set or characteristic function (e.g. increasing production capacity, introducing cost-cutting technology, mergers or acquisitions) implies a change of the game.

Given the clear logic and sparse formalism of cooperative game theory Brandenburger and Stuart (1996) used its modeling techniques under the structure-conduct-performance paradigm to formulate the added value approach to strategy. The aim was to build a formal model for studying the way value creation and competition shape firms' performance, i.e. value appropriation. Drawing on the value chain concept (Porter, 1980) authors emphasized the need for symmetrical treatment of customers and suppliers, since both categories of players together with the focal firm form the vertical chain of value creation. According to proposed framework value created by those players is defined as the difference between willingness to pay of customers and opportunity cost of suppliers, both calculated with the reference to alternative opportunities outside the game. However, a somewhat ambiguous distinction between players and alternatives can be attributed to the fact that the approach does not specify any rules for determining the boundaries of a game. Such relaxed attitude is in line with the argument formulated by Ford et al. (2011), according to which boundary of business network is an artificial concept due to the fact that all agents are in fact directly or indirectly related to each other. Thus, defining contours of a game or business network is a matter of convention, the aim of a particular analysis.

Further, in order to provide an answer to the core question of how much value a given firm may capture, the Brandenburger and Stuart (1996, p. 6) introduced the concept of added value[6] of a player defined as "the value created by all the players in the vertical chain minus the value created by all the players except the one in question." It has been assumed that added value of a player determines the maximum amount of value appropriable for that player. Firm can achieve a positive added value by creating competitive asymmetries with respect to the willingness to pay of customers and opportunity cost of suppliers (value-based strategies). However, having a positive added value is a necessary, yet not sufficient condition for a player to capture value. The second component, which determines division of value created, is unrestricted bargaining (all players are able to identify and seek out all favorable deals) between players. According to the rules of the formulated model the ability to capture value should diminish due to the existence of competition, i.e. alternative players.

---

6   Brandenburger and Stuart (1996) distinguished the concept of added value applied in the strategy context from value added term used in accounting and conveying quite different meaning.

A cooperative approach with unrestricted bargaining induces two main issues, i.e. identification of a subset of players which generates most value (most favorable deal) and description of created value distribution (payoffs) among participating entities. In their seminal work Brandenburger and Stuart (1996) discuss the most prominent model for unrestricted bargaining, namely the core.[7] The core is defined as a payoff distribution among the players such that no subset configuration of players can make them better off (Stuart, 2001). The core is used as an indicator of stability of cooperative games (Chatain & Zemsky, 2011) as it conveys the notion of "unbridled competition" (Aumann, 1985, p. 53). The core does not implicate a single point solution, rather a set of undistinguishable allocation vectors. Given the range of values specified by the core, the minimum is interpreted as the value guaranteed due to the existence of competition, while the difference between the minimum and the maximum (positive added value of a player) is recognized as a residual bargaining problem (Stuart, 2001).

Acknowledging the fact that business strategy concerns not only exploiting an existing game but also exploring and designing new games Brandenburger and Nalebuff (1995) introduced a value-net framework, which combined both cooperative and competitive ways for changing the game (coopetition). In contrast to added value approach based on the classical value chain concept, value-net framework is based on the assumption that value is created within the complete net of relationships, across both vertical and horizontal dimensions. In order to break the narrow view of business interdependencies and to direct attention toward searching opportunities for cooperation, instead of traditionally defined competitors (strong confronting connotation) the horizontal axis of the value net involves substitutors (alternative players for customers and suppliers) and complementors (players offering complementary products to customers or acquiring complementary resources from suppliers). Brandenburger and Nalebuff (1995) conceptualized process of value creation and distribution in a cooperative setting. They assumed that the quality of cooperation between players determines the amount of value each participant

---

7   The core is not the only solution for cooperative games, however it is the most widely utilized model in the game theory scholarship. Second prominent solution commonly applied to economic analyses is the Shapley value. In contrast to the core the Shapley value provides a single distribution vector defined as a player's average marginal contribution to all possible subsets of players. This solution is commonly perceived as a fair allocation because of its assigned properties (Henkel & Hoffman, 2014, p. 7): efficiency (the total value is distributed among the players), symmetry (players with the same contribution receive the same value), additivity (combining two cooperative games into a single game is described by the sum of the two original characteristic functions), null player (players without contribution do not capture any value). Due to its relatively high predictive accuracy it has been quite extensively used in economics as a predominant solution to cost-sharing problems (Henkel & Hoffman, 2014).

can appropriate. Hence, it implies a joint consideration of value capture and value creating strategies in terms of a trade-off: enlarging the individual share or the whole size of the pie. According to this framework business strategies concern changing one or more components of the game in order to achieve either positive-sum or zero-sum gains. Firm can redesign the game by changing players, players' contributions and perceptions of the risk-return payoffs, rules structuring the game, and boundaries of the game (Brandenburger & Nalebuff, 1996).

Building on the idea that business strategy embraces both exploitation and exploration of business games Brandenburger and Stuart (2007) introduced a hybrid game form labeled as a biform game. This type of game allowes for modeling situations in which players can choose what business game to be in. In a biform game consequences of decisions made are not vectors of payoffs (at least not directly) but complex business situations modeled again as cooperative games (Stuart, 2001). Hence, biform game is a two-stage game, in which the first stage is non-cooperative and provides insight into strategic moves of the players, while the second stage is cooperative and is designed to describe the distribution of power and subsequently value (payoffs) in a given setting of players (Brandenburger & Stuart, 2007).

With above mentioned approaches it became more feasible to actually formalize the concept that business strategy shapes the competitive environment (Gans & Ryall, 2015) . This research stream has provided appealing frameworks that integrated value creation, value appropriation and competition, yet maintained a clear distinction between all categories. Research advances inspired many management scholars to underpin competitive strategy conceptualizations with game theory insights. Recent proposition of value appropriation model (VCM) presented by Ryall (2013) follows the idea of value network and builds on the core assumption of the added-value approach that the amount of value available to capture in a given setting is bounded by asymmetries between participating players and alternative opportunities for value creation located outside of a network. Nevertheless, the framework is still under development as it requires further studies for input variables identification and empirical verification.

Although game theory conceptualizations substantially enriched and enhanced the discussion on value appropriation, many authors have argued that proposed models are quite vulnerable to real-life situations (Foss & Foss, 2002; Lippman & Rumelt, 2003; Cygler, 2009; Pitelis, 2009). Indeed, game theoretical modeling implies simplification with underlying assumptions of complete information, rational behavior, frictionless bargaining, extreme form of competition, unitary perception of value. However, as pointed by MacDonald and Ryall (2004), Aumann (1985), or Chatain and Zemsky (2011), those assumptions should not be attacked in attempt to disregard the resulting theoretical model, but instead the focus should be on refinement of over simplistic assumptions in order to bring the logic of conceptualizations more closely to empirical applications. Studies on incomplete information (Aumann & Mascheler, 1995), introduction of the concept of frictions into a formal value-based model (Chatain & Zemsky, 2011), or application of value-based approach to investigate the interplay between competition, capability heterogeneity and product market performance (Chatain, 2010) to name a few, are visible examples of such direction. Besides, it has to be underlined that although „the cooperative game theory has a long history in economics, it is relatively recently that this methodology began being applied to the central questions in strategic management" (Gans & Ryall, 2015). Bearing in mind that the economic theory is based on the *ceteris paribus* assumption, moving the context for research to the strategic management field implies a pervasive deviation of that assumption, hence requires further theoretical and empirical work to match the *mutatis mutandis* approach circumscribing managerial dimension.

2.2.3 RESOURCE BASED VIEW

The resource based view of the firm (RBV) emerged in 1980s in reaction to limitations of IO tradition to provide explanation on persistent performance differences between firms operating within similar competitive structures. The industry level analysis viewed firms as "black boxes" in a given market structure, hence it ignored the strategic relevance of firm resources (Barney, 1991). As a growing number of studies confirmed importance of firm-specific idiosyncrasies in explaining intra industry heterogeneity, the strategic management scholarship experienced a major shift toward an internal dynamics of an organization and a resource-level analysis under the RBV framework. Nevertheless, it did not imply the preeminence of the inward-looking approach to strategy, or substitution of the industry-level analysis. Although the RBV has provided a distinct and powerful explanation of performance differentials, it has been argued that it pertains to a different level of analysis (Peteraf & Barney, 2003). Thus, despite of a common tendency to excessively explore either industry structure or firm's characteristics, resource-based and market-based frameworks are not to be perceived as opposite ends of a single continuum,[8] but rather complementary concepts each providing a partial view and explanation (Wernerfelt, 1984; Mahoney & Pandian, 1992; Peteraf & Barney, 2003; Bridoux, 2004; Kraaijenbrink et al., 2010; Schmidt & Keil, 2013). Collis and Montgomery (1995) have captured the idea by emphasizing that "resources cannot be evaluated in isolation, because their value is determined in the interplay with market

---

8   Especially considering conceptual similarities and shared assumptions, e.g. rationality of organizational actors, models of competition, focusing on economic rather than social exchanges (Fahy, 2000).

forces." Hence, the strategic management literature provides a growing number of interesting investigations confirming the importance of the interdependency between firm-specific resources and the industry environment[9] (Bednarczyk, 1996; Hawawini et al., 2003; Schmidt & Keil, 2013). Moreover, directing scholarly attention toward the intersection of internal and external dynamics has given rise to a dynamic capabilities perspective, which is thoroughly discussed in Chapter 3 (Teece et al., 1997; Eisenhardt & Martin, 2000).

Since the seminal works of Wernerfelt (1984), Rumelt (1984), and Barney (1986) a vast amount of the research effort has been done to develop a sound theoretical foundation of the RBV[10] (Barney, 1991; Dierickx & Cool, 1989; Grant, 1991; Peteraf, 1993; Foss & Knudsen, 2002; Peteraf & Barney, 2003; Newbert, 2007; Schmidt & Keil, 2013). A central premise of the RBV is that firms compete on the basis of heterogeneous resource endowments, which may persist over time due to imperfect mobility of resources (Barney, 1991; Peteraf & Barney, 2003). Thus, the main focus is not on a structural but on a resource position of a firm determined by heterogeneity and scarcity of controlled resources. Drawing on those basic assumptions numerous authors developed more or less elaborated sets of conditions underlying persistent performance differentials (Table 2.2). Nevertheless, the insight into the content of proposed criteria allows for a conclusion that most of them can be derived from the generic conditions of heterogeneity and scarcity.[11] A resource heterogeneity is understood not as much in terms of input differentials across firms but rather differential levels of efficiency of various resources (Peteraf, 1993). Efficiency with respect to resources is viewed broadly in the sense of cost reduction as well as use value enhancement (Barney, 1991; Peteraf & Barney, 2003). Given that value created is defined as a difference between perceived use value and resource costs, it has been concluded that control over superior resources enable firm to increase value created, and consequently achieve a competitive advantage. However, sustainability of such an advantage is determined by the scarcity of controlled superior resources, which refers to a limited (fixed or quasi-fixed) supply of a particular resource in relation to demand for its services (Peteraf & Barney, 2003). Scarcity in turn depends on an effective protection of those superior resources against competitive duplication, i.e. imitation, transfer, substitution (Wernerfelt, 1984; Rumelt, 1984; Dierickx & Cool, 1989; Barney, 1991).

---

9   For example, according to an investigation conducted by Hawawini et al. (2003), industry factors tend have a dominating impact on performance of "stuck in the middle" firms, while for firms characterized by above and below average performance levels firm-specific factors prevail. Thus, obtained research findings confirmed a nonlinear dependency between firm performance and either of defined groups of factors.

10 For a detailed overview of intellectual roots of the RBV, see Fahy (2000).

11 However, some authors, e.g. Nanda (1996) or Foss and Knudsen (2002), argue that heterogeneity is a supportive but not a necessary condition for rent generation, since heterogeneity can be derived from more basic condition of scarcity.

Table 2.2 Conditions and characteristics of resources underlying sustainable competitive advantage

Author	Conditions / characteristics of resources	Description
Dierickx & Cool (1989)	nontradeable	There are no markets for such assets
	inimitable	Limited opportunities for accumulating similar asset stocks due to time compression diseconomies, asset mass efficiencies, interconnectedness of asset stocks, asset erosion, casual ambiguity
	nonsubstitutable	Limited opportunities for applying alternative asset stocks
Barney (1991)	valuable	Resource enables exploitation of opportunities and/or neutralization of treats in a firm's environment
	rare	Resource is not present among firm's current and potential competition
	imperfectly imitable	Resource cannot be easily replicated by other firms due to unique conditions, causal ambiguity or social complexity
	nonsubstitutable	Resource does not have strategically equivalent alternatives
Peteraf (1993)	heterogeneity	Resources exhibit differential levels of efficiency
	ex post limits to competition	Factors that preserve the condition of heterogeneity: imperfect imitability and imperfect substitutability
	imperfect mobility	Resources are nontradable or less valuable to other users (idiosyncrasy, co-specialization, transaction costs) and cannot be bid away readily from the firm
	ex ante limits to competition	Imperfections in strategic factor markets that prevent costs from offsetting the rents
Amit & Schoemaker (1993)	complementarity	The strategic value of each asset's relative magnitude may increase with an increase in the relative magnitude of other strategic asset
	scarcity	Asset is not present among firm's current and potential competition
	low tradability	Assets are difficult to buy and sell
	inimitability	Assets cannot be easily replicated by competitors
	limited substitutability	It is hard to replace an asset using alternatives
	appropriability	Economic returns generated from assets are appropriable by the firm
	durability	life-span of assets which reduces investments required to offset their depreciation
	overlap with strategic industry factors	Applicability of an asset to a particular industry setting

Author	Conditions / characteristics of resources	Description
Collis & Mont-gomery (1995)	inimitable	It is hard to copy the resource, which has at least one of the key characteristics: physical uniqueness, path dependency, casual ambiguity, economic deterrence.
	durable	Resource is able to sustain competitive advantage over time
	controlled by the company	Resource is inextricably bound to the company
	nonsubstitutable	It is hard to replace a resource using an alternative
	superior	Competitive superiority of a resource defined through an external assessment of the value generated by a resource

Source: Author's own work.

Given that according to the RBV not all resources matter equally when considering a firm's sustainable competitive advantage (Fahy, 2000), a great deal of the research effort has been directed toward investigating and categorizing the exact types of resources that can meet the criteria of superiority. The difficulty of the task stems not only from the relatively large amount of resources that may meet these criteria, unclear boundaries between them, but also from the fact that resources in question may exhibit different effectiveness under different circumstances. Thus, the literature provides an impressive collection of various typologies of resources, starting with Penrose's (1959) proposal of two categories, i.e. physical and human resources, Ansoff (1965) who distinguished physical, monetary and human resources, or Barney (1991) with similar approach of physical, human and organizational resources, and ending up with more elaborated proposals formulated by Grant (1991) with five categories of financial, physical, technological, human and reputational resources, or Teece et al. (1997) with eight categories of technological, complementary, financial, reputational, structural, institutional, market and boundary assets. Nevertheless, the usability of those typologies has been questioned. As pointed by Kraaijenbrink and Groen (2008), most of proposed resource categorization schemes do not provide rationale for distinguishing particular types of resources, and bear no direct relationship with criteria defined for evaluating superior resources (Miller & Shamsie, 2006). In order to address those shortcomings Miller and Shamsie (2006) formulated a distinct typology based on the key criterion of inimitability of resources. Hence, they distinguished "property-based resources" – specific and well-defined assets or processes that can be protected by property rights, and "knowledge-based resources" – processes or skills protected by knowledge barriers. It is quite interesting and uncommon that physical and intangible assets are not isolated but classified under the same category Moreover, each category can be further decomposed into discrete/stand alone resources (e.g. exclusive contracts, individual technical skills) and bundled/systemic resources (e.g. units of a distribution system; team skills). According to that proposal property-based resources should be most useful in stable, predictable environments, while less specific and more flexible knowledge-based resources should be of the greatest utility in dynamic, unpredictable environments. Thus, contradictory to other studies (Hall, 1993; Castanias & Helfat, 1991) it is assumed that depending on the dynamics of the environment and the extent of effective usage of a given protection mode, superior resources may be found among physical and intangible assets. This proposition seems more appealing to the RBV assumptions and further to the conceptualizations developed under the profiting from technological innovation perspective (PI).

Bowman and Swart (2007) formulated another interesting categorization scheme which also addresses the problem of ambiguous boundaries and ownership of resources. They distinguish separable, embodied and embedded forms of resources. Separable resources embrace all tangible, physical assets and intangible intellectual property (patents, trademarks) that can exist independently from the individuals that work with them. In contrast, embodied resources are primarily explicit and tacit skills (human capital) and as such cannot exist separately from the individuals. The third form, embedded resources, occur in the relationship between the two aforementioned categories: "embedded capital exists where there is ambiguity surrounding the rent creating contributions of human capital due to synergistic interactions between separable and embodied capital that are difficult to disentangle" (Bowman & Swart, 2007, p. 494). Conceptualization of embedded resources provides a sound ground for analyzing not only casual ambiguities of the value creation process but also bargaining power asymmetries between employees, managers, shareholders that influence value appropriation at the intra-organizational level.[12] It highlights the struggle of ownership of resources between internal actors involved in value capture, since the problem of appropriability arises when the scope of property rights lacks precise definition (Grant, 1991).

Although both aforementioned proposals clearly express a close relation with the theoretical framework of the RBV and include stand alone as well as systemic resources, it needs to be underlined that they are based on an all-inclusive definition of resources, which does not distinguish assets from actions undertaken upon those assets. In the early works the unit of analysis was a single resource while "the processes through which particular resources provide competitive advantage remain[ed] in a black box" (Barney, 2001, p. 33). In 1995 Barney improved his original VRIN (valuable, rare, inimitable,

---

12 Mazur (2011) applied that conceptualization in a thorough study of value appropriation at intra-organizational level.

nonsubstitutable) framework for analyzing internal resources by introducing an additional component, namely organizing context (VRIO) for absorbing, applying and capturing value generated by strategic resources. Subsequent exploration derived more comprehensively from Penrose's (1959) conceptualization and the focus has moved from merely possession and accumulation of individual resources toward development, configuration and deployment of resource bundles (Grant, 1991; Amit & Schoemaker, 1993; Teece et al., 1997). Scholars have begun to assert more clearly that possession of heterogeneous and scarce resources is a necessary but insufficient condition for explaining a firm's competitive position (Newbert, 2007; Kraaijenbrink et al., 2010). The literature has provided a growing number of insightful contributions regarding processes to which resources should be subjected to in order to generate expected value (Grant, 1991; Kogut & Zander, 1992; Amit & Schoemaker, 1993; Teece et al., 1997; Eisenhardt & Martin, 2000). Hence, many authors departed from an inclusive way of defining resources and introduced a distinction between resources (possession) and capabilities (action) (Table 2.3). Such an approach enabled breaking the endless loop in which activity of deploying a resource is conceived as a resource as well (Priem & Butler, 2001). Broadening the scope of analysis with capabilities and organizing context has substantially leveraged the discussion by providing the missing link between resource possession and resource exploitation (Mahoney & Pandian, 1992). Discussion has been further enriched by influential contributions from the evolutionary perspective (Nelson & Winter, 1982), organizational learning (Kogut & Zander, 1992), entrepreneurial perspective on strategy (Schumpeter, 1934; Lewin & Phelan, 2002). Scholars have actively responded to advances in those diverse streams of literature and as pointed by Newbert (2007) since the beginning of 2001 the research attention has shifted towards capabilities and their importance in shaping a firm's competitive position. Hence, the field has been continuously expanding from a resource-characteristics oriented approach toward a theory of dynamic resource management.

Although many RBV scholars have referred to a competitive advantage and superior performance in an interchangeable manner, it is important to emphasize that those are distinct concepts characterized by quite different relationship with the resource position of an organization (Coff, 1999; Bridoux, 2004; Newbert, 2007). As Ma (2000) pointed out, having a competitive advantage does not necessarily lead to a higher performance, as well as it is possible to achieve a superior performance without having a competitive advantage. Interchangeable treatment of those constructs would imply an assumption that the residual value generated through services yielded by a given resource/resource bundle is fully captured by the firm. When considering resources as bundles of property rights (Alchian & Demsetz, 1973) it becomes more apparent that firms rather often fail to appropriate all created value, since "one

Table 2.3 Seminal definitions of resources and capabilities

Author	Type of definition	Description
Wernerfelt (1984)	inclusive, neutral	By a resource is meant anything which could be thought of as strength or weakness of a given firm. More formally, a firm's resources at a given time could be defined as those (tangible and intangible) assets which are tied semi-permanently to the firm.
Barney (1991)	inclusive, positive	Firm resources include all assets, capabilities, organizational processes, firm attributes, information, knowledge, etc. controlled by a firm that enable the firm to conceive of and implement strategies that improve its efficiency and effectiveness. Firm resources are strengths that rims can use to conceive of and implement their strategies.
Grant (1991)	distinctive, neutral	Resources are inputs into the production process – they are the basic units of analysis. On their own, few resources are productive. Capability is the capacity for a team of resources to perform some task or activity.
Amit & Schoemaker (1993)	distinctive, neutral	Resources are stocks of available factors that are owned or controlled by the firm. Resources are converted into final products or services by using a wide range of other firm assets and bonding mechanisms. Capabilities refer to a firm's capacity to deploy resources, usually in combination, using organizational processes to effect a desired end. They are information-based, tangible or intangible processes that are firm-specific and are developed over time through complex interactions among the firm's resources.
Teece et al. (1997)	distinctive, positive	Factors of production are undifferentiated inputs available in disaggregate form in factor markets (they lack a firm-specific component). Resources are firm-specific assets that are difficult if not impossible to imitate. Organizational competences are distinctive activities enabled by integrated clusters of firm-specific assets that span individuals and groups.
Makadok (2001)	distinctive, neutral	Resources are tangible and intangible assets that can be valued and traded. Capability is a firm-specific capacity with a primary purpose to enhance the productivity of resources that the firm possesses. Capacity is embedded in organization and its processes, thus it is not easily transferable.

Source: Author's own work.

firm may have the right to consume a resource, even while another has the right to obtain income from the same resource and yet another has the right to alienate some of the resource's attributes" (Kraaijenbrink et al., 2010, p. 365).[13] In order to bring more clarity on the subject Peteraf and Barney (2003) provided a refined definition of the concept, according to which in order to have a competitive advantage a firm needs to be able to create more value than the marginal competitor (capable of breaking even). Thus, a competitive advantage is viewed not in terms of a final outcome but rather a firm's potential to best rivals with respect to specific features of value created. This line of reasoning is fundamental for investigating the issue of value appropriation, because it implies that although "competitive advantage leads to rent creation, it does not necessarily ensure that a firm can capture those rents in the form of higher returns" (Peteraf & Barney, 2003, p. 312). Hence, it separates on a conceptual ground value creation from value distribution, with the former one being linked to a competitive advantage and the latter to a performance.

The key explanatory challenge concerns differences between firms in turning a competitive advantage into superior performance, i.e. in translating created value into captured streams of value. It has been argued that resource position of a firm not only determines the value creation process but also influences value appropriation as it underpins the bargaining position of a firm on both product and factor markets. According to the RBV the bargaining position of a focal firm on a product market, i.e. versus its competitors and customers, is shaped by the way inimitable and nonsubstitutable resource bundles are being deployed (Blyer & Coff, 2003). It is the extent of uniqueness of deployed resources that has a direct impact on the spread between the willingness to pay and the firm's cost – the amount of value the focal firm can capture (Bowman & Ambrosini, 2000; Becerra, 2008). The firm's bargaining position against customers weakens when competitors are able to duplicate its strategic resources, which allow offering comparable products. With a growing number of alternative offerings a focal firm is being forced to provide higher customer surpluses on the basis of similar resource endowments. Hence, a firm needs to compete by decreasing the share of appropriable value (Bowman & Ambrosini, 2000; Becerra, 2008). Nevertheless, as pointed out by Chatain (2010), not all firms with superior resources face the same competitive pressure. He argues that the existence of highly client-specific value creation has a direct impact on the competitive landscape of a focal firm. When a client-specific knowledge is instrumental in delivering a service or customized product to that client in such a way that new client needs are more likely to be fulfilled by firms that are already providing other services to that client, then the number of relevant

---

13 Such conclusion follows the assumption that property rights over resources are multi-faceted, hence can be partitioned and held separately with respect to usage, purchasing and selling (Kim & Mahoney, 2006).

competitors can be reduced according to buyer's existing supplier relationships (Chatain, 2010, p. 77). Thus, highly client-specific value creation changes the reference point for evaluating the resource position of a focal firm.

Discussing competition on the product market scholars in the RBV focus on mechanisms that can prevent a competitive replication of strategic resources. Those mechanisms are commonly labeled as isolating mechanisms (Rumelt, 1984), resource position barriers (Wernerfelt, 1984) or impregnable bases (Penrose, 1959) and are defined as any knowledge, physical or legal barriers that may restrict the extent to which competitors are able to mimic any value-creating task, product or service of a focal firm (Lepak et al., 2007). The RBV scholarship provides a wide spectrum of different isolating mechanisms (Rumelt, 1984; Reed & DeFillippi, 1990; Barney, 1991; Mahoney & Pandian, 1992; Collis & Montgomery, 1995; Lavie, 2007) that can be embedded in the characteristic of individual and bundled resources (e.g. complexity, firm--specificity, path dependency, casual ambiguity) or can constitute additional resources that preserve uniqueness of other resources (e.g. patents). Given the variety of isolating mechanisms it is important to note that most firms implement more than one mechanism at a time, and depending on particular activities performed by the firm some mechanisms complement each other (e.g. trade secrets and lead time advantages) and some act like substitutes (e.g. patents and secrecy) (Fischer, 2011; Najda-Janoszka, 2014a, b).

According to the management literature a product-market competition does not necessarily overlap with a factor-market rivalry, since resources may "trigger rivalry between firms that provide unrelated offerings in different product markets" (Markman et al., 2009, p. 439). Given that competition on factor markets determines value that accrue to resource owners (Barney, 1986), the analysis concerns distribution of value between a focal firm, suppliers and providers of complementary assets. Relaxing the assumption about perfect competition on factor markets has brought the discussion closer to economic reality, where employees and other resource owners are able to capture some proportion of value created attributable to the resources they control. According to the RBV the bargaining position of a focal firm on the strategic factor market is determined by the degree of competition with respect to a given resource (Peteraf, 1993; Sojer, 2010) and ex-ante evaluation of the value creation potential of that particular resource (Barney, 1986; Makadok, 2001; Schmidt & Keil, 2013). Considering the first determinant in the case of a scarce resource acquisition, a split of value attributed to that resource depends on the number of potential purchasers. The more limited opportunities to an effective use of a scarce resource outside of a focal firm, the stronger is the bargaining position of that firm against a supplier. However, actual bargaining will be also determined by a firm's dependency on a supplied resource – risk of hold up (Bowman & Ambrosini, 2000). On the other hand, if that scarce resource can be used in an equally efficient manner by other firms, then the resource price can be bid up to the point, where a supplier captures a full value creation potential of a resource (Peteraf, 1993). The same logic can be applied to an intra-organizational competition for a residual value. Firstly, the bargaining position of internal claimants is shaped by the extent of a possible identification of the individual contribution to productivity (Bowman & Swart, 2007). If the increased productivity can be unambiguously attributed to the individual, then this person is in a favorable position to appropriate a substantial proportion of the generated value. The second factor concerns the extent of possible use of employee skills outside of a focal firm. If the skills being applied offer a similar productivity to other firms, i.e. skills are not firm-specific, then the individual is in a relatively strong position to bargain for its share of residual value (Bowman & Swart, 2007).

A firm attributes value to a resource prior its acquisition or development and that value reflects incremental payments a firm expects to generate in the product market to which that resource is deployed (Lippman & Rumelt, 2003). Due to uncertainty it is argued that "rivalry in factor markets is less predictable than in product markets" (Markman et al., 2009, p. 439). The decision upon an investment in purchase or development of a particular resource depends on its ex-ante evaluation, which in turn is shaped by (Makadok, 2001; Sirmon et al., 2007; Schmidt & Keil, 2013):
  − ex-ante resource base of a firm, which allows for complementarities and idiosyncrasies while deploying a new resource,
  − information asymmetry between market players and access to privileged information, and
  − managerial knowledge and experience.

Under the regime of uncertainty it is possible to underestimate or overestimate the value creating potential of a resource, and either of those misleading expectations may jeopardize the share of appropriable value. Hence, a firm's resource valuating capability is important not only for successful value creation but equally for optimizing value appropriation (Makadok & Barney, 2001).

Acknowledging that inter-organizational arrangements are becoming an important vehicle for value creation, it is important to analyze the impact of a resource position of a firm on the way a value generated through collaboration is distributed among participating firms (Dyer et al., 2008; Zakrzewska--Bielawska, 2013). In case of the inter-organizational collaboration value is generated in two main forms, i.e. common benefits that refer to common objectives of a particular arrangement and are available to all participants, and private benefits that are realized only by the individual participant (Khanna et al., 1998). Dyer et al. (2008) argue that those distinct forms of gains can be explained through different theoretical approaches. According to their proposal the distribution of common benefits among collaborating parties is

supported by the resource dependence perspective, since it is assumed that partners investing more critical resources to the relationship should be able to capture a higher proportion of generated common value. However, the distribution of common benefits set in ex-ante negotiations (Pfeffer & Salancik, 1978) can change substantially in due course of a relationship. The bargaining power of a focal firm based on its resource position in an inter-organizational arrangement can change substantially if partners acquire/learn firm's critical resources or if a focal firm makes greater investments in transaction-specific assets relative to other partners. In order to explain distribution of private benefits a firm can generate from a collaboration Dyer et al. (2008) suggest a combination of three theoretical perspectives:
- Related resources perspective – ability of a firm to generate private benefits depends on the level of complementarity between ex-ante resource base and resources acquired through collaboration, and on the level of its absorptive capacity together with effective organizational routines to facilitate resource transfers.
- Structural holes perspective – ability of a firm to generate private benefits depends on the structure of firm's network of relationships, the location of the firm in that network, and effective organizational routines to exploit resource and information differentials.
- Resource development perspective – ability of a firm to generate private benefits depends on the superior access to market information through collaborative relationships and effective firm's sense-making capabilities (capacity to understand, organize and exploit incoming knowledge) to determine which resources to develop in the future.

Given that firms participating in inter-organizational collaborative arrangements are likely to obtain a certain proportion of both private and common benefits, the key challenge is to maintain an adequate balance between them in order to maintain desired longevity and stability of a particular collaboration (Zakrzewska-Bielawska, 2013; Czakon & Rogalski, 2012; Cygler, 2009; Stańczyk--Hugiet, 2011; Jankowska, 2012). Most of factors that drive differential payoffs from inter-organizational collaborations change over time as well as refer to firm's capacities to manage resources, therefore a comprehensive analysis of value appropriation in such structures inevitably requires incorporation of the dynamic capability perspective (DCP), the approach that introduced a dynamic dimension into a static theoretical landscape of the RBV (Priem & Butler, 2001).

Resuming, the RBV yields interesting and quite broad insights on performance differences between firms operating in similar environmental conditions. Provided explanations refer to distinctive resource positions resulting from ownership and implementation of strategic resources with characteristics serving as isolating mechanisms. Those isolating mechanisms support firms in capturing value on product and factor markets. Nevertheless, theory has been commonly criticized for providing a static view based on an assumption that necessary, unique resource configurations are already under control of a given firm. The missing parts concern a solid explanation of how resources are bundled and used to generate competitive advantage (Priem & Butler, 2001) and whether ownership of resources is a necessary condition for capturing a lion's share of created value (Lavie, 2007). This critique has triggered further studies aiming at addressing those unsolved issues. One strand of literature has been focusing on exploring the impact of resource position of a firm on the way a value generated through interorganizational collaboration is distributed among involved parties (Lavie, 2007; Dyer et al., 2008; Cygler, 2009; Zakrzewska-Bielawska, 2013). Presented research findings and discussions have relaxed the resource ownership rule proclaimed in the early works of the RBV, since firms may create and capture value using resources provided by collaborating partners. Studies contributing to the second strand of literature have been addressing the unsolved issues referring to resource management process. Theoretical and empirical exploration of underlying processes of acquiring, accumulating, bundling, deploying and divesting of resources in a given environmental context has lead to development of the dynamic capabilities perspective, which has reintroduced Penrose's seminal contribution to the RBV: "a firm may achieve rents not because it has better resources, but rather the firm's distinctive competence involves making better use of tit s resources" (Penrose, 1959, p. 54, after: Foss, 2005, p. 207). Enriched with a dynamic dimension the RBV provides a sound conceptual foundation for investigating managerial challenges in value appropriation.

2.2.4 PERSPECTIVE OF PROFITING FROM TECHNOLOGICAL INNOVATIONS

Scholarly works in the tradition of the RBV have provided a broad, generic picture of the competition for value created, while literature on profiting from technological innovations presents a more narrower, yet more detailed and nuanced view on the fundamental lever of value creation, i.e. innovation. The understanding of the relationship between value appropriation and innovation investments is by no means critical in a world characterized by strings of continuous innovations, since innovation process provide opportunities for both innovating pioneers and followers (Table 2.4). There is a rich pool of empirical evidence confirming that a successful completion of the innovation process not necessarily guarantees profits from the developed innovation (Teece, 1986; Schnaars, 1994; Teece, 2001; Shenkar, 2010), as bluntly stated by Gibson "the trouble with being a pioneer is that the pioneers get killed by the Indians" (Schnaars, 1994, p. 20).

Table 2.4 Advantages of first-movers and followers

First-movers	Followers
• Image derived from early entry • Creating brand loyalty • Technological leadership, experience effects • Setting product standards • Determining distribution channels • Legal protection of innovation	• Image created through fast adapting to market development • Lowering the price and improving the quality through product upgrading • Lower costs of educating customers • Technological leapfrogging • Avoiding lock-in with irreversible investments before development of the dominant design • Lower R&D expenditures and shifting capital to marketing • Use of knowledge leakages, inventing around, reverse engineering

Source: Najda-Janoszka (2012, p. 59).

Thus, given that firm's ability to appropriate value generated from innovation determines its performance, scholars contributing to the PI investigate availability and efficiency conditions of various mechanisms enabling both protection of innovations against imitation and capturing an adequate proportion of innovation returns. Most of contributions to the profiting from innovations stream of the literature are built on or derive in large extent from the basic framework formulated by Teece (1986). According to his proposal there are three main components that influence the share of value created an innovator can capture in comparison to its followers and suppliers: the appropriability regime, specialized complementary assets, and the dominant design paradigm.

The appropriability regime is govern by two dimensions, the nature of the technology and the efficacy of legal protection of intellectual assets (Teece, 1986). Characteristics of technology refers mainly to the degree of its transparency to current and potential rivals. Exposition to competitive duplication is a function of an inherent replicability of a given technology defined as susceptibility to redeployment or transfer from one economic setting to another (Teece, 2001, p. 16). From the perspective of an innovator replicability acts as a double sword, as on the one hand it generates opportunities for dynamic growth, product line expansion, learning and improvement, but on the other hand it raises the risk of competitive duplication, i.e. replication performed by other market players. An effective replication requires a deep process understanding that involves codification of the underlying tacit knowledge, as highlighted by Teece (2002, p. 18) "if the knowledge is highly tacit, it indicates that the phenomenon is not well understood." At the same time, the higher the range codified knowledge embedded within the innovation, the greater the likelihood of imitation. Therefore, according to Teece (1986) in order to keep the benefits from replicability and at the same time prevent imitation, enterprises should implement legal instruments for protecting their intellectual property.

Intellectual property embracing various creations of the mind and symbols used in commerce can be protected by the relevant intellectual property legislation. Intellectual property legislation confers exclusive rights on owners of a particular intellectual property to exploit it and prevent its unauthorized use (Adamczak & Du Vall, 2010). Provided legal enforcement mechanisms labeled as Intellectual Property Rights (IPR) or formal protection mechanisms are divided into industrial property rights (patents, industrial designs, utility models, trademarks), copyrights (for literary and artistic works, and computer software) and know-how (trade secrets).[14] Those legal mechanisms differ not only with respect to the nature of protected intellectual assets but also with regard to the implementation procedure (registration and disclosure requirement), duration and geographical scope of protection, costs incurred for obtaining, maintaining and enforcing the right (Table 2.5). Moreover, the characteristics and the extent of possible application of a particular mechanism may differ depending on the national law of a given country. For example, in the EU computer software is excluded from the patentable subject matter, while in the USA computer programs as well as business methods can be registered for patent protection.

The main generic function of IPR is to exclude other parties from exploiting results of one's own innovative activities, i.e. prevent imitation of the created new value. Hence, firms that implement formal protection mechanisms are expected to enjoy a strong bargaining position in the competition for value created because they are equipped with enforcement mechanisms for pursuing infringers for a certain time period. Meanwhile, empirical studies have provided a less enthusiastic picture, as most of them have confirmed a relatively limited effectiveness of protection provided by formal mechanisms (Cohen et al., 2000; Fischer, 2011). Those findings specifically concern patents, which are often invented around (Cohen et al., 2000; Teece, 2001; Fischer, 2011; Neuhäusler, 2012). Nevertheless, the number of patent applications is not decreasing because firms tend to exploit patents also for strategic purposes, such as (Cohen et al., 2000; Hall & Ziedonis, 2001; Neuhäusler, 2012):

- blocking competition – patents are used to exclude competitors from technology adjacent to firm's own innovations,
- generating licensing revenues – patents are used for enabling markets for technology while maintaining ownership exclusivity,
- cross-licensing – using own patents for accessing technologies possessed by competitors and thus enhancing a freedom to operate,
- deterrence of legal attacks – own patents are used for threatening counter-litigation,
- increasing firm's reputation – patents are used to attract customers and investors.

---

14 A thorough analysis of the nature and distinct characteristics of intellectual property rights protection mechanisms is presented in a collective study edited by Adamczak and Du Vall (2010).

Table 2.5 Main intellectual property rights provided by Polish legislation

	Patent	Industrial design	Utility design	Trademark	Copyright	Secret know-how
Protected property	Invention *(novelty and usefulness)*	Appearance *(novelty and usefulness)*	Technical process *(novelty and usefulness)*	Distinctive sign *(distinctiveness)*	Expression of idea *(originality and authorship)*	Secret information *(confidentiality)*
Registration requirement	Yes	Yes/No	Yes	Yes/No	No	No
Protection date	Date of a decision of National Patent Office	Date of an application	Date of a decision of National Patent Office	Date of a decision of National Patent Office	Fixation of an idea in a tangible medium of expression	Date of conception or receipt of secret information
Disclosure requirement	Yes	Yes	Yes	No	No	No
Duration of protection	20 years	5x5 years	10 years	10 years + voluntarily extended	Life of author + 70 years	Until disclosure
Geographical scope of protection	Country of registration	Country of registration	Country of registration	Country of registration	No limits	No limits
Cost of obtaining and maintaining protection	High	High	High	Moderate	Low	Low
Cost of enforcing rights	High	High	High	Moderate	Moderate	High

Source: Author's own work based on information provided by Polish Patent Office (http://www. uprp.pl, accessed 03.05.2015).

Thus, considering strategic purposes for using patents it is not a single patent that matters but the size of controlled patent portfolio. While discussing trends in using patents it is important to acknowledge a recent phenomenon of patent trolls, i.e. entities specializing in value appropriation without contributing to value creation (Fischer, 2011). Patent trolls hold on patents with no intention to manufacture products or license patented technology ex-ante to other market players. Instead those entities purposively wait until other firms infringe patents with successfully commercialized products. Then, patent trolls threaten a costly lawsuit by putting at risk further distribution of those products. Thus, the higher the importance of patented technology to final products that infringed the patent, the stronger the bargaining position of patent trolls in competition for value created by other firms. Activity of patent trolls is in a large extent concentrated in the software industry, because of the high complexity of computer programs that makes it difficult to clearly determine the owners of individual lines of the source code (Henkel & Baldwin, 2009; Fischer, 2011; Najda-Janoszka, 2012).

According to the business practice innovating firms may experience varying levels of legal protection. It is due to the fact that not every new value created by a firm can be protected by the intellectual property rights (Jennewein, 2005), as well as availability and efficacy of formal mechanisms of protection vary with respect to different factors embracing specificity of a given innovation, firm and sector/industry characteristics (Teece, 2001; Jennewein, 2005; Fischer, 2011). Moreover, as evidenced by numerous empirical investigations the spectrum of instruments used by firms to protect innovations and maximize expected returns is much wider than the scope of mechanisms enforced by law (Table 2.6). Some of those instruments, commonly labeled as informal mechanisms, refer directly to the problem of inherent replicability of an innovation (e.g. secrecy, complexity) and as such were included in Teece's (1986) original concept of appropriability regime. Table 2.6 presents a summary of key results from earlier studies that describe the influence of those factors on the use of formal and informal protection mechanisms.

Teece (1986, 2001) argues that depending on a characteristics of a particular invention and efficacy of legal mechanisms of protection in prohibiting spillovers, appropriation regime can be tight or weak. Tight appropriation regime is the most desirable one, because it provides sufficient conditions for capturing at least some proportion of the value generated by innovation. With a lack of similar products on the market innovators are not forced to compete by offering high customer surpluses. However, given that a tight appropriation regime requires a low inherent replicability of innovation together with a highly effective legal protection, in the economic reality such conditions are rather an exception than a rule (Teece, 1986, 2001). Most often firms have to manage value appropriation in weak appropriability regimes. According to Teece (1986), when the underlying technology is inherently easy to replicate and legal protection mechanisms are hardly available or ineffective, then the opportunity for capturing at least a positive fraction of created value depends on the access to complementary assets necessary for successful implementation of innovation. In case of a tight appropriability regime control over complementary assets enhances an already favorable position of an innovator (Figure 2.4). Technological innovations are characterized by a strong functional interrelatedness and dependencies between their internal sub-systems and incumbent solutions. Therefore successful innovation requires a careful management of those linkages to complementary services (e.g. marketing, manufacturing, after-sales support) and technologies, e.g. entering the market with new data storage technology requires availability of its complementary readers.

Table 2.6 Factors influencing the use of protection mechanisms

Survey studies			
Kitching & Blackburn (1998) – small firms in the UK operating in four high-tech sectors	Arundel & Kabla (1998) – European R&D performing firms	Cohen et al. (2000) – R&D performing manufacturing firms in the USA	Hall & Ziedonis (2001) – firms operating in semiconductor industry in the USA
Arundel (2001) – innovative manufacturing firms in 7 European countries	Blind et al. (2006) – innovative manufacturing firms in Germany	Tether & Massini (2007) – service and manufacturing firms in the UK	Leiponen & Byma (2009) – technology-intensive small firms in Finland
Hurmelinna-Laukkanen & Ritala (2012) – R&D performing firms in Finland	Neuhäusler (2012) – innovative manufacturing firms in Germany	Thomä & Bizer (2013) – innovative small firms in Germany	Najda-Janoszka (2014a,b) – small tourism firms in Poland

Factors	Description of influence	Relevant study
Firm size	SMEs face higher resource constraints in effective implementing formal mechanisms and in enforcing property rights. Large firms exhibit higher proficiency in conducting patenting procedures and enforcing property rights	Kitching & Blackburn (1998); Arundel & Kabla (1998); Cohen et al. (2000); Arundel (2001); Leiponen & Byma (2009); Thomä & Bizer (2013)
	U-shaped relationship between size of a firm and a number of patent applications: large and small firms are very active while medium sized firms provide a negligible contribution to the number of patent applications	Neuhäusler (2012)
	Low propensity of smaller firms to adopt IPRs is related to the specific nature of their innovation regime	Thomä & Bizer (2013); Najda-Janoszka (2014a,b)
	Small firms exhibit different motivation for strategic use of formal appropriability mechanisms aiming at reputation enhancement, acquiring financing and alliance partners. Large firms focus mainly on blocking competition, cross-licensing and providing incentives for R&D personnel	Cohen et al. (2000); Hall & Ziedonis (2001); Blind et al., (2006); Neuhäusler (2012)
Research intensity	R&D intensity is positively related to the likelihood to patent innovations	Blind et al. (2006); Leiponen & Byma (2009); Neuhäusler (2012)
Cooperation in R&D	Inter-organizational cooperation in R&D increases the value of formal mechanisms, as patent portfolio is used as a strong argument in bargaining over ownership of cooperative output	Cohen et al. (2000); Arundel (2001)
	Innovative SMEs that engage in cooperative R&D do not perceive secrecy and formal methods of protection as effective and important. SMEs prefer a quick market launch	Leiponen & Byma (2009)

Factors	Description of influence	Relevant study
Internationalization	Importance of patents increases with the number of foreign markets a firm operates in.	Neuhäusler (2012); Thomä & Bizer (2013)
	Firms more active on an international scale use patents more frequently for strategic purposes	Neuhäusler (2012)
	Formal protection mechanisms play a key role in affecting the likelihood of service-oriented firms to internationalize	Hurmelinna--Laukkanen & Ritala (2012);
Sector/industry specificity	Firms in discrete product industries (e.g. chemicals) tend to use patents to block development of substitutes by rivals. Firms operating in complex product industries (e.g. semiconductors) tend to use patents to force rivals to negotiations. Patent portfolio races are observable in complex product industries	Cohen et al. (2000)
	There is an increasing "complexity" in all sectors. Sector differences can only be observed selectively with regard to strategic motives for using protection mechanisms.	Blind et al. (2006)
	Firms operating in industries characterized by a short product life cycle and fast pace of technological advance are more prone to use informal protection methods (e.g. lead time)	Hall & Ziedonis (2001)
	Service firms are less inclined to use formal protection mechanisms than manufacturing firms	Tether & Massini (2007); Leiponen & Byma (2009); Najda--Janoszka (2014a, b)
	Manufacturing and service industries differ by the average number of protection method used. Manufacturing firms tend to use more complex combinations of protection methods	Tether & Massini (2007)
Innovation type	Process, marketing and organizational innovations tend to be protected by informal protection mechanisms	Najda-Janoszka (2014a, b)
	Firm introducing more than one type of innovation tend to use complex protection strategies involving several formal and informal protection methods	Tether & Massini (2007)

Source: Author's own work.

Teece (1986) differentiated among three different types of complementary assets: generic, specialized, and co-specialized. Assets defined as generic can be easily contracted in the market on competitive terms, since do not require any major adjustments to a given innovation. On the contrary specialized and co-specialized assets are those that are somehow tailored to a particular innovation. The former type exhibits an unilateral dependence with the innovation, that is either the complementary asset depends on the innovation or the innovation depends on the complementary asset. The latter category, the co-specialized assets are those for which dependence goes in both directions simultaneously.

In most cases innovators are not endowed with all necessary complementary assets as it is impossible to keep pace in all complementary areas of technology. The strategic choice for an innovator that aims at strengthening its bargaining position in competition for value created is to either expand by integrating into complementary assets (build internally or acquire) or engage in contractual relation with providers of such assets (Teece, 2001). While acquiring generic assets usually does not cause major problems, gaining access to specialized and co-specialized complementary assets is more challenging and time consuming. Specialization of assets implies special purpose, irreversible investments that raise the risks for the engaged party. Thus, the control over complementary assets gains in importance with a greater degree of asset specialization. In weak appropriability regimes owners of co/specialized complementary assets are expected to capture a lion's share of the value generated by the innovation (Ceccagnoli & Rothaermel, 2008). When given innovation can be easily imitated an innovator is not afforded enough time to build or acquire specialized/co-specialized complementary assets. Hence, in a competition for value created such an innovator often loses out to imitators or assets providers (Figure 2.4). Further, it is argued that for an innovator introducing a new value in a regime of a weak appropriability, opportunities for capturing a positive fraction of value created are determined by a lead time and ex-ante positioning in the necessary co/specialized complementary assets (Teece, 1986).

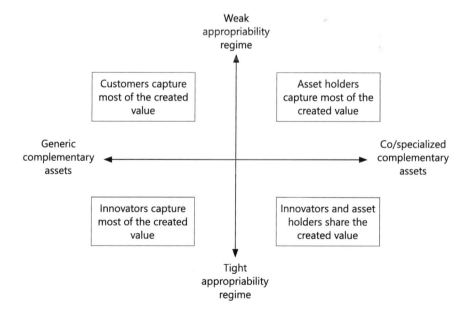

Figure 2.4 Profiting from technological innovations according to Teece
Source: Author's own work based on Teece (1986, 2001).

When an innovator does not possess required co/specialized complementary assets, but the regime of appropriation remains tight, a viable option is to co-develop a new product under a contractual agreement with the provider of necessary assets. High barriers to imitation are the key argument in deciding on irreversible investments on both sides of that contract. At the same time "the situation is one open to opportunistic abuses on both sides" (Teece, 1986, p. 294). Cooperative interorganizational structures initiated to jointly commercialize innovations usually involve capability transfer that further triggers learning races between engaged parties (Hamel, 1991). As pointed out by Ceccagnoli and Rothaermel (2008), due to their larger resource portfolio, holders of co/specialized assets are more advantageously positioned to learn and acquire innovation capabilities. According to the existing empirical evidence on contractual arrangements in pharmaceutical industry, the holder of specialized complementary assets is more likely to acquire upstream technological capabilities than the other way around (Rothaermel & Deeds, 2004; Ceccagnoli & Rothaermel, 2008). Moreover, with the competence-destroying technological discontinuities, i.e. radical innovations, that emerge exogenous to incumbent industries, a strategic positioning and performance of incumbent holders of complementary assets improve either due to their financial strength in case of necessary generic capacities or due to R&D capabilities in case of specialized assets required for commercialization of a breakthrough innovation (Rothaermel & Deeds, 2004).

Resuming, the distribution of value generated from innovation commercialized in contractual arrangements depends strongly on the bargaining power of each party engaged in a contract (Teece, 1986). This bargaining power is determined not only by the size of involved partners but also by the stage in the evolutionary development of a given industry or a branch. Drawing on the work of Dosi (1982), Abernathy and Utterback (1978), Teece (1986) differentiated two basic stages, the preparadigmatic and paradigmatic one. At the preparadigmatic stage there is no single generally accepted technological content and/or design of newly introduced products, hence, firms compete for developing a dominant design. The second stage in the evolutionary development of an industry, the paradigmatic stage, begins once a dominant design emerges. Acceptance of agreed upon standards results in a shift in a competitive struggle away from design towards prices (Teece, 1986). In both stages the critical factor is the time, either for performing necessary trials (preparadigmatic stage) or for accessing necessary generic and co/specialized complementary assets. In the case of a tight appropriability regime innovators are afforded a comfortable time advantage regardless of the industry development stage. Conversely, in a weak appropriability regime innovators struggle with a limited time and generally also disadvantageous position against providers of complementary assets.

Discussion on the preparadigmatic and paradigmatic stage sheds more light on the importance of the time of entry to the market. Temporal advantage of an innovator is considered a highly effective mechanism for capturing value from innovations, often evaluated as more efficient relative to patents, trademarks or business secrets (Fischer, 2011, p. 29–30). With a temporal advantage innovators can strengthen their ability to capture value generated from innovation, since they are afforded necessary time for strengthening bargaining power in relation to customers (limited competition, raising switching costs), strategic positioning on the market of complementary assets, moving along learning curve (Fischer, 2011, p. 28). Innovators taking advantage of a temporary monopoly can intensify marketing activities to maximize market exploitation of an innovation and at the same time invest in development of subsequent new solutions before competitors manage to imitate already implemented innovation (Jennewein, 2005, pp. 180–181). Hence, a lead time advantage is particularly important for firms operating in sectors characterized by a short life cycle of technology and products (Najda-Janoszka, 2012).

Although the definition of appropriability regime proposed by Teece has been widely recognized in the literature, recent studies have challenged the way appropriability regime should be conceptualized and understood. Drawing on the extant literature and conducted empirical research Hurmelinna--Laukkanen and Puumalainen (2007) introduced a new conceptual framework for investigating appropriability regime. They claim that, since appropriability regime reflects "the extent to which innovators can be protected from imitators" (Hurmelinna-Laukkanen & Puumalainen, 2007, p. 96), it should embrace all appropriability mechanisms besides the nature of the core knowledge and intellectual proprerty rights (IPRs). Consequently, Hurmelinna-Laukkanen and Puumalainen (2007) proposed a new categorization of appropriability regime consisting of five mechanisms: nature of knowledge (tacit, codified), institutional protection (IPRs, formal contracts, labor legislation), human resource management (communication control, (im)mobility of human resources), practical/technical means (passwords, secrecy, access), lead time (market entry, continuous development). Moreover, this extended conceptualization is based on an assumption that availability and efficacy of a given protection mechanism is shaped not only by external factors but also other mechanism that constitute appropriability regime. Thus, that new proposal provided a more comprehensive picture of appropriability regime, that enhances the understanding of the dynamic nature of the concept.

Usefulness of that new conceptualization introduced by Hurmelinna--Laukkanen and Puumalainen (2007) is evident when considering results of the extant empirical investigations confirming that firms tend to use more than one mechanism to protect streams of value generated by developed innovation, i.e. different elements of an innovation are protected by different protection instruments and/or mechanisms employed vary in subsequent phases of the innovation process (Cohen et al., 2000; Hussinger, 2006). Given that the degree to which firms profit from innovation is shaped by the interplay between imitation-related factors, the understanding of the logic of the relationship between appropriability and innovation investment is critical for making strategic managerial decisions concerning allocation of resources for parallel processes of new value creation and appropriation. As emphasized by Baden-Fuller and Haefliger (2013, p. 424), the choice of a business model of a firm, which reflects its logic for creating and appropriating value "influences the way in which technology is monetized", yet "the business model may need to change in order to appropriate features of [developed] technology." It has been observed that in order to retain freedom to operate and maximize returns from innovations a growing number of firms has departed from a traditional approach focused on basic protective function of intellectual property rights toward a more strategic use of available protection mechanisms. This reorientation manifests itself not only in a dynamic trend of patent portfolio development, or a common use of informal protection mechanisms, but also in a relatively recent phenomenon of know-how externalization under the open innovation paradigm (Chesbrough, 2003). According to the open innovation paradigm firms make a greater strategic use of external knowledge (outside-in approach) and simultaneously decide to externalize certain components of their intellectual property. By opening up an innovation process to third parties (customers, suppliers, universities, competitors), a formerly protected know how becomes a means for knowledge exchange, which is expected to ultimately lead to additional monetary and strategic benefits (Powell et al., 1996; Chesbrough, 2003). However, intellectual property release under the open innovation paradigm implies giving a particular know-how away for free. Thus, there is no contractual definition of compensation. Benefits to be obtained through know-how release are much more uncertain, time-extended and difficult to estimate. Nonetheless, the literature on open intellectual property approaches distinguishes three main motives for releasing proprietary know-how:

- economic – maximizing profits by providing complementary products and services (installation, trainings, consultancy, maintenance) and lowering internal R&D costs,
- technological – improvement of quality and applicability of technology through knowledge in-sourcing, promoting developed technological standard (dominant design),
- social – enhancing corporate reputation, gaining social legitimacy.

Given that open innovation model does not imply externalization of all possessed knowledge assets, a given firm needs to develop a coherent strategy for simultaneous protecting and sharing its proprietary components of know-how. In order to solve this managerial dilemma Henkel and Baldwin (2009) formulated a concept of Intellectual Property Modularization (IPM) built on the idea of a modular production system (Tu et al., 2004). They assumed that modularization[15] can be equally effectively applied to products, processes, task forces as to knowledge assets. Thus, according to the developed concept of IPM, a modular system of knowledge implies a division of knowledge into components that are subject to a different treatment in the sphere of intellectual property (different IP status). Given that one of the basic guidelines of a modular system design is to encapsulate strongly interdependent elements in one module, Henkel and Baldwin (2009) claim that a single knowledge module should contain only compatible elements with regard to their IPR status. Further, with a modular system of knowledge as a baseline, a firm should design its product, process and task force modules in accordance with corresponding modules intellectual property (Henkel & Baldwin, 2009). Open innovation models together with modular production systems have been considered quite problematic for value appropriation, since both concepts encourage new players (i.e. potential competitors) to enter the market (Teece, 2001. Meanwhile, a modular approach to knowledge enhances management of outgoing and incoming intellectual property in open innovation systems (Najda--Janoszka, 2011), and reduces the risk that partners innovating on product modules would compete away the rents (Henkel & Baldwin, 2009). Extending modularization from physical production process to intellectual property allows for managing a right balance between systemic and autonomous innovations triggering product development. Although partners may innovate on modules, a focal firm maintains proprietary those areas of knowledge that are sensitive and necessary for innovating at the product architecture level, or the other way around when a focal firm decides to keep modules proprietary, while discloses system of interfaces (Henkel & Baldwin, 2009). Nevertheless, despite the discussed opportunities, intellectual property modularization always comes at cost. Hence, a decision on opening the innovation system and introducing a modular system of knowledge involves critical strategic trade-offs to be thoroughly considered. Nevertheless, there is a lack of a sound empirical evidence evaluating whether open or closed approach generates an overall greater innovative performance. Similarly, the question of openness frontier, a point where openness becomes counterproductive, has not been examined yet.

Extant literature on profiting from technological innovations provides valuable and detailed insights into factors affecting the potential of firms to capture value generated from innovations. Presented discussions and

---

15 Modularity describes "the degree to which a system's components can be separated and recombined, and it refers both to the tightness of coupling between components and the degree to which the rules of the system architecture enable (or prohibit) the mixing and matching of components" (Schilling, 2000, p. 312).

empirical investigations reach beyond the narrow, protective approach. A number of studies confirms that protection mechanisms are indeed utilized more widely than just as barriers to imitation. Thus, the strategic approach gains in importance. Firms tend to use those protection mechanisms as means for direct creation of value and as strategic tools that enable competitive position enhancement. Emergence of open innovation paradigm fits perfectly into this strategic shift. Nevertheless, given the number of diverse factors influencing in various ways the efficacy of protection mechanisms (Table 2.6), there is a need for further studies focused on potential nonlinearities in protective and strategic effectiveness of those mechanisms. Those nonlinearities may substantially affect the optimal resource configuration for successful value appropriation (Fischer, 2011).

2.3 RECAPITULATING STRATEGIC MANAGEMENT PERSPECTIVE ON VALUE APPROPRIATION

The theoretical grounding for discussing the problem of value appropriation is wide-ranging and rich with useful, enlightening insights. Although the aim of this study is to contribute to development of the strategic management theory, it is necessary to map those broad intellectual roots in order to assess the state of art on the subject matter. According to the discussion presented in this Chapter current view of the problem of value capture in the management field is shaped in a great part by the economic understanding of the notion of value and residual claimacy. This economic insight is the salient point of departure to the management field that provides a collection of subsequently developed, complementary concepts that build one upon another (Figure 2.5). Thus, the aim of this Chapter was to present a comprehensive picture of that diverse collection.

The discussion has embraced the input of industrial organization scholarship concerning the impact of structural conditions and a firm's positioning on the value appropriation potential. Then, the focus has been shifted toward a different conceptual lens provided by game theory frameworks in order to provide more clear ramifications of interaction between value capture actions of positioning and restricting competitive forces. Further, guided by the main objective of strategic management as to explain performance differentials between firms, the discussion has reached a different level of the analysis that enabled opening of the "black box" and exploration of firms' resource endowments and isolating mechanisms that support firms in capturing value on product and factor markets. Building on the notion of isolating mechanisms the theoretical picture has been enriched by the concept of profiting from innovations and insights informing on the strategic approach to the use of formal and informal protection mechanisms.

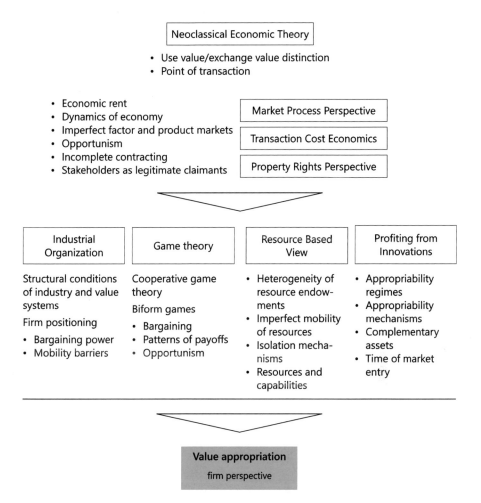

Figure 2.5 Theoretical foundations of value appropriation
Source: Author's own work.

Concluding, the Chapter has highlighted most relevant features of a broad collection of ideas developed mainly in the field of management but also in economics. The aim was not to generalize complex streams of the scholarly work but to provide useful insights into subtle points pertinent to the problem of value appropriation. Therefore, the result is a persuasive illustration of interconnected theoretical contributions that build current understanding of value appropriation at an organizational level.

3   DYNAMIC CAPABILITIES PERSPECTIVE

The dynamics of the environment, observed and experienced through a more and more intensive globalization, integration and interdependence of markets, forces firms toward incorporation of that dynamics into their strategic management in order to grow, and most importantly to survive (D'Aveni, 1994; Banaszczyk & Cyfert, 2007). A strategic attempt to effectively exploit changes in the environment needs to be supported by inevitable modifications in deployed patterns of action. Thus, a thorough understanding of development of competitive advantages in such unstable conditions requires an approach that directly addresses the problem of change. An emerging concept of dynamic capabilities represents a relatively new and promising approach to explore strategic renewal (Cyfert, 2012), since it is characterized by an inherent focus on change. The field has been generating a significant and systematic growth of scholarly attention. Outcomes of that research effort confirm a substantial move forward on a developmental path of dynamic capabilities from a vague and obscure concept toward a cohesive paradigm. However, despite that remarkable flow of research, the framework still retains some unsolved issues and inconsistencies regarding its core elements. Thus, this Chapter aiming at providing a comprehensive view of the state of art is organized as follows. Firstly, the discussion concerns a theoretical grounding of the dynamic capabilities perspective in order to capture the complexity of the framework by recognizing multisource flows of theoretical contributions. Further, this broad base of theoretical foundations of the dynamic capabilities perspective is used as a point of departure for analyzing terminological issues. Clarification on key concepts and terms used in the dynamic capabilities perspective is followed by a thorough operationalization of the construct. Based on a review of seminal approaches presented in the literature a cohesive interpretation is attributed to relations between the overall construct and its components, and among the components as well. Finally, the Chapter presents an overview of the extant empirical studies on dynamic capabilities in order to characterize main directions of exploration in the field and to identify underdeveloped areas.

3.1 DEFINING DYNAMIC CAPABILITIES

It is quite challenging to define a newly introduced concept such as the dynamic capabilities perspective in a way that is at once precise and comprehensive. For one part, the perspective is still at a relatively early stage of development, for the other part its development is driven by contributions from diverse fields. Thus, in order to describe the logic of the dynamic capabilities perspective, as well as limitations and directions of further development, it is fundamental to recognize the theoretical grounding of the perspective in the first place. Accordingly, this chapter begins with a discussion on the main theoretical streams of contributions that shape the multidimensional nature of dynamic capabilities. It is followed by a thorough review of existing approaches to defining dynamic capabilities.

3.1.1 INTELLECTUAL ROOTS OF THE DYNAMIC CAPABILITIES PERSPECTIVE

The concept of dynamic capabilities is embedded within a broad context of scientific discussion concerning firm's survival and growth (Figure 3.1). Presented description of intellectual roots of the dynamic capabilities perspective entails those concepts and ideas, whose contribution has been unambiguously acknowledged in the most influential research works on dynamic capabilities.

In most scholarly works the dynamic capabilities perspective is recognized as an extension of the resource base view of the firm (RBV) (Eisenhardt & Martin, 2000; Wang & Ahmed, 2007), since it emerged on the theoretical grounding of the RBV. Both approaches share fundamental assumptions regarding heterogeneity of resource bundles in the context of the competitive advantage of a firm, yet the dynamic capabilities concept has been developed to overcome substantial shortcomings of the static perspective exhibited in the RBV. While the RBV stresses that the basis for a competitive advantage is located in unique bundles of special resources (valuable, rare, inimitable, non-substitutable), the dynamic capabilities framework concentrate on change, on creating, extending and reconfiguring resources over time. Thus, the dynamic capabilities perspective with its dynamic efficiency nicely complements the main prescription of the RBV that concerns the importance of allocative efficiency for achieving a sustainable competitive advantage.

Refocusing research efforts toward changes in productive opportunities of firms was triggered by a fundamental distinction emphasized by Penrose (1959) between stocks – resources defined as inputs in the production process, and flows – services that may be obtained from resources. In other words,

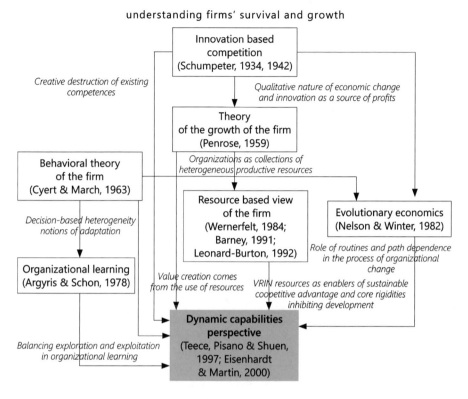

Figure 3.1 Theoretical background of the dynamic capabilities perspective
Source: Author's own updated version of Najda-Janoszka (2015, p. 36).

resources can be understood as bundles of potential services and "the services [actually] yielded by resources are a function of the way in which they are used" (Penrose, 1959, p. 25). Hence, according to Penrose, unused resources should be viewed as "concealed form of unused abilities" (Penrose, 1959, p. 54). This logical distinction provided the rationale for introducing the concept of capabilities as notions of aforementioned services and potential sources of inter-firm heterogeneity. Given that services rendered by resources reflect the knowledge and experience of the firm gained over time (path-dependency), they are expected to encapsulate the key idiosyncrasies underlying firm heterogeneity. Moreover, the optimal growth of the firm reaches beyond a mere resource superiority ex ante and a defined pool of services yielded by those resources. Economic growth requires a delicate balance between exploitation of existing resources and development of new ones, which is nourished by a dynamic tension between internal knowledge development and external knowledge acquisition (Penrose, 1959). Hence, those important insights have triggered a discussion on effective management of resources involving a balanced sequence of resource development, acquisition, absorption, deployment, and release, further explored and conceptualized as processes and routines underlying dynamic capabilities. Penrose's canonical intellectual input (Cockburn et al., 2000) refers also to the recognition of managerial capacities as constraints setting limits to firm's growth and acknowledgement of the role of entrepreneurs in discovery of productive opportunities (Augier & Teece, 2008). Nevertheless, although Penrose's direct and intentional contribution does not refer to strategy prescriptions for creating sustainable streams of value, provided brilliant analysis of processes through which firms grow has substantially informed the descriptive building blocks of firstly the RBV and then the dynamic capabilities perspective (Rugman & Verbeke, 2002).

Given that the conceptual focus of the dynamic capabilities perspective is on a continuous integration, development and reconfiguration of firm-specific resources, a thorough exploration of those processes requires a sound understanding of an organizational and technological change provided by the theory of entrepreneurial management. In the context of rapidly changing environments open to global competition, firm strategic behavior involves more than mere control and coordination of certain resources. A broader set of tasks embracing proactive search, opportunity identification and evaluation is expected to be performed under an entrepreneurial function of management (Bratnicki, 2011). The research effort under the dynamic capabilities framework is directed toward identifying ways in which firms can effectively adjust to or even shape market shocks and discontinuities in their competitive environment (Teece et al., 1997; Helfat, 1997). By aiming at processes of renewal and reconfiguration of the resource base, dynamic capabilities support development of corresponding innovations and realization of Schumpeterian rents (Teece et al., 1997). Hence, the intellectual roots of dynamic capabilities perspective reach down to Schumpeterian innovation-based competition and "a creative destruction" process, which implies that introduced isolating mechanisms can provide only a temporary protection of a competitive advantage (Schumpeter, 1934, 1942). Many scholars emphasize a clear and close link between entrepreneurship and the dynamic capabilities perspective (e.g. Teece et al., 1997; Madsen, 2010; Bratnicki, 2011).

According to the dynamic capabilities perspective the strategy of a firm is conceptualized as an integration of evolutionary processes with an intentional design (Augier & Teece, 2008). Thus, the approach emphasizes the role of managers, their strategic choices that shape the performance of a firm. Locating managers at the core of the concept, giving priority to adaptation over determinism, reveals an evident influence of the behavioral theory of the firm, that "takes the firm as a basic unit, the prediction of firm behavior with respect to such decisions as price, output and resource allocation as its objective, and an explicitly emphasis on the actual process of organizational decision making as its basic research commitment" (Cyert & March, 1963, p. 19). The behavioral theory explains functioning of firms by analyzing individual bargaining that leads to setting of organizational goals; the way bounded rationality affects gathering and interpretation of information, which in turn form organizational expectations; decision making through the use of operating procedures in line with current aspiration levels for specified goals; and resulting choice affected by the past experience (Cyert & March, 1963). According to Cyert and March (1963) each firm is uniquely defined by its distinctive goals, expectations and standard operating procedures. Thus, the key contribution to development of the dynamic capability perspective refers to the assumption of decision-based fundamental heterogeneity of firms (Augier & Teece, 2008). The behavioral theory has provided important insights into the inward tension between inherent organizational rigidity and adaptation. Decision processes are affected on the one hand by the dynamic nature of aspirations that enable generating new decision alternatives, on the other hand by the path-dependent nature of standard operating procedures that provide internal consistency and stability, yet hamper flexibility of a firm's strategic behavior. Those standard operating procedures are built from the entirety of previous experience of a firm and as self-enforcing characteristic cannot be easily altered or modified. At the same time they are inherently heterogeneous across firms and have a critical influence on the unique character of a firm. According to Augier and Teece (2008) this implies that adaptation of standard operating procedures to the dynamic environment is possible, albeit difficult, and firms may exhibit different abilities to introduce changes into their strategic behavior. Thus, the dynamic capability perspective directly draws on and develop further the concept of standard operating procedures.

Standard operating procedures formed the conceptual basis for exploring the role of underlying organizational routines as enablers and constraints of organizational change (Nelson & Winter, 1982). According to Nelson and Winter (1982), those self-sustaining patterns of interactions in a group behavior define how firms solve observable problems. Given that firms tend to work out similar problems by deploying successful approaches used in the past, organizational routines serve as storages of the organizational memory. This implies that organizational routines contain collective and, for most part, highly tacit knowledge of a firm. Hence, according to evolutionary economics those routines are unique to a firm and form the basis for rent seeking strategies of firms. Nevertheless, while a continuous redeployment of organizational routines strengthens their existence in a firm, it also makes them quit difficult to change. As firms are expected to respond and adapt to environmental changes, those repetitive patterns of activity need to be altered to fit new strategic circumstances. Discussing the possibility for changing operational routines Nelson and Winter (1982) turned toward organizational learning processes and distinguished ordinary-static routines that enable effective replication of previously performed tasks, and dynamic routines aimed at learning and generating innovations. Thus, it lead to a conclusion that firms can alter routinized responses through search and learning, yet those critical processes are also expected to be conducted in a patterned fashion based on previous experience (Besanko et al., 2010, pp. 455–456). By shedding light on the enduring problem of path dependency in the strategic behavior of firms, Nelson and Winter (1982) provided an appealing framework for analyzing opportunities and constraints determining strategic renewal of a firm. All seminal conceptualizations developed under the dynamic capabilities perspective have been greatly inspired by the concept of path-dependent organizational routines. By recognizing that "organizational learning is accomplished through and embedded in routines/procedures" (Pierce et al., 2002, p. 88) scholars that contributed to development of the dynamic capabilities perspective reached for useful insights provided by the theory of organizational learning (Argyris & Schon, 1978) in order to explain how dynamic capabilities are created and developed. Drawing on the ideas of a single-loop and double loop learning and balancing knowledge exploration with exploitation (Argyris & Schon, 1978; March, 1991), the subsequent research works have considered learning either as a fundament that originates and drives the evolution of dynamic capabilities (Eisehnardt & Martin, 2000; Zollo & Winter, 2002) or as a dynamic capability itself (Teece et al., 1997).

This broad base of theoretical foundations of the dynamic capabilities perspective briefly outlined above, undoubtedly "reflects the breadth and complexity of the issues under consideration" (Helfat & Peteraf, 2003, p. 93). Hence, the conceptualization and operationalization of dynamic capabilities is recognized as a quite challenging task (Wang & Ahmed, 2007; Helfat & Peteraf, 2003; Ambrosini & Bowman, 2009; Zahra et al., 2006). Nevertheless, as an outhgrowth of discussed intellectual streams, the theoretical content of the concept of dynamic capabilities provides a sound ground for enhacing the undertstanding of managing a delicate balance between system stability and adaptability to changing circumstances.

3.1.2 TERMINOLOGICAL CHALLENGES

Since the seminal article written by Teece et al. (1997), the field of dynamic capabilities has been generating a significant and systematic growth of scholarly attention. According to ABI/INFORM database by the mid-2014 the number of scientific works referred directly to "dynamic capabilities" reached a remarkable level of 6885 (as of 20 June 2014). Hence, existing literature provides a wide spectrum of definitions as well as distinct views on the concept resulting from different research backgrounds of scholars contributing to the field of dynamic capabilities.

Table 3.1 Key definitions of dynamic capabilities presented in the most cited articles

Source	Citations of the article*	Definition
Teece et al. (1997)	4 419	Firm's ability to integrate, build, and reconfigure internal and external competences to address rapidly changing environments.
Eisenhardt & Martin (2000)	2 107	The firm's processes that use resources – specifically the processes to integrate, reconfigure, gain and release resources – to match and even create market change. Dynamic capabilities thus are the organizational and strategic routines by which firms achieve new resource configurations as markets emerge, collide, split, evolve, and die.
Zahra & George (2002)	1 343	Dynamic capabilities are embedded in organizational processes and (...) enable the firm to reconfigure its resource base and adapt to changing market conditions in order to achieve a competitive advantage.
Zollo & Winter (2002)	1 080	A dynamic capability is a learned and stable pattern of collective activity through which the organization systematically generates and modifies its operating routines in pursuit of improved effectiveness.
Teece (2007)	670	These (dynamic) capabilities can be harnessed to continuously create, extend, upgrade, protect, and keep relevant the enterprise's unique asset base. Dynamic capabilities can be disaggregated into the capacity (1) to sense and shape opportunities and threats, (2) to seize opportunities, and (3) to maintain competitiveness through enhancing, combining, protecting, and, when necessary, reconfiguring the business enterprise's intangible and tangible assets.
Winter (2003)	574	Those (capabilities) that operate to extend, modify or create ordinary capabilities.

* Web of Science Core Collection (as of 30 June 2014)
Source: Najda-Janoszka (2015, p. 38).

Successively introduced definitions, built on the initial one (Teece et al., 1997) and incrementally improved on the basis of generated cumulative knowledge, reflect the evolvement of the research on dynamic capabilities. Consequently, the existing literature provides a considerable amount of definitions exhibiting different degree of conciseness and comprehensiveness with regard to the logic of dynamic capabilities. Nevertheless, the dynamic capabilities perspective is an emerging field of inquiry, still at an early stage of development from "an approach" toward "a theory" (Helfat & Peteraf, 2009). Hence, bearing in mind other examples of emerging theories, i.e. transaction cost theory, proliferation of definitions is a common occurrence at early stages of theory development and reaching a consensus takes rather a long time (Helfat & Peteraf, 2009). As exhibited on Table 3.1, main definitions presented in the most cited articles referring to "dynamic capabilities" vary in several aspects indicating existence of distinct perspectives on the nature of dynamic capabilities. On the basis of a thorough review of definitions presented in the extant literature Madsen (2010) has distinguished three main approaches to defining dynamic capabilities: (1) thorough results, which commonly refer to competitive advantage (e.g. Griffith & Harvey, 2001; Zahra & George, 2002); (2) by focusing on the presence of external conditions (e.g. Teece et al., 1997; Eisehnardt & Martin, 2000); (3) by focusing on activities which make a firm dynamic (e.g. Winter, 2003; Zahra et al., 2006). However, a growing number of studies have questioned the assumptions proclaimed by the first two approaches (Madsen, 2010; Helfat et al., 2007; Barreto, 2010) by emphasizing an indirect relationship between dynamic capabilities and firm performance (Eisenhardt & Martin, 2000; Helfat & Peteraf, 2003; Ambrosini & Bowman, 2009), intrinsic impossibility to isolate an individual impact of a single dynamic capability (Madsen, 2010), applicability of the concept to conditions of relatively stable environments (Eisenhardt & Martin, 2000; Helfat & Winter, 2011), as well as to internally generated changes (Madsen, 2010; Helfat & Winter, 2011). Hence, it can be observed a tendency in the recent research to define and explore dynamic capabilities in accordance with the latter approach, which links the concept with the organizational dynamics (e.g. Helfat et al., 2007; Pavlou & El Sawy, 2011; Kuuluvainen, 2013). Accordingly this study builds on this perspective, which conceive dynamic capabilities in terms of capacity to purposively transform the resource base of an organization in response to internal and external signals.

Although there is a general agreement on the idea that dynamic capabilities involve an intentional reconfiguration of the resource base of an organization, yet an overview of main definitions indicates some important areas of ambiguity. Aiming at explaining the nature of dynamic capabilities scholars use a broad array of terms: abilities, processes, routines, competences. Defining dynamic capabilities as ability raised arguments of tautology, whereas referring to a process and routine without further explanation of the distinction between used terms escalated criticism against the concept as being vague and elusive (Williamson, 1999; Wang & Ahmed, 2007). Thus, in the subsequent studies scholars have put much effort to address those concerns and provide an unambiguous terminology (Wang & Ahmed, 2007; Helfat & Winter, 2011; Helfat & Peteraf, 2015). At the base line all the main approaches to dynamic capabilities draw on the fundamental distinction between resources (stocks) and capabilities (flows) (Penrose, 1959; Amit & Schoemaker, 1993; Grant, 1991). It is assumed that resources as inputs into the production process are the sources of capabilities (Grant, 1991). Resources are reservoirs of potential services and in order to generate value they need to be bundled, activated and coordinated. Hence, capabilities are notions of services yielded by resources (Penrose, 1959). As suggested by Grant (1991), organizational capabilities can be identified by referring to functional areas of firm's activity such as human resource management, financial control, market research etc. Recognizing that firm's activities can be performed according to various approaches, it is argued that, in contrast to ad-hoc initiatives, capabilities involve patterned and collective behavior that enable repeated and reliable performance (Grant, 1991; Helfat & Winter, 2011). Such a view of capabilities was largely informed by the concept of organizational routines introduced by Nelson and Winter (1982). Given that organizational routines are defined as repeatable patterns of interdependent actions, they are regarded as a fundamental construct that aggregates individual activities into a collective behavior of an organization (Nelson & Winter, 1982; Teece et al, 1997; Grant, 1991; Karpacz, 2014; Stańczyk-Hugiet, 2015). Hence, routines involve the quasi-modular knowledge in a form of individual skills and the non-modular knowledge referring to relational and organization-specific skills learned only through experience in the specific organization (Dosi, Faillo & Marengo, 2008, p. 1170). The concept of routines refers to simple decision rules based on low levels of information processing and also to automatic behaviors that do not involve a presumption and conscious choice but high levels of repetitive information processing (Dosi et al., 2008). As resources are the basic units while analyzing stocks, routines are the basic units while analyzing flows in organizations. Therefore, it is commonly assumed that organizational routines are the building blocks of a higher level construct labeled as an organizational capability, yet not the only building blocks (Dosi, Nelson & Winter, 2000). As pointed out by Dosi et al. (2000), capabilities involve also other components, which are neither routines nor do resemble routines, e.g. a customer database for a marketing capability (Figure 3.2). Thus, an organizational capability, whether operational or dynamic, is conceptualized as a set of routines and their contextual requisites that enable both the performance and coordination of individual tasks (Helfat & Peteraf, 2003; Dosi et al., 2000).

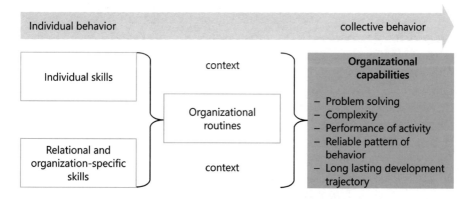

Figure 3.2 Routines as building blocks of organizational capabilities
Source: Author's own work based on Dosi, Faillo, and Marengo (2003, pp. 1165–1185).

The extant literature on dynamic capabilities provides another term with an overlapping meaning, i.e. competences. A review of the available studies suggests that there are two approaches to the understanding of the terms. Authors representing the first approach emphasize the distinction between capabilities and competences, which is basically confined to a scale of observation. Some scholars provide a more broad interpretation of the notion of competences (Bratnicki, 2000; Czakon, 2012), which concerns a wider range of organizational behavior than capabilities (Rokita, 2005). According to Rokita (2005), capabilities refer to a specific business unit or problem, while competences pertain to a more broad strategic context and involve corporation level activities. This is a dominating perspective in the Polish literature on management (Czakon, 2012). Conversely other scholars introduce a narrower view, which places competences between single routines and firm-wide capabilities (Dosi et al., 2008). Thus, it is argued that capabilities encompass the entire value chain, while competences refer to a technological and production expertise at specific points along the value chain (Stalk et al., 1992, p. 44), i.e. competences "capture 'chunks' of organizational abilities identified in terms of performed tasks and knowledge bases upon which they draw" (Dosi et al., 2003, p. 6).

According to the second approach to the understanding of capabilities and competences, both categories can be used interchangeably (e.g. Grant, 1991; Liebermann & Montgomery, 1998; Sanchez, Heene & Thomas, 1996; Drejer, 2002; Burmann, 2002) as "the distinction between competencies and capabilities is purely semantic" (Hamel & Prahalad, 1992, p. 164). It has been argued that the differences presented in the literature appear not very distinct (Drejer, 2002). As pointed by Drejer (2002) the observed divergence of perspectives derives mainly from a different theoretical background of a particular study, e.g. recognition of prior works of Penrose or Hamel and Prahalad. Given that this approach prevails in the world literature on management, in this work capabilities and competences are also considered equivalent terms, which represent a collective capacity of an organization for undertaking a coordinated deployment of resources. Nevertheless, as the concept of competencies is most often applied in the context of a firm's corporate diversification strategy, it is important to underline that authors refer, then, to a specific type of competencies, namely core competencies (Prahalad & Hamel, 1990, 1994). While dynamic capabilities are currently defined in terms of a capacity, a potential for expected outcomes, which exhibits certain cross-firm and/or cross-industry commonalities (Eisenhardt & Martin, 2000; Helfat et al., 2007), the notion of core competences implies an element of uniqueness in firms that contributes largely to a competitive advantage of those firms (Prahalad & Hamel, 1990; Bratnicki, 2000, p. 23). Core competencies exhibit strategic asymmetries between the company and its competitors and are conceived as non-product centric capabilities of an organization that involve multiple lines of company functions and span multiple lines of product markets (Prahalad & Hamel, 1990). This construct is always valued relative to other market players, indicating what a firm does extremely good. Hence, in order to avoid confusion over the terminology used, in this study it is assumed that organizational capabilities and competencies emphasize the same behavioral aspects of a strategy, yet specific types labeled as core competencies and dynamic capabilities are conceived as distinct concepts.

Besides referring to routines or competences some authors define dynamic capabilities also in terms of organizational processes (e.g. Eisenhardt & Martin, 2000; Ambrosini & Bowman, 2009). Nevertheless, dynamic capabilities are not organizational processes per se as they are embedded in processes (Helfat et al., 2007; Wang & Ahmed, 2007). Managerial and organizational processes are the mechanisms that enable development and deployment of dynamic capabilities, and thus, the performance of dynamic capabilities depends on those processes (Helfat et al., 2007). Dynamic capability is an aggregated construct involving distinct capacities enabling modification of the resource base of an organization. Each of those capacities is associated with one or more managerial and organizational processes, e.g. a component commonly labeled as opportunity sensing is developed and deployed through scanning, interpretative and creative processes (Teece, 2007). Definitional confusion emerges from the fact, that "when we observe a dynamic capability in use, we are observing the underlying processes" (Helfat et al., 2007, p. 31).

According to all definitions presented in the literature dynamic capabilities reflect an organizational capacity to create new solutions in ambiguous situations.Hence, it is argued that dynamic capabilities enable a firm to overcome an organizational inertia generated by path dependences and core rigidities in the firm's organizational processes (Teece et al., 1997; Helfat et al., 2007). However, as pointed out by Korhonen and Niemelä (2005), all organizational capabilities entail an infrastructural component (technology, structure, culture) that releases the knowledge embedded in the organization and a bundling process component (stabilizing, creating, trimming) that integrates knowledge with given resources. Since it has somehow questioned the logic for distinguishing dynamic capabilities, in order to solve the controversy concerning phrases such as "capability to change capabilities" authors turned to discuss firm capabilities and routines in a hierarchical order (Table 3.2), thus defining dynamic capabilities as those that alter the resource base / operational capabilities (Zollo & Winter 2002; Wang & Ahmed, 2007; Ambrosini & Bowman, 2009). It has been argued that dynamic capabilities representing a higher order capabilities are characterized by performative aspects concerned with putting resources into action, while operational capabilities involve not only performative but also ostensive aspect that captures structural view of underlying routines (Feldman & Pentland, 2003). However, Helfat & Winter in their article published in 2011 argue that although dynamic and operating capabilities can be distinguished on the basis of their purpose and intended outcomes, the line between them is in fact blurry due to the fact that change is always occurring at least to some extent and it is impossible to unambiguously link dynamic capabilities with only radical changes. Moreover, Schreyögg and Kliesch-Eberl (2007) present a very interesting argumentation contesting integration of a dynamic dimension into the capability construct. In their view conceptualizing dynamic capabilities by merging two contradictory dimensions of exploitation and exploration leads to a serious theoretical dilemma since "the same process cannot comprise concurrently stabilizing and destabilizing forces" (Schreyögg & Kliesch-Eberl, 2007, p. 925). Adding dynamic feature to the static problem-solving-architecture (concept of organizational capabilities) dissolves the replicable essence of routinized action patterns. Schreyögg and Kliesch-Eberl (2007) emphasize that focusing on a continuous change inevitably means lessening the stress on the reliable replication (2007). Therefore, they propose a dual-process model that recognizes "capability evolvement and system dynamization (…) as two separate countervailing processes, which are performed simultaneously" (Schreyögg & Kliesch-Eberl, 2007, p. 925). Although the proposition provides an interesting, alternative logic for defining the nature of dynamic capabilities, the workability of the model is to be explored. Meanwhile, Feldman and Pentland (2003) drawing on the idea of adaptation (Cyert & Marchi, 1963) and mutation (Nelson & Winter, 1982) of routines, argue that every organizational routine, and consequently also capability, can be regarded as a source of both inertia and change. The point of departure for this perspective is the recognition of a routine as a social phenomenon that embodies a duality of structure and agency. Thus, organizational behavior is conceived as an outcome of a complex interaction between the abstract idea of a routine (structure) and actual performances of a routine by employees in a certain context (agency). By shifting the focus from a structure toward agency, Feldman and Pentland (2003) emphasize the importance and impact of subjective and self-reflective behavior across repetitive patterns of actions.[1] Since there are manageable limits to routine specification, "there are always contextual details that remain open (…) for the routine to be carried out" (Feldmand & Pentland, 2003, p. 101). Thus, the performance of a routine always involves the aspect of interpretation and improvisation that may lead to resistance of expectations and introduction of an alternative course of action. Accordingly, changes in routines do not have to be triggered only by external pressures from management. As pointed out by Feldmand and Pentland (2003) organizational routines conceived as collective human activities exhibit an inherent capacity for endogenous changes.

---

1 For further discussion on individual-level microcomponents of organizational routines is presented, see Felin and Foss (2009).

Table 3.2 Hierarchy of capabilities

Collis (1994)	Winter (2003)	Zahra, Sapienza & Davidsson (2006)	Wang & Ahmed (2007)	Ambrosini & Bowman (2009)
First category Resources enabling performance of the basic functional activities of the firm	*Zero-level* Operational capabilities enabling firms to earn their current living	*Substantive capabilities* Set of abilities and resources that go into solving a problem or achieving an outcome	*Zero-order* Resources *First-order* Capabilities of deploying resources *Second-order* Core capabilities strategically important to competitive advantage at a certain point of time	*Resource base*
Second category Dynamic improvements to the activities of the firm *Third category* Capability to recognize the intrinsic value of other resources or to develop novel strategies before competitors	*First-order* Dynamic capabilities that alter zero-level capabilities	*Dynamic capabilities* Dynamic ability to change or reconfigure existing substantive capabilities	*Third-order* Dynamic capabilities enabling renewal, reconfiguration and re-creation of resources, capabilities and core capabilities to address the environmental change	*Incremental dynamic capabilities* Dynamic capabilities enabling incremental adjustments of the resource base in relatively stable context *Renewing dynamic capabilities* Dynamic capabilities enabling renewing the nature of the resource stock due to rapid changes in the environment
Meta-capabilities Learning-to-learn capabilities	*Higher-order* Dynamic capabilities that alter routinized responses to familiar types of change			*Regenerative dynamic capabilities* Dynamic capabilities allowing the firm to move away from previous change practices towards new dynamic capabilities
Ad infinitum meta-capabilities				

Source: Author's own work.

At first sight an assumption that all organizational capabilities can be considered as sources of stability and change may appear somehow contradictory to the logic of the dynamic capabilities perspective. However, generating endogenous alternations through improvisation represents an ad hoc problem solving, which is an alternative and distinct approach from the one defined as dynamic capability (Winter, 2003). The dynamic capabilities perspective provides a patterned way for introducing changes into organizational behavior. Thus, as "change and adaptation do not necessarily require the intervention of »dynamic« capabilities as intermediaries" (Helfat & Peteraf, 2003), it is possible for a firm to use either of those two approaches depending on a particular context.

In order to highlight a distinctive character of dynamic capabilities several definitions presented in the literature include also an explicit purpose for the construct, ranging from responding to rapidly changing environments (Teece et al., 1997), creating market change (Eisenhardt & Martin, 2000), improving organizational effectiveness (Zollo & Winter, 2002), to attaining and sustaining competitive advantage (Wang & Ahmed, 2007; Augier & Teece, 2009). Although, the dynamic capabilities perspective was originally formulated within the context of rapid technological change (Teece et al., 1997), further studies confirmed that the construct applies also to more stable environments (Eisenhardt & Martin, 2000; Helfat & Winter, 2011) and triggers of change may be generated also internally (Helfat & Winter, 2011). Therefore, acknowledging those contributions subsequently formulated definitions received a more general form without referring to external conditions (Helfat et al., 2007; Barreto, 2010).

The second group of purposes included in definitions derived from the assumption that dynamic capabilities are the main source of competitive advantage (Teece et al., 1997). Defining dynamic capabilities by their direct impact on firm's performance was broadly criticized for being tautological (Williamson, 1999; Eisenhardt & Martin, 2000; Cepeda & Vera, 2007; Barreto, 2010). Given that dynamic capabilities may exhibit varying degrees across different organizations and are not synonymous with superior performance, new proposals referred dynamic capabilities to "a capacity" that reflects "a potential for adequate performance" and repeatability of action patterns (Helfat et al., 2007, p. 5). According to that line of reasoning "change in the resource base of an organization implies only that the organization is doing something different, but not necessarily better, than before" (Helfat et al., 2007, p. 5). Therefore, a growing number of scholars refer to an approach that assumes a "purposeful" character of changes induced by dynamic capabilities without specifying resulting outcome of those changes (Helfat et al., 2007). It underlines a necessity for a minimal degree of intentionality that distinguishes dynamic capability from pure luck (Helfat et al., 2007).

It can be concluded that through the years dynamic capabilities have been defined in many different ways, reflecting the advances in knowledge on the subject matter. Subsequent contributions have responded to the criticism and substantially enhanced the understanding of the concept. The importance of maintaining explicitness, universality and stability of terminology used should not be underestimated. It is worth recalling at this point an important consideration shared by Maria Romanowska and Ewa Stańczyk-Hugiet during the Conference on Strategic Choices under Conditions of Uncertainty held in Poznań (Poland) in October 2015. In fact it was a call for a more careful and cautious introduction of new terms and concepts into the management field. Such introduction should be supported by a thorough review and recognition of already existent terms with a commonly acknowledged meaning. This is of special importance when discussing phenomena difficult to extract and observe such as capabilities. Therefore, defining dynamic capabilities by making a clear and direct reference to commonly used terms in the management scholarship, is a valuable contribution of this work.

Recently, an elegant definition put forward by Helfat et al. (2007) is gaining support. According to this proposition "a dynamic capability is the capacity of an organization to purposefully create, extend, or modify its resource base" (Helfat et al., 2007, p. 4). Definition is precise, yet comprehensive enough to capture the very nature of dynamic capabilities. Hence, it addresses all above-mentioned contentious issues. Firstly, it highlights the intentionality and patterned character of performed actions, yet used terms imply only a potential for expected outcomes. There is no a priori link to a superior performance. Further, the function of dynamic capabilities is not limited to providing an appropriate response to environmental change. Conversely, definition leaves open the possibility that organizational changes introduced by dynamic capabilities may be triggered by signals coming from both external and internal environments. Given that the definition proposed by Helfat et al. (2007) captures all the necessary features of dynamic capabilities in a clear and precise manner, it is considered suitable for guiding understanding of the concept in this study.

3.2   OPERATIONALIZATION OF DYNAMIC CAPABILITIES

The fact that dynamic capabilities constitute an aggregate and highly abstract construct raises important and difficult challenges for the empirical research. The performative character of dynamic capabilities makes it quite difficult to unambiguously separate the construct from its antecedents and consequences. Thus, there is a need for a cohesive and comprehensive operationalization of the concept in order to eliminate existing methodological discrepancies.

The following paragraphs present the state of art with regard to the conceptual decomposition of dynamic capabilities.

3.2.1 DEVELOPMENT TRAJECTORY OF DYNAMIC CAPABILITIES[2]

Although most authors agree that dynamic capabilities are built rather than bought in the market (Makadok, 2001) there is a scarcity of studies that explicitly and comprehensively explain how dynamic capabilities are created and developed. On the basis of the evolutionary economics contribution it is generally assumed that dynamic capabilities are developed through learning mechanisms (Eisenhardt & Martin, 2000), thus are path-dependent (Zollo & Winter, 2003; Teece et al., 1997) and embedded in the organization (Eisenhardt & Martin, 2000). However, the extant literature presents a fragmentary picture of the problem, since discussions are in general not supported by any clear conceptual model providing a common language and logic of capability development. Meanwhile, in order to explain the relationship between organizational capabilities and firm heterogeneity, it is necessary to understand how those capabilities evolve over time and become to a large extent idiosyncratic. Helfat and Peteraf (2003) have addressed the need and formulated the concept of capability lifecycle by drawing on the logic of a product lifecycle. Given that the management scholarship on the dynamic capabilities perspective does not provide an equally comprehensive alternative, further discussion on the problem of dynamic capability development is based on the concept of capability lifecycle.

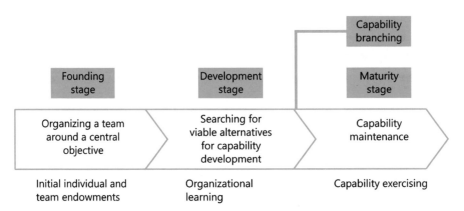

Figure 3.3 Capability lifecycle
Source: Author's own based on Helfat & Peteraf (2003, pp. 997–1010).

2   This section was presented as a separate article on the conference „Restructurization..." held in Krynica-Zdrój, Poland, in 2015. It is expected to be published in Conference Proceedings in 2016.

The point of departure for analyzing development patterns of organizational capabilities is an assumption that all capabilities can accommodate change, yet some of them are purposively designed to deal with adaptation and alteration. In other words organizational change may occur with or without intervention of dynamic capabilities. Accordingly, the concept of capability lifecycle provides a general framework that describes development trajectories of any type of organizational capability (Helfat & Peteraf, 2003). Nevertheless, it is important to note that the pace of induced change should not be regarded as the sole criterion for distinguishing operational and dynamic capabilities. The key task is to assess comprehensively the extent, nature and speed of change enabled by a particular capability (Helfat & Winter, 2011, p. 1249).

Conceptualization distinguishes several stages in the evolution of organizational capability by referring to the corresponding logic of a product life cycle. Such a line of reasoning is supported by the fact that products and capabilities are indeed two sides of the same coin (Wernerfelt, 1984, after: Helfat & Peteraf, 2003, p. 998). The life cycle of a new capability begins with a founding stage (Figure 3.3). Given that intentionality constitutes a key feature of capabilities, the stage starts with an objective the achievement of which involves creation of a capability. Then, the second requirement of the founding stage concerns organizing a group of individuals around that central objective in order to provide the necessary collective-level effort. Formation of teams does not occur in a vacuum. It is strongly affected by the organizational history of created and managed processes, systems and structures (Teece, 2007), as well as human and social capital of organized teams (Helfat & Peteraf, 2003; Ambrosini & Bowman, 2009). Given that the endowments present at the founding stage entail not only tangible inputs but also individual experience, knowledge, skills, social ties, it is argued that those endowments provide important sources of heterogeneity between subsequently developed capabilities (Helfat & Peteraf, 2003).

Once the team has been organized around the central objective, the development stage of capability evolution begins. According to the concept of capability lifecycle capability develops through a search for plausible alternatives that would enable achieving the central objective (Winter, 2003; Helfat & Peteraf, 2003). Teams may generate initial alternatives by considering variations with regard to the types and quantity of resources required, nature and complexity of tasks to be performed, form of a necessary coordination. The range and content of generated propositions is greatly affected by diverse stimuli supplied by the external environment, endowments at founding stage and experience accumulated over time. Consequently, capability development is constrained and guided by past and present actions. Thus, it is possible that generated alternatives may include formerly used solutions and/or involve completely new processes. Pursuing either of available alternatives is challenging, as each proposition entails new sets of activities not practiced by a team. Therefore, during the development stage initial alternatives undergo continuous evaluation and improvement until a satisfactory level of skillfulness or technical limits are reached. This improvement path is shaped by organizational learning (Teece, 1997; Eisenhardt & Martin, 2000; Zollo & Winter, 2002). Given that most scholars recognize the underpinning function of organizational learning, available studies present a variety of different perspectives on drivers of successful organizational learning that contribute to development of organizational capabilities (Cordes-Berszinn, 2013). Therefore, responding to the need for a coherent and general framework Zollo and Winter (2002) formulated a recursive cycle of three core learning mechanisms that enhance development of all kinds of capabilities, namely: (1) experience accumulation through a repeated execution of similar tasks, (2) knowledge articulation (collective discussions, performance evaluation) that enhances understanding of action-performance links, and (3) knowledge codification that supports the entire knowledge evolution process. This cyclical movement from exploration to exploitation and back again, is triggered by internally and externally generated stimuli. Organizational and external environments provide a substance for critical reflections on current organizational behavior and possible improvements of performed activities (Zollo & Winter, 2002). Thus, development of a new capability proceeds via an iterative process of trials and revisions based on the feedback and accumulated experience (Helfat & Peteraf, 2003).

As it was mentioned before at some point a continuously developed capability attains a satisfying level of functionality or reaches its technical limits. Then, further development is ceased and capability enters its maturity stage. During that stage the focus is shifted towards maintenance of the capability, that involves its regular exercising. Capabilities that are repeatedly used become more embedded in an organization and less susceptible to organizational forgetting, yet more habitual and tacit in nature (Helfat & Peteraf, 2003, p. 1003).

A current development trajectory may be either enforced or altered depending on signals coming from internal and external environments. Those signals Helfat and Peteraf (2003) describe as selection effects. In extant literature scholars discussing the development of dynamic capabilities refer to antecedents of dynamic capabilities (Rothaermel & Hess, 2007). It is argued that understanding the incentives, motivation and limitations to developing dynamic capabilities is a requisite to address the notion of purpose and intentionality of the construct. According to Rothaermel and Hess (2007), antecedents can be classified into three general categories: intra-organizational level (individual), organizational level, and inter-organizational level. At the first level antecedents embrace personal characteristics, individual cognition, expertise, mental processes and mental maps that affect individual behavior, perception of risk, opportunities and decision making (Rothaermel & Hess, 2007; Ambrosini & Bowman, 2009; Helfat & Peteraf, 2015). Although most works focus on the cognition and behavior of the top management, recent studies have extended the exploration over ordinary employees to capture a collective mind set undergirding development of dynamic capabilities (e.g. Sprafke & Wilkens, 2014). Organizational level antecedents involve organizational structure, design and culture characteristics. Within this level scholars emphasize the role of social capital (Blyer & Coff, 2003), multi-dimensional cultural interaction within the organization (Hong et al., 2008), degree of organizational centralization and formalization (e.g. Karim, 2009), project management orientation (e.g. Newell & Edelman, 2008), resource endowments (e.g. Verona & Ravasi, 2003). The individual and organizational level factors generate internal pressures toward change. The last group of antecedents belongs to the inter-organizational level and entails environmental factors concerned with conditions of the institutional environment, demand, competition, and technological development (e.g. Eisenhardt & Martin, 2000; Teece, 2007) and factors related to inter-organizational relationships such as network position of an organization, accessibility of complementary resources (Teece, 2007), opportunities for cross-organizational knowledge sharing and transfer (Kale & Singh, 2007). Recognizing such a broad spectrum of distinct but correlated factors it is important to emphasize that antecedents appear across all three levels of analysis. The overview of research findings on antecedents of dynamic capabilities enhances understanding of the complex nature of the concept and the contextual embeddedness of its development trajectory.

Whether caused by inward motivated managerial decisions or by changes in demand, technology, lifecycle, branching may occur only with regard to activity that "has reached at least a minimum threshold of functionality" (Helfat & Peteraf, 2003, p. 1005) and can be qualified as a capability. Hence, a current trajectory may be altered not only at the maturity stage but also at the development stage. Helfat and Peteraf (2003) distinguished six branches of capability lifecycle, that reflect organizational response to selection effects (Figure 3.4): retirement, retrenchment, replication, renewal, redeployment, and recombination. Choice over one or more of available branches at a time depends on the nature of opportunities and threats generated by selection effects. A firm may decide to reduce production or even to shut down the whole production line, when it faces threatening signals from the market that put in question a current level of production. In that situation retirement and retrenchment are viable options, because reduced utilization of a capability inevitably leads to its degradation. However, instead of a gradual or total cessation a firm may also consider replication of the capability in question in other geographical markets, that provide more favorable conditions for carrying out activities.

Moreover, disturbing signals from internal and external environments may in fact provide new opportunities for capability growth. Three other branches of renewal, redeployment in different product-markets and recombination involve new development stages, as all imply significant alternations of the capability and thus also require searching for most suitable adaptations and improvements.

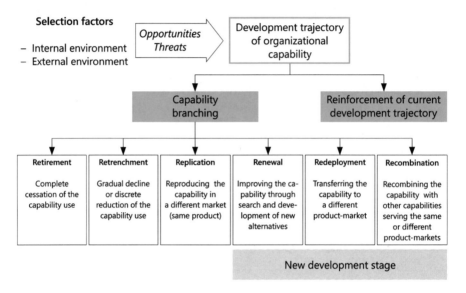

Figure 3.4 Capability branching
Source: Author's own work based on Helfat & Peteraf (2003, pp. 997–1010).

According to the concept of capability lifecycle, shifts in current development trajectory are always accompanied by some kind of transformation of the original capability. Early conceptualizations of dynamic capabilities assumed a direct link between organizational change and dynamic capabilities, i.e. dynamic capabilities were considered a necessary mechanism to alter operational capabilities. Moreover, the main purpose of dynamic capability was to address a rapid technological change (Teece et al., 1997). Further exploration of the field discarded those assumptions and the current understanding of the nature and function of dynamic capabilities is clearly reflected in the concept of capability lifecycle. According to presented framework firms may use dynamic capabilities to introduce changes, however the undertaken course of action may address various events occurring in internal and external environments. It corresponds with an interesting observation made by Eisenhardt and Martin (2000) that dynamic capabilities apply also to environments characterized by lower rates of change. Authors pointed out that structural patterns of dynamic capabilities depend on the market dynamisms in such a way that in high-velocity markets dynamic capabilities consist of mostly simple and unstable routines, while in moderately dynamic markets those structural patterns become more complicated and detailed (Eisenhardt & Martin, 2000).

In the concept of capability lifecycle dynamic capabilities are not considered as indispensable factors determining the evolutionary path of other organizational capabilities (Winter, 2003; Helfat & Peteraf, 2003, p. 1008). An overview of the capability lifecycle provides a more clear picture of the scale of efforts required for developing a capability. It is not only time but also substantial cognitive, managerial and operational costs (Ambrosini & Bowman, 2009). Thus, it can be concluded that dynamic capabilities are not automatically involved in every reaction to environmental change and a decision on development and deployment of dynamic capabilities depends on the balance of costs and benefits derived from their deployment in comparison to other non-routinized responses (Winter, 2003). Although the intended function of dynamic capabilities is to facilitate branching of other capabilities, management may turn to other plausible ways for accommodating change depending on particular circumstances.

Further in this vein, it is worth noting that with regard to path-dependency of dynamic capabilities scholars point at a quite important paradox. On the one hand it is assumed that dynamic capabilities represent the main approach to overcome lock-in situations resulting from path dependencies in organizations (Teece et al., 1997). On the other hand, dynamic capabilities are commonly defined as path-dependent processes, hence are subject to evolutionary mechanisms of variation-selection-retention and are characterized by three main principles of path-dependent processes: history matters, increasing returns and the risk of lock-in (Schreyögg & Kliesch-Eberl, 2007; Cordes-Berszinn, 2013). Thus, it has been argued that in order to respond to unfamiliar triggers an organization needs a frame breaking approach instead of a patterned course of action (Schreyögg & Kliesch-Eberl, 2007). Thus, such observation brings back the importance of non-routinized, ad hoc interventions and improvisations in organizational behavior.

Given that this study is focused on dynamic capabilities, and core discussion concerns the applicability of the dynamic capabilities concept to the problem of value appropriation, the illuminating insights provided by the capability lifecycle framework provide unique perspectives that guide and enhance the reliable theoretical and empirical exploration of the subject matter. Hence, the line of reasoning of the study acknowledges the critical role of initial endowments, experience accumulation over time and regular practice for capability development and maintenance. Accordingly, the empirical part of the study entails a qualitative case study research that enable a fine-grained analysis of organizational history and provides opportunity for capturing peculiarities in development trajectories of investigated capabilities.

3.2.2 MEASUREMENT APPROACHES

A review of the extant literature on the dynamic capabilities perspective suggests a common agreement on the understanding of dynamic capabilities as the capacity of a firm to purposively build, integrate and reconfigure its resource base (which includes operational capabilities). Thus, as it has been presented in the previous section dynamic capabilities are conceived in terms of a higher-order capability defined at a higher level of abstraction. The fact that dynamic capabilities constitute a meta-level aggregate (Burmann, 2002) raises important and difficult challenges for the empirical research. In order to verify the concept and move forward beyond the theoretical debate, the "black box" of dynamic capabilities needs to be opened and thoroughly described. Lacking a proper operationalization, it is impossible to solve the tautology problem of the link between dynamic capabilities and firms' performance (Priem & Butler, 2001; Barreto, 2010, Kraaijenbrink et al., 2010). It is a fundamental requisite to shift from viewing dynamic capabilities as an independent variable to a dependent one that needs to be explained in itself (Sprafke & Wilkens, 2014).

Although scholars emphasize theoretical usefulness of the dynamic capabilities perspective a review of the extant literature suggests that the concept remains quite difficult to operationalize (Barreto, 2010; Helfat & Winter, 2011; Peteraf et al., 2013). A breakthrough advance in the research concerns breaking the aggregate construct into a limited number of distinct but correlated components. Most important contributions are presented in Table 3.3. According to existing conceptualizations of the dynamic capabilities perspective there is no one single dynamic capability. Given that dynamic capabilities are embedded in organizational processes and act upon resources and operational capabilities, an organizational behavior may involve a quite wide range of different dynamic capabilities. An overview of distinguished categories constituting components of the aggregated construct of dynamic capability, confirms that different types of dynamic capabilities may be activated simultaneously across different dimensions of a business activity. However, it is not only the nature but also a particular spatial and temporal context that determines the way a given dynamic capability actually work. Thus, firms may use the same dynamic capabilities in different organizational areas, for different purposes (Helfat et al., 2007).

A wide spectrum of components presented in Table 3.3 also reveals a considerable divergence of conceptualizations, which is deeply rooted in versatility of the theoretical backgroud behind presented approaches to the dynamic capabilities perspective. According to some authors the key component of dynamic capabilities involve ensuring efficient and effective coordination of resources (e.g. Whitley, 2003; Pavlou & El Sawy, 2011; Protogerou et al., 2012). Meanwhile, Burmann (2002) emphasize that the coordination of resources should not be regarded as a constitutive and distinguishing feature of dynamic capabilities, since it is a general characteristic that can be applied to all types of organizational capabilities including operational ones. Moreover, it is quite questionable to identify adaptive capability as a component involving a capacity to find and use opportunities to align with external demand (e.g. Wang & Ahmed, 2007), when such description applies to the whole construct of dynamic capabilities. Another controversy concerns conceptualizing innovation capability as a tool for renewing capabilities (e.g. Wang & Ahmed, 2007). In contrast to such proposition there is a general stance in the literature to conceive dynamic capabilities as determinants of innovation (e.g. Eisenhardt & Martin, 2000; Zott, 2003; Teece, 2007). It is commonly assumed that the purpose of innovation described as producing customer value through new products/services, is mediated by dynamic capabilities. Hence, this work follows the dominant perspective that considers dynamic capabilities as sources of innovations, i.e. mechanisms that explain creation and implementation of innovative solutions. Further, there are propositions that recognize organizational learning as a dynamic capability itself (e.g. Whitley, 2003; Pavlou & El Sawy, 2011), while other conceptualizations conceive learning processes as specific processes that underpin and guide the evolution of dynamic capabilities (e.g. Eisenhardt & Martin, 2000; Burmann, 2002). Similarly, distinguishing absorptive capability as a standalone component next to innovative capability is also disputable (e.g. Wang & Ahmed, 2007), since in the extant literature notions of both categories are often overlapping – i.e. innovation capability is considered as a part of absorptive capability (Cohen & Levinthal, 1990) or absorptive capability is considered as a driver of innovation (Zhou & Wu, 2010). Undoubtedly, existence of those contradictory views stem from the fact that the dynamic capabilities perspective is still at an early stage of development, yet in order to unpack the conceptual black box and empirically investigate the concept, it is necessary to provide a clear distinction between diverse forms of the overall construct and its underlying processes. Given that the understanding of dynamic capabilities in this study is guided by the definition provided by Helfat et al. (2007) and the capability life cycle concept put forward by Helfat and Petraf (2003), organizational learning is not considered as a dynamic capability itself but as an underlying process that enable and shapes development of operational and dynamic capabilities. This approach is consistent with den Hertog, van der Aa, and de Jong (2010), who emphasized that learning is linked to all dimensions of dynamic capabilities and as such cannot be conceived and measured as a distinct capability. Further, since it is assumed that dynamic capabilities act upon operational capabilities it is necessary to emphasize those features of the concept that best capture its distinctiveness. Hence, this study follows the arguments put forward by Burmann (2002) and recognize coordination of resources as an inherent characteristic of any type of organizational capability.

Table 3.3 Decomposition of dynamic capabilities

Author(s)	Decomposition criteria	Secondary components	Characteristics
Eisenhardt & Martin (2000)	Organizational function	Dynamic capabilities for integration of resources	The ability to improve or adapt a business concept when resources are introduced, combined or modified – e.g. product development, strategic decision making.
		Dynamic capabilities for reconfiguration of resources	Transfer processes, coevolving, patching processes.
		Dynamic capabilities for gaining resources	Alliancing and acquisition processes.
		Dynamic capabilities for releasing resources	Dynamic capabilities that enable jettisoning outdated, obsolete resources.
Burmann (2002)	Organizational learning processes	Replication	Mastering integration processes relating to familiar tasks through knowledge codification and transfer.
		Reconfiguration	Recombining resources through knowledge abstraction (decontextualization of knowledge to make it applicable in other contexts) and knowledge absorption (internalization).
Whitley (2003)	Organizational function	Coordinating dynamic capabilities	Dynamic capabilities that focus on the gathering and integration of information about internal and external processes.
		Organizational learning capabilities	Dynamic capabilities that focus on joint problem-solving and continuous improvement of production and related processes through incremental innovations.
		Reconfiguring capabilities	Dynamic capabilities that involve the transformation of organizational resources and skills to deal with rapidly changing technologies and markets.
Branzei & Vertinsky (2006)	Pay-off schedule and capability life-cycle stage	Assimilation capabilities	Dynamic capabilities that focus on maintenance and adjustment of existing absorption and incorporation routines.
		Acquisition capabilities	Dynamic capabilities that involve experimentation with new types of information search and absorption routines.
		Deployment capabilities	Dynamic capabilities that focus on replication and refinement of existing product development or commercialization routines.
		Transformation capabilities	Dynamic capabilities that involve discovery of different knowledge generation or recombination routines.

Author(s)	Decomposition criteria	Secondary components	Characteristics
Teece (2007)	Organizational function	Sensing and shaping opportunities and threats	Scanning, creation, learning, interpreting and investing in research.
		Seizing opportunities	Addressing opportunities through new products, processes, or services.
		Reconfiguring organizational assets	Continuous alignment and realignment of specific tangible and intangible assets.
Wang & Ahmed (2007)	Organizational function	Adaptive capability	Ability to adapt in a timely fashion through flexible use of resources and by aligning resources and capabilities with environmental changes.
		Absorptive capability	Ability to recognize the value of new, external information, assimilate it and apply it to commercial ends.
		Innovative capability	Ability to develop new products and/or markets, through aligning strategic innovative orientation with innovative behaviors and processes.
Schienstock (2009)	Organizational function	Knowledge creating capabilities	Dynamic capabilities that create new knowledge internally.
		Absorptive capabilities	Dynamic capabilities that identify and exploit external sources of knowledge and related opportunities.
		Combinatory capabilities	Dynamic capabilities that combine newly created or acquired knowledge with an existing knowledge base.
		Transformative capabilities	Dynamic capabilities that recognize and exploit available in-house knowledge and related technological opportunities, i.e. transform knowledge into technological innovations.
Ambrosini, Bowman & Collier (2009)	Degree of organizational change	Incremental dynamic capabilities	Dynamic capabilities that introduce a limited extent of change in a form of incremental adjustments and improvements to the resource stock (resource stock would not be transformed).
		Renewing dynamic capabilities	Dynamic capabilities that refresh and renew the nature of the resource stock and therefore enable sustaining a rent stream in changing environments.
		Regenerative dynamic capabilities	Dynamic capabilities that change the way a firm creates, extends or modifies its resource base, i.e. change previous change practices.

Author(s)	Decomposition criteria	Secondary components	Characteristics
Madsen (2010)	Strategic orientation of performed activities (exploitation vs. exploration, internal vs. external)	External observation and evaluation	Dynamic capabilities that monitor the environment, provide impulse to new ideas, discover new possibilities and evaluate these.
		Internal resource renewal	Dynamic capabilities that integrate new resources in original and effective resource configurations.
		External resource acquisition	Dynamic capabilities that acquire and/or link the firm to external resources.
		Internal resource reconfiguration	Dynamic capabilities that reconfigure or restructure internal resources.
Barreto (2010)	Organizational function	Propensity to sense opportunities and threats	Managerial framing of opportunities and threats.
		Propensity to change the resource base	Creating, extending and reconfiguring the resource base.
		Propensity to make timely decisions	Quickly accomplishing reconfiguration and transformation ahead of competitors.
		Propensity to make market-oriented decisions	Focusing on ways to provide superior value to customers.
Pavlou & El Sawy (2011)	Organizational function	Sensing capability	Dynamic capability focused on spotting, interpreting, and pursuing opportunities.
		Learning capability	Dynamic capability focused on revamping existing operational capabilities with new knowledge.
		Integrating capability	Dynamic capability focused on embedding new knowledge into operational capabilities with collective sense-making.
		Coordinating capability	Dynamic capability focused on deploying tasks, resources and activities in reconfigured operational capabilities.

Author(s)	Decomposition criteria	Secondary components	Characteristics
Protogerou, Caloghirou & Lioukas (2012)	Impact of firm's performance	Coordination	Firm's ability to assess the value of existing resources and integrate them to shape new competences.
		Learning	Principal means enabling organizations to explore and learn new ways while at the same time to exploit what they have already learned (i.e. strategic renewal).
		Strategic competitive response	Firm's ability of the firm to scan the environment, identify new opportunities, asses its competitive position and respond to competitive strategic moves.
Sprafke & Wilkens (2014)	Sequences of actions and interactions between individual and organizational level	Cooperation	Activities targeted at purposefully building and maintaining relationships with other actors on the market in order to expand the organization's options to act, and to reinforce intra-organizational collaboration.
		Reflection and Adaptation	Activities of analyzing, evaluating and adjusting the effectiveness of organizational development processes, structures and projects.
		Creative Problem-Solving	Activities targeted at experimenting with novel approaches, integrating new strategies, and using creativity techniques to create new problem solutions.
		Dealing with Complexity	Activities of observing, absorbing and structuring environmental change, sensible selection and systematical elaboration of information, and the regulation of responsibilities.

Source: Author's own work.

By indentifying key components of dynamic capabilities scholars acknowledge that at a certain level of abstraction dynamic capabilities exhibit commonalities that stretch over a range of firms or even industries. The initial view of dynamic capabilities that embraced a vast array of firm-specific organizational and managerial processes and routines proved to be overly complex, hard to operationalize and too narrow and idiosyncratic in application to develop a generalizable theory (Williamson, 1999; Galunic & Eisenhardt, 2001). Disaggregating the construct into a parsimonious set of distinct components reflecting common and measurable features of dynamic capabilities at high level of abstraction, directly addresses formulated concerns (Barreto, 2010; Helfat et al., 2007). This assumption of common characteristics within dynamic capabilities indeed enabled development of general frameworks of the dynamic capabilities perspective. Given that in order to become a theory a concept needs to reach a certain level of generality, it can be concluded that this advancement in research is a milestone on the development trajectory of the dynamic capabilities perspective.

Conceptualizations of dynamic capabilities presented in the literature decompose the meta-level construct into coherent sets of also aggregated components. Hence, distinguished constitutive components are also highly abstract and embrace a plethora of various organizational capabilities and processes. In order to address the need for a better empirical grounding of the dynamic capabilities perspective, operationalization of the concept requires breaking those aggregated components down to organizational routines, processes, structures, and behavior of individuals within an organization, i.e. micro-level analysis of dynamic capabilities (Teece, 2007; Felin et al., 2012). A review of the extant studies suggests that the field remains in a great part fragmented with regard to underlying processes, procedures and actions. Undoubtedly, challenges for a cohesive operationalization are grounded in the fact that dynamic capabilities are conceptualized as a notion of causal ambiguity in organizational behavior. Hence, dynamic capabilities appear incomprehensible to outside observers as well as to the organization itself. Because the literature does not provide a commonly accepted measurement tool, introducing an operationalization for this study requires reviewing existing empirical approaches presented in the extant research works. Literature provides a quite wide spectrum of distinct measurement approaches. Although it is a common argument that empirical studies on dynamic capabilities are dominated by a qualitative research with a negligible usage of quantitative methods, a thorough review of the extant empirical studies conducted by Eriksson (2013, 2014) indicated a relatively comparable number of qualitative and quantitative studies. Presented approaches vary from in-depth case studies focused on subjective identification of idiosyncrasies of dynamic capabilities in a given context (e.g. Danneels, 2011), to analyses of input-output factors (e.g. Dutta et al., 2005) and finally qualitative and quantitative assessments of distinct clusters of activities performed at the micro-level (e.g. Teece, 2007; Alsos et al., 2008). Most of single case studies provide an overly detailed and context specific picture of the concept, which is deduced post hoc from firm's performance. Focusing only on retrospective collection of data makes it almost impossible to distinguish between existence of dynamic capability and its outcomes, thus leads to significant methodological discrepancies that link current status of dynamic capabilities with the past performance (Zahra et al. 2006; Eriksson, 2013). On the other hand, operationalizing dynamic capabilities in terms of input and output factors falls very closely to the success factor analysis based on a quite simplistic assumption that organizational capabilities represent a sole intermediate step between selected resources and planned, identifiable outcomes (Dutta et al., 2005). Hence, it underscores the complex nature of capabilities and contextual embeddedness of performed activities as well as it does not explain the heterogeneity of capabilities across firms. Bearing in mind that dynamic capabilities are a meta-level highly abstract and aggregated construct, it should be remembered that "the ease of measurement must not be put before the content of the measures" (Eriksson, 2013, p. 317). Therefore, in order to capture the theoretically postulated complexity of dynamic capabilities and identify both idiosyncrasies and commonalities of the construct, the latter group of operationalizations focused on clusters of activities performed at the micro-level were chosen to serve as a point of reference for this study (Table 3.4).

Scholars implementing the micro-level measurement approach commonly refer to microfoundations of dynamic capabilities. As pointed out by Felin et al. (2012), the notion of microfoundations has been developed through long debates in the economics and management fields on the role of individuals and collectives in shaping organizational behavior. In the extant literature discussion on microfoundations means explanatory reduction from the macro- to micro--level, in order to explain wholes in terms of their components (e.g. Felin et al., 2012; Helfat & Peteraf, 2015; Piórkowska, 2014). Hence, it is assumed that "each analyzed level is influenced by lower level mechanisms or entities in time" (Felin et al., 2012, p. 1353). However, as emphasized by Hodgson (2012) social phenomena such as organizations cannot be entirely explained by a complete micro-reduction to the most elementary particles. In case of organizations, which involve emerging relations and interactions through time, Hodgson (2012) calls for a multiple-layered ontology and respectively a multi-level analysis. Accordingly, exploration of microfoundations of dynamic capabilities should not be focused on searching for "sole units in terms of which everything can be explained" (Hodgson, 2012, p. 1393). Thus, although it is important to understand individual characteristics and motivations when investigating organizational capabilities, it is not necessary to reduce explanations completely to the level of individuals. Accordingly recent research on microfoundations

Table 3.4 Measurement variables of dynamic capabilities

Authors	Perspective	Secondary components	Primary components
Teece (2007)	Organizational perspective Theoretical approach	Sensing and shaping opportunities and threats	Analytical systems (and individual capacities) to learn and to sense, filter, shape and calibrate opportunities: • Processes to direct internal R&D and select new technologies • Processes to tap supplier and complementor innovation • Processes to tap developments in exogenous science and technology • Processes to identify and target market segments, changing customer needs and customer innovations
		Seizing opportunities	Enterprise structures, procedures, designs and incentives for seizing opportunities: • Delineating the customer solution and the business model (selecting the technology and product architecture, designing revenue architectures, selecting target customers, designing mechanisms to capture value) • Selecting decision-making protocols (recognizing inflexion points and complementarities, avoiding decision errors, anti-cannibalization proclivities) • Selecting enterprise boundaries to manage complements and control platforms (calibrating asset specificity, controlling bottleneck assets, assessing appropriability, recognizing, managing and capturing co-specialization economies) • Building loyalty and commitment (demonstrating leadership, effectively communicating, recognizing non-economic factors, values and culture)
		Reconfiguring assets	Continuous alignment and realignment of specific tangible and intangible assets • Decentralization and near decomposability (adopting loosely coupled structures, embracing open innovation, developing integration and coordination skills) • Governance (achieving incentive alignment, minimizing agency issues, checking strategic malfeasance, blocking rent dissipation) • Co-specialization (managing strategic fit so that asset combinations are value enhancing) • Knowledge management (learning, knowledge transfer, know-how integration, achieving know-how and intellectual property protection)

Authors	Perspective	Secondary components	Primary components
Wang & Ahmed (2007)	Organizational perspective Theoretical approach	Adaptive capability	• Strategic flexibility • Ability to align internal resources with external demand • Ability to scan the market, customers and competitors • Ability to respond quickly to changing market conditions
		Absorptive capability	• Ability to recognize the value of new external information • Ability to integrate and apply external information • Sharing new information within multidisciplinary teams • Development and usage of complementary knowledge
		Innovative capability	• Ability to introduce new products and services • Ability to introduce new methods of production • Discovering new sources of supply • Developing new organizational forms
Alsos, Borch, Ljung-gren & Madsen (2008)	Organizational perspective Empirical study Managerial insight	Observation and evalu-ation (external-explo-ration)	Systemic approach to search for new business opportunities through observation and benchmarking, backed up by resource transfer and formal (written) strategy develop-ment
		Resource acquisition (external-exploitation)	Active searching for new partners and cooperation with customers, suppliers, uni-versities in innovation and R&D; exploitation of personal networks of managers and employees as knowledge resources.
		Resource renewal (internal-exploration)	R&D investment and managerial engagement in development of plans, processes and routines for R&D; employees contribution to exploration of new opportunities
		Resource reconfiguration (internal-exploitation)	Allocating and reconfiguring of resources to enhance competences of employees; de-veloping routines for systematization of experiences; directing efforts toward efficiency gains

Authors	Perspective	Secondary components	Primary components
Pavlou & El Sawy (2011)	Organizational perspective Empirical study Managerial insight	Sensing capability	• Market intelligence generation • Disseminating market intelligence • Responding to market intelligence
		Learning capability	• Acquiring knowledge • Assimilating knowledge • Transforming knowledge • Exploiting knowledge
		Integrating capability	• Contributing individual input to the collective business • Disseminating individual input to the collective business • Interrelation of individual input to the collective business
		Coordinating capability	• Assigning resources to tasks • Appointing the right person to the right task • Identifying complementarities and synergies among tasks and resources • Orchestrating collective activities
Protogerou, Caloghirou & Lioukas (2012)	Organizational perspective Empirical study Managerial insight	Coordination	Managerial and organizational processes that relate with the coordination and integration of different activities and different skills, through certain organizational practices and internal policies, encouraging efficiency: • integration and standardization of business processes, • adoption of the latest management tools and techniques, • systematic implementation of business planning
		Learning	Knowledge creation and development processes, knowledge sharing and integrating processes as well as procedures of experience-based learning: • systematic in-house learning and knowledge development • team-working • on-job training
		Strategic competitive response	Processes aiming at understanding and adapting to environmental trends: • benchmarking • systematic formulation of long-term strategy • timey response to competitive strategic moves • flexible adaptation of human resources to technological and competitive changes

Authors	Perspective	Secondary components	Primary components
Alinaghian (2012)	Organizational perspective Empirical study Managerial insight	Sensing	• macro factor sensing • network sensing
		Shaping	• business shaping • network configuration • intra-firm configuration • processes shaping
		Seizing	Decision making • prioritization • selection • resource allocation
		Transforming	• network configuration • intra-firm configuration • transforming processes
Ali, Peters & Lettice (2012)	Organizational perspective Empirical study Managerial insight	Integration capabilities	• Interconnecting work tasks/outputs among firm's departments and group members, • Structuring resources through acquiring, accumulating and divesting, • Bundling resources through stabilizing, enriching and pioneering, • Organizing resources by arranging and allocating human and material resources within and among a firm's departments
		Reconfiguration capabilities	• Patching resources by realigning of business processes to match-up the changing market conditions and opportunities • Effective benchmarking • Transforming competencies into novel combinations • Transforming markets by forgoing existing ones and targeting future markets • Consolidating resources, • Leveraging resources through mobilizing, replicating and deploying resources needed to capitalize on opportunities in the market
		Renewal/recreation	• Adaptation and recreation of resources and capabilities in search of enhancing business processes • Exploitation and exploration of resources and capabilities in search of enhancing business processes

Authors	Perspective	Secondary components	Primary components
Sprafke & Wilkens (2014)	Individual perspective Empirical study Employee insight	Cooperation	Cooperation at an individual level – actions aiming at a flexible adapting to different persons, demanding but also offering help, dealing constructively with conflicts, holding on to commitments
		Reflection and adaptation	Reflection and learning at an individual level – actions of reflecting and evaluating conducts and acts, inviting and putting feedback into practice, and adapting others strategies for own improvements
		Creative problem-solving	Creative problem solving at an individual level – actions of applying own knowledge to various problem situations, using creative methods and striking out on new paths to develop problem solutions
		Dealing with complexity	Dealing with complexity at an individual level – auctions of planning, priority setting and monitoring of tasks and steps, managing time and goals effectively, getting one's ideas across
Janssen, Castaldi & Alexiev (2015)	Organizational perspective Empirical study Managerial insight	Sensing user needs and technological options	Staying up to date with promising new services - systematic observation, analysis and evaluation of customer needs, technologies of competitors and own services using different information sources
		Conceptualizing	Innovative approach to developing new ideas for new service concepts and aligning new service offerings with current business and processes
		Coproducing & orchestrating	Initiating and maintaining partnerships to improve and introduce new services (coordinating innovation activities across organizational boundaries)
		Scaling & stretching	Stretching successful innovations over organization following developed branding strategy
Helfat & Peteraf (2015)	Individual perspective Theoretical approach Top management insight	Sensing opportunities	Cognitive capabilities for sensing opportunities: • Perception – mental processes that organize and interpret information • Attention – mental processes responsible for awareness and selection of information
		Seizing opportunities	Cognitive capabilities for seizing opportunities • Problem solving and reasoning involving automatic and controlled mental processing
		Reconfiguring assets	Cognitive capabilities for reconfiguring and orchestrating assets • Language and communication used to affect workers response to change initiatives • Social cognition for inducing cooperation among members of an organization

Source: Author's own work.

of dynamic capabilities in a great part comply with the multiple-layered ontology by focusing not only on individuals but also on processes, structures and interactions between them (Table 3.4). Those approaches that refer solely to the individual perspective should be conceived as a complementary input, since authors do not claim that identified cognitive and behavioral microfoundations exhaust the *explanantia*.

The review of measurement approaches allows for concluding that there is an emerging consensus on constituent components of dynamic capabilities. Most of subsequently developed measurement approaches build on the notion of the initial operationalization proposed by Teece (2007), that entails all overarching categories of microfoundations, i.e. individuals, processes and structures, and interactions between them, across three main activity clusters of dynamic capabilities – sensing, seizing and reconfiguring. Scholars drawing on that operationalization either:

- apply clusters of activities originally defined by Teece using the same labels (e.g. Alinaghian, 2012), or
- use the content of clusters developed by Teece under different nomenclature (e.g. Wang & Ahmed, 2007), or
- develop distinct variables to clusters defined by Teece by shifting accents between different categories of microfoundations (e.g. Helfat & Peteraf, 2015), or
- extend the initial proposition by introducing additional secondary components while maintaining the original logic of the approach (e.g. Pavlou & El Sawy, 2011; Sprafke & Wilkens, 2014).

Hence, it should be emphasized that the operationalization proposed by Teece (2007) proved to be valid for investigations conducted at the organizational and individual level of analysis. Moreover, a qualitative case study research (e.g. Kuuluvainen, 2012) as well as large sample quantitative studies (e.g. Pavlou & El Sawy, 2011) confirm a high reliability of this formative model. A growing number of studies referring to the salient framework provided by Teece (2007), reflects an emergent trend toward organizing developed knowledge base in a more structured manner, hence, consolidating the plethora of explanations into a cohesive, generalizable, yet composite construct. Introduced decomposition maintains the right balance between the required general character of the concept (relevant across diverse sectoral contexts) and the necessary level of specificity (salient idiosyncratic properties at the micro-level). Thus, on the one hand it allows for a disclosure of an "elusive black box" of dynamic capabilities (Pavlou & El Sawy, 2011), while on the other hand it preserves a somewhat opaque view on their microfoundations (Teece, 2007). This incompleteness stems from the assumption that "idiosyncrasy in details" of dynamic capabilities determine the cross-organizational heterogeneity and the potential for achieving a competitive advantage (Eisenhardt & Martin, 2000; Teece, 2007; Peteraf et al., 2013).

Given that the formative model proposed by Teece (2007), and subsequently developed by other scholars through empirical investigations, has emerged as a dominant framework for exploring dynamic capabilities, this study also builds on that accumulated knowledge and operationalize dynamic capabilities into three main activity clusters of sensing, seizing and reconfiguring. Such approach should contribute to the integration of the previous research of dynamic capabilities. Further, recognizing the central role of management in the concept of dynamic capabilities and adopted organizational perspective on the process of value appropriation, investigated primary indicators reflect the organizational level of analysis and managerial insight.

3.2.3 OUTCOMES OF DYNAMIC CAPABILITIES

The line of reasoning for developing the dynamic capabilities framework was to overcome limitations of the RBV to provide explanation of how strategic resources are bundled and used to generate a competitive advantage. Thus, the relationship between dynamic capabilities and firm performance has been a central foci for most studies in the field since its origins. Guided by this main objective that led to development of the dynamic capabilities perspective, early works on dynamic capabilities assumed a direct link to performance by concerning dynamic capabilities as the main source of competitive advantage (Teece et al., 1997). The dominance of such approach was reflected in a number of definitions formulated at that time, in which dynamic capabilities were conceived as those capabilities that produce superior performance in dynamic environments (e.g. Teece et al., 1997; Griffith & Harvey, 2001; Zahra & George, 2002). This tendency to define the concept in terms of its results was broadly criticized for being tautological. Thus, addressing the criticism much effort was directed toward resolving the confusing relation between the concept and the main proposition. Although Teece (2007, p. 1320) has continuously emphasized that "dynamic capabilities lies at the core of enterprise success (and failure)," other scholars have exhibited a less radical perspective by pointing out that dynamic capabilities are not a sole, exhaustive source of competitive advantage. Eisenhardt and Martin (2000) underlined that a long-term competitive advantage of a firm depends on the way dynamic capabilities are implemented (in comparison to competition) and on resulting resource configurations. In other words, according to that perspective "dynamic capabilities are necessary but not sufficient, conditions for competitive advantage" (Eisenhardt & Martin, 2000, p. 1106). In contrast, Winter (2003), Helfat and Peteraf (2003) argued that development and use of dynamic capabilities induces substantial costs and firms may decide to use alternative means for generating necessary change. Hence, firms can accumulate change and achieve a high level performance also through ad hoc problem solving. It lead to a conclusion that a competitive advantage and superior performance cannot be conceived as indicators of dynamic capability usage. Attempts to verify a direct impact face difficult methodological and conceptual challenges concerning the problem of extracting the influence of dynamic capabilities from a plethora of other performance determinants together with a delay in observing expected outcomes (Zahra et al., 2006). Hence, as pointed by Peteraf et al. (2013, p. 1407) "regardless of the level of market dynamisms or the nature of dynamic capabilities, dynamic capabilities may enable firms to attain a sustainable competitive advantage *in certain conditional cases*." A wide recognition of this understanding has been reflected in subsequent contributions and introduced definitions free from any explicit or implicit reference to overall performance or competitive advantage (Zott, 2003; Helfat & Peteraf, 2003; Helfat et al., 2007; Ambrosini & Bowman, 2009; Barreto, 2010).

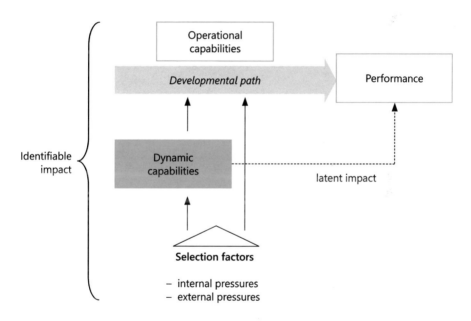

Figure 3.5 Mediation model of interaction between dynamic capabilities and firm performance
Source: Author's own work.

As the notion of dynamic capabilities and performance has been decoupled (Helfat et al., 2007), the focus of research has shifted toward a two-step casual chain assuming an indirect impact of dynamic capabilities through intermediate outcomes (Figure 3.5). Such understanding is consistent with commonly discussed arguments that dynamic capabilities may operate as a key antecedent of firms' strategic choices (e.g. entry strategies, diversification) (Teece et al., 1997; Eisenhardt & Martin, 2000). Accordingly, as dynamic capabilities are commonly depicted as means to change operational capabilities through integrating, reconfiguring and releasing resources in response to internally or externally generated pressures, it has been argued that identifiable outcomes of dynamic capabilities refer to the resulting resource and capabilities configuration (Zahra et al., 2006; Wang & Ahmed, 2007). Thus, the performance effect is explained directly by a technical dimension of how operational capability performs its intended function, i.e. a purposeful set of activities. This internal measure of capability performance depends on the characteristics of the available resource base as well on the way dynamic capabilities are deployed in terms of the time-cost efficiency. Therefore, a technical fitness of a given dynamic capability (Helfat et al., 2007) can achieve various levels, yet as an absolute measure of capability it must exceed zero to reflect a minimum capacity to perform a given task (Helfat et al., 2007, p. 9).

Nevertheless, acknowledging that dynamic capabilities are context depended, it can be concluded that produced change may not necessarily turn out to be valuable in terms of the overall performance of a firm (Winter, 2003; Helfat et al., 2007). Technical fitness of a dynamic capability does not always match "the demand for the product to which the capability contributes" (Helfat et al., 2007, p. 8) as well as a wide distribution of similar dynamic capabilities among firms increases competition and in result renders obsolete the value of those capabilities (Zahra et al., 2006). Moreover, there can be a negative interaction between various capabilities resulting in unsatisfactory outcomes at the level of a firm (Helfat et al., 2007). Thus, a high technical fitness of dynamic capabilities can be understood as a potential for matching changing environmental circumstances, yet not a guarantee of success. According to Helfat et al. (2007, p. 14) there are three main conditions for dynamic capabilities to match the context in which a firm operates, i.e. confer a competitive advantage:
- heterogeneity across firms in technical fitness of dynamic capabilities of the same type,
- demand for services provided by dynamic capabilities,
- rarity of dynamic capabilities in relation to demand for their services.

Given that the value of dynamic capabilities is determined by the context in which they are employed, it becomes clear that dynamic capabilities do not necessarily lead to a competitive advantage (Stadler et al., 2013). As argued by Helfat et al. (2007, p. 7), the bottom line of evolutionary fitness of dynamic capabilities, i.e. "how well a dynamic capability enables an organization to make a living by creating, extending or modifying its resource base," is reflected in firm's survival. Although, depending on the circumstances, dynamic capabilities may contribute to the growth of an organization, the base line concerns warding off decline and survival in the face of change.

Although empirical studies providing a reliable and comprehensive verification of the link between dynamic capabilities and firm performance are scarce, there are a few works that comply with a two-step mediation model and confirm a positive influence of dynamic capabilities on the operational level capabilities and further positive impact of reconfigured operational capabilities on firm performance (e.g. Morgan et al., 2009; Pavlou & El Sawy, 2011; Protogerou et al., 2012; Stadler et al., 2013). Implementing a mediation model has enabled a more cohesive discussion on theoretical and empirical issues of the dynamic capabilities perspective. It brings both dimensions to the common assumption of three essential elements of the dynamic capabilities perspective: "(1) the ability to solve a problem (an operational capability), (2) the presence of rapidly changing problems (environmental characteristics) and (3) the ability to change the way the firm solves its problems (a dynamic capability)" (Zahra et al., 2006, p. 921). Thus, the evolving understanding of the relationship between dynamic capabilities, firm performance and competitive advantage has allowed to address the concerns of tautology and provided a sound conceptual ground for validating the relevance of dynamic capabilities. Acknowledging the logic of mediation model and an emerging consensus on that line of reasoning among scholars, this study also builds on the two-step causal chain in both the theoretical discussion and empirical investigation.

4 DYNAMIC CAPABILITY-BASED FRAMEWORK OF VALUE APPROPRIATION

Given that value creation and value appropriation are conceived as intertwined yet distinctive processes, the development path of the former may not necessarily comply with the course of action exhibited by the latter one. According to the discussion presented in the Chapter 2 of this study value capture involves a multilevel, complex pattern of actions that extend far beyond the single point of transaction (Coff, 2010). In fact, as emphasized by Moran and Ghoshal (1997, p. 7), any specific resource deployment should be preceded not only by the existence of a resource and opportunity itself but also by the reasonable expectation "for some value to be realized from the deployment." Hence, it has become a common recognition that receiving and retaining value streams involves a wide range of resources and organizational capabilities developed across organizational functions (Fischer, 2011). Recalling that organizational capabilities are path dependent sets of routines (and their contextual requisites) brings in the issue of organizational inertia. On the one hand this experience based, path-dependent nature of operational capabilities used for value appropriation provides an internal consistency and stability of organizational behavior, on the other hand as self-enforcing characteristics cannot be easily modified and thus may hamper adaptation of an organization to the dynamics of the environment. Changes in technology, demand, legal regulations, competition or internal pressures generated by changes in the organizational structure, human capital, available resources, value creation processes, may require substantial reconfiguration of resources and existent practices of value capture to ensure not only growth but also survival of an organization. Therefore, although it appears quite challenging, firms facing internal and external pressures toward change need to respond to them by altering or introducing new ways for capturing value i.e. extend, modify, retrench or cease various elements of this complex pattern of activity (Katkalo et al., 2010). Guided by the understanding of the dynamic capabilities perspective adopted in this study it can be stated that an organization may generate necessary alternations by using dynamic capabilities or by turning to other plausible ways for accommodating change based on ad hoc problem solving. Given that capability development and deployment involves substantial cognitive, managerial and operational costs, it can be assumed that dynamic capabilities are not automatically involved in every reaction to environmental change and a decision on using a particular mechanism for accumulating change depends on the cost-benefits analysis in a given context. Accordingly, the developed dynamic capability-based framework of value appropriation is build on this assumption of existence of alternative modes for introducing change into current practices of value appropriation (Figure 4.1).

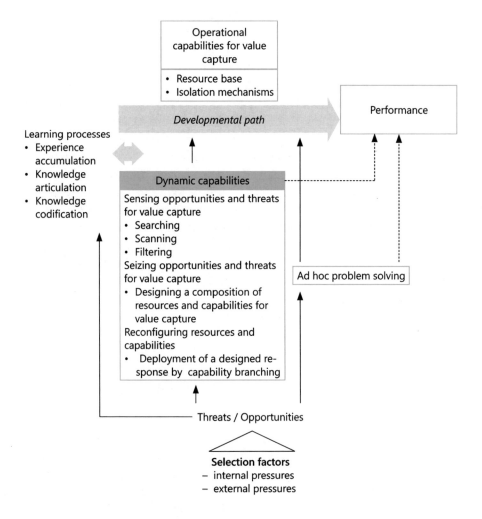

Figure 4.1 Dynamic capability-based framework of value appropriation
Source: Author's own work.

Building on the assumption that change can be accumulated by different mechanisms and dynamic capabilities are not synonymous with success, the adopted line of reasoning follows a two-step casual chain introduced in a mediation model of interaction between dynamic capabilities and firm performance. Further, formulated framework draws on the operationalization of dynamic capabilities proposed by Teece (2007), hence dynamic capabilities for value capture are decomposed into three main activity clusters of sensing, seizing and reconfiguring. The specific indicators used for evaluating those clusters in the context of value appropriation activities were developed on the basis of extant theoretical and empirical research on dynamic capabilities and value appropriation. Following sections of this chapter provide a more detailed discussion on that matter.

Given that it is generally assumed that the development trajectory of operational as well as dynamic capabilities is greatly affected by the experience accumulated over time, formulated framework includes organizational learning as an underlying process that underpin and guide the evolution of all kinds of organizational capabilities. Following Zollo and Winter (2002) organizational learning is conceived as a recursive cycle of exploration and exploitation involving three types of processes: (1) experience accumulation through repeated execution of similar tasks, (2) knowledge articulation that enhances understanding of action-performance links, and (3) knowledge codification that supports the entire knowledge evolution process. Dynamic of those processes is driven by external and internal factors stimulating critical reflections on current organizational behavior and possible improvements of performed activities (Zollo & Winter, 2002).

Dynamic capability-based framework of value appropriation was formulated on the basis of a cumulative knowledge generated from a wide range of theoretical and empirical studies on value capture and dynamic capabilities and further was verified and improved during the empirical investigation. The following sections present a more detailed picture of main elements of the framework.

4.1 PATH DEPENDENCY

Conceptualizing value appropriation through the dynamic capabilities perspective implies that organizational capabilities involved in receiving and retaining streams of value are shaped not only by firm's strategic and unique resources, but also available strategic paths. It is a common observation that despite a growing demand for flexibility firms often remain inert and locked in behavioral and decision making patterns shaped by the past experience (Romanowska, 2002). As pointed out by Leonard-Barton (1992) firm's most important capabilities may become its core rigidities as a firm becomes overly focused on successful patterns of behavior to anticipate discontinuities that undermine the usefulness of heavily used, embedded knowledge. This tension between inherent organizational rigidity and adaptation can be observed also in practices of value capture. Hence, a path dependency provides not only consistency and stability of the course of action, it is also widely recognized as an isolating mechanism that underlies casual ambiguity and prevents replication of particular behavior of a given firm (Rumelt, 1984). Nevertheless, drawing on historical imprinting may increase an organizational inertia. From a strategic perspective rigidity resulting from path dependency is a notion of potential inefficiency. Particular action pattern may work successfully for a certain time and in certain environmental and organizational contexts, yet potential inefficiency becomes realized when an organization facing change pressures generated by altered internal or external circumstances is unable to provide an adaptive response that extends beyond current patterns of behavior (Sydow et al., 2009). Thus, for exploring value appropriation under the dynamic capability-based framework it is necessary to clarify the conditions and dynamics of organizational path dependency.

The point of departure for discussing the concept of path dependency is recognizing that historical imprinting of a rational choice is to a large extent a common characteristics of decision processes (Sydow et al., 2009). Hence the notion of the concept is broader than past dependency. Arguments of history matters encapsulated in a famous phrase "bygones are rarely bygones" (Teece et al., 1997, p. 522), provide just a partial explanation. Analogically, an early investment restricts the future scope of action, yet not all investments bring about path dependency. In extant literature scholars refer to related concepts that appear very similar, yet underlying assumptions and content are quite distinct from the concept of path dependency. An overview on main differences and possible areas of convergence is presented on the Table 4.1.

Confrontation with related concepts has revealed a considerably complex nature of organizational path dependency. Undoubtedly, more deep insights are necessary to enhance understanding of a dynamic nature of the process. The evolutionary economics literature provides a great support for the discussion, by conceiving path dependency as a complex process driven by distinct but interrelated self-reinforcing mechanisms such as learning, complementarity (e.g. Nelson & Winter, 1982). Building on manifold contributions from evolutionary economics, innovation studies, and economic history Sydow et al. (2009) developed an appealing framework that conceptualizes an emergent process of path dependency along three developmental phases governed by different causal regimes: pre-formation phase, formation phase, and lock-in phase (Figure 4.2).

Table 4.1 Path dependency and related concepts

Related concepts	Path dependency
Imprinting • Initial cognitive schemes and organizational context imprint organizational processes • Replicated pattern is present as a ready-made scheme at the founding stage. Initial scheme persists and influence organizational processes	• Patterned content of an organizational path is not clear at the beginning • Unfolding process of path formation ⇨ Acknowledging the role of imprinting in explaining restrictions during organizational path development
Escalating commitment • Focus on courses of actions raising inefficiencies at a very beginning No positive feedback	• Assumption of an accidental beginning and of a relatively long phase of successful outcomes • Self-reinforcing mechanisms based on positive feedback ⇨ Replication of inefficient solutions despite of negative feedback at the lock-in phase
Sunk costs An early investment restricts the future scope of action	• Escalation of self-reinforcing processes ⇨ Not all investments bring about path dependency, yet irreversibilities influence organizational path development
Structural inertia • Focus on organizational feature that develops in the course of structuring an organization No structural dynamics	• Assumption of an accidental beginning and of a relatively long phase of successful outcomes • Self-reinforcing mechanisms based on positive feedback ⇨ Establishing reliable organizational structures is an universal requirement for all organizations
Reactive sequences • Focus on sequences of modular events governed by singular cause-and-effect relationships No assumption that causal reactions reproduce a specific action pattern	• Processes explained by self-reinforcing mechanisms • Casual logic of lock-in ⇨ Explaining singular events while analyzing evolvement of historical processes

Source: Author's own work based on Sydow et al. (2009, p. 696–698).

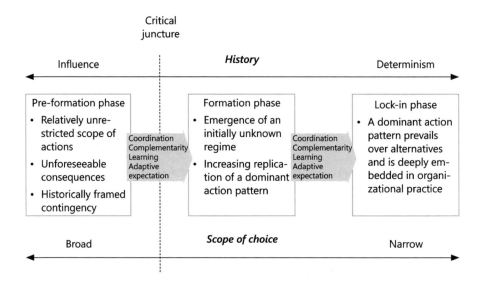

Figure 4.2 Concept of path dependency
Source: Author's own work based on Sydow et al. (2009, pp. 691–695).

According to Sydow et al. (2009), the pre-formation phase provides a relatively broad scope of action influenced by institutional imprints, since in organizations all initial actions are embedded in an institutional heritage. Initial, triggering activities characterized by unforeseeable consequences are considered in terms of contingency rather than causal determinants. This first phase ends when a critical juncture occurs. It is a moment when triggering activities transform into self-reinforcing dynamics. This dynamics becomes a causal regime of the second phase. During the formation phase a dominant action pattern emerges narrowing the scope of possible alternatives. The path is evolving as it becomes more and more difficult to reverse the initial action pattern. Eventually, when the behavior becomes highly inflexible and predominant mode prevails over any available alternatives, regardless of the differences in efficiency, then it can be concluded that the process has reached the lock-in phase. However it is important to emphasize that the lock-in phase may differ depending on the level of analysis. In contrast to the market level implications (e.g. dominant design – see Teece, 2001; Howells, 2005), in an organizational setting lock-in does not imply a complete rigidity. There are always some variations of the replication practice due to individual interpretations of the core pattern.

Development of organizational path dependency along phases is driven by self-reinforcing dynamics of four distinct but related mechanisms:

coordination effects, complementary effects, learning effects, and adaptive expectation effects (Sydow et al., 2009). Coordination effects refer to increasing benefits of a rule-guided behavior, as following the same set of rules enhances internal consistency of an organization and reduces costs of coordination (e.g. using FIDIC conditions of contracts for procuring work or consultancy services). Complementarity effects stem from using sets of interrelated practices that produce additional surplus when deployed in combination (e.g. modular production systems supported by intellectual property modularization, Computer-aided Design CAD, robotic automation, CNC machinery). Self-reinforcing learning effects refer to accumulated skills and experience through a subsequent repetition of activities (e.g. focus on improving currently produced solution at the expense of experimentation with a completely new technology). Adaptive expectation effects are related to the tendency of individuals to follow preferences of others (e.g. subscribing to the mainstream practices of providing an open source code of produced software).

A thorough explanation of the logic of organizational path dependency provides a salient ground for analyzing the problem of breaking the action pattern that turned out to be inefficient when confronted with changing circumstances. Although it is commonly argued that organizational paths can be unlocked through externally or internally generated factors (e.g. Winter, 2003; Helfat & Peteraf, 2003; Sydow et al., 2009), the extant literature provides also contradictory observations evidencing that discontinuous change strengthens rigidity by narrowing the scope of alternative actions (Gilbert, 2005). As pointed out by Gilbert (2005), in order to solve the confusion, the issue needs to be described by a more precise set of determinants. Accordingly he identified two key determinants of an organizational lock-in by decoupling the motivation from the structure of a response (Gilbert, 2005, p. 741):

- resource rigidity defined as "a failure to change resource patterns," and
- routine rigidity described as "a failure to change organizational processes that use those resource investments."

The importance of that distinction is supported by a differential content, antecedents and thus generated response to a discontinuous change. While a resource rigidity builds predominantly on resource dependency and reinvestment incentives to preserve market power, a routine rigidity strengthens due to a deeply embedded logic, tacit cognition and purposeful design of routines, which are further performed by a variety of individuals. The different notion of determinants implies that they can move independently, even in opposite directions. Hence, heavy investments in response to unforeseeable market change may be accompanied by only negligible adaptation of underlying routines. Moreover, research findings presented in the literature suggest variation of response depending on the perception of a particular disruptive event (Krupski, 2014). It has been observed that individuals exhibit a higher propensity to increase resource investments when the change factor is perceived as a threat than opportunity (Gilbert, 2005). Conversely, with regard to a routine rigidity it is an opportunity-driven response that unlocks the dominant logic, while a threat-induced response tend to increase rigidity (Gilbert, 2005). Given that the scope of this study concerns path-breaking responding to various selection factors, those insights have informed greatly the logic of conducted investigation. Hence, recognizing perception of a particular triggering event has been included as a key element of the formulated dynamic capabilities-based framework of value capture. Whether a response is opportunity- or threat--driven, it is expected to have an important influence on the way an organization accumulates change within the process of value appropriation. Moreover, following the idea that "resource rigidity is concerned with movement along line, while routine rigidity deals with the trajectory of the line" (Gilbert, 2005, p. 757), adopted line of reasoning acknowledges the interaction between both determinants of organizational lock-in. Response to a particular selection factor can induce tension between determinants, as a growing investment in VRIO resources may increase constraints on altering the underlying logic of organizational capabilities for value capture. Thus, the formulated framework embraces both determinants in order to provide a more refined view into the way organizations introduce change into value appropriation practice through different problem-solving mechanisms.

4.2   ACTIVITY CLUSTERS OF DYNAMIC CAPABILITIES

Given that a dynamic capability of a firm is defined in terms of an organizational capacity to purposefully create and modify the available resource base, it is conceived as an aggregate construct that needs to be decomposed in order to be empirically verified. Operationalization introduced in this study draws on the formative model proposed by Teece (2007), and subsequently developed by other scholars through theoretical and empirical investigations. The following sections present a more detailed picture of three main activity clusters of sensing, seizing and reconfiguring.

4.2.1 SENSING OPPORTUNITIES AND THREATS

In order to introduce changes an organization needs first to sense the triggers. Sensing involves a complex set of interrelated activities of environmental scanning, searching and making sense of gathered information by evaluating area, scale, importance of the influence and by deciding whether the issues of concern are the domain of loss (threats) or the domain of gain (opportunities). Outcomes of those actions have a direct impact on the form and content of an organizational response to changing circumstances. Sensing builds on a conscious linkage between organization and its environment. According to the logic of the dynamic capabilities perspective the focus of the component defined as sensing is on events that require alternation along a developmental path of an organization. It emphasizes the notion of discontinuity and complies with the entrepreneurial perspective on organizational behavior (Bratnicki, 2011) and strategy (Krupski et al., 2009). Nevertheless, the understanding of discontinuous change adopted in the dynamic capabilities perspective is not affected by either a positive or negative evaluative bias. It is the perception of an event in given circumstances that gives the meaning of an opportunity or a threat (Gilbert, 2005; Krupski, 2007; McMullen & Shepherd, 2006; Davidsson, 2015). Thus, undertaken activities embrace identification of events and making sense of them by recognizing either possibilities of gains due to supportive context, or risk of loss by acknowledging existing vulnerabilities. Meanwhile, as pointed out by Davidsson (2015), extant literature provides a quite blurred theoretical picture of the problem, because in most studies opportunity construct is applied to discuss both circumstances that create a room for new economic activities and evaluation of those circumstances. It leads to a confusion when discussing a negative perception of competitive imperfections. In order to maintain clarity around notions of enabling events, opportunities and threats, this study builds on a fundamental distinction between the content and evaluation of the content (Davidsson, 2015). Hence, terms opportunity and threat are used when referring to perception of a particular situation.

A review of contributions from the fields of entrepreneurship and strategic management suggests that there are two dominant views of circumstances that create a room for new economic activities (Alvarez & Barney, 2007; Zahra, 2008; Short et al., 2010; Krupski, 2011, 2012). According to the first view, which prevails in strategic management, such conditions are conceived in terms of concrete realities that exist independently of an entrepreneur. It means that specific circumstances for new activities arise exogenously from changes in the context within which an organization exists (Shane, 2000; Alvarez & Barney, 2007). Those changes disrupt the competitive equilibrium on product and factor markets (Alvarez & Barney, 2004). Hence, opportunities for value capture can be formed by environmental changes concerning technology, demography, regulations, etc. (Kirzner, 1973) as well as can arise from underutilized or unemployed tangible and intangible resources (Alvarez & Barney, 2004). Those competitive imperfections may also undermine current value appropriation practices by rendering obsolete possessed patents, tacit knowledge protected by secrecy, complementary assets, etc. (Teece, 2001; Krupski,

2013). It is assumed that as objective phenomena, competitive imperfections need to be first discovered in order to be further acted upon. On the contrary, the second view, represented predominantly by entrepreneurship scholars, advocates that competitive imperfections are not discovered but created during an entrepreneurial process (Ardichivili, et al., 2003; Alvarez & Barney, 2007). Thus, it suggests that actions undertaken by entrepreneurs represent the essential source of opportunities for value appropriation, yet may also generate risks of losing certain streams of value. Hence, threats may be created by members of an organization either purposefully (e.g. malicious acts of sensitive knowledge disclosure) or accidentally (e.g. sensitive knowledge leakage due to careless behavior while using digital databases) (Najda-Janoszka & Wszendybył-Skulska, 2015).

Those two abovementioned perspectives have important implications for the way sensing activities are performed. The first one suggests focusing on searching the environment for hidden opportunities or threats created by exogenous shocks. Since it is assumed that opportunities or threats wait for being discovered, a competitive challenge for an organization concerns alertness, i.e. becoming timely aware of opportunities by capitalizing on information asymmetry, differentials in risk perception, cognition, etc. (Shane, 2003). According to the second, the creative perspective, issues of concern are being formed and therefore, managers are to a large extent unable to make reliable estimations of probability distributions related to undertaken decisions (Alvarez & Barney, 2007; Davidsson, 2015). Thus, sensing internally created threats involves for the foremost continuous monitoring of key resources and individual behavior, however in case of purposefully created threats additional challenges concern the fact that the whole process is intentionally kept secret (Najda-Janoszka & Wszendybył-Skulska, 2015). On the contrary, when sensing opportunities, undertaken activities draw on experimentation and continuous scanning of the knowledge and experience generated on an on-going basis from the process of enacting an opportunity (Alvarez & Barney, 2007; Krupski, 2011).

Despite the fact that discussed perspectives are build on distinct assumptions about the nature of reality (Alvarez et al., 2010), they both provide valuable insights for investigating an activity cluster of sensing opportunities and threats of value appropriation. The underlying logic of the framework of this study provides a fruitful ground for acknowledging complementarities between those standpoints. Given that according to both perspectives circumstances, which create possibilities for new activities, exist when a competitive imperfection occur in product or factor markets and the goal of entrepreneurs is to form and exploit those conditions, it can be concluded, following Short et al. (2010, p. 54), that some opportunities and threats are discovered whereas others are created. Zahra (2008) also supports an integrative approach by implying that discovered competitive imperfections usually generate further changes and lead to creation of new possibilities for new activities. Hence, it suggests that the whole process should be conceived as a recursive cycle of discovery and creation. Moreover, in attempt to address the problem of inconsistency and fragmentariness of the picture Alvarez et al. (2010, p. 28) discuss an evolutionary realist approach, which integrates both perspectives by assuming that "knowledge may be constructed by individuals, but it is validated through social cross-validation." This study acknowledges those integrative efforts and indicated complementarities by examining the context under which entrepreneurs/decision-makers operate.

It is assumed that sensing involves not only scanning and searching across technologies and markets but also filtering and giving the meaning to gathered information in terms of opportunities and threats. Given that discontinuity triggers may arise from internal and external changes, searching needs to embrace environmental circumstances as well as the internal resource base. Including an inward perspective enhances identification of critical knowledge areas and enables defining resource and capability gaps that may negatively affect the value capture potential of a firm (Cepeda & Vera, 2007). Considering external environment, searching activity may have a more or less precisely defined focus. Thus, usually preceded by an internal gap analysis, searching may be narrowed to pattern-matching solutions (focused search) or as undirected scanning may reach beyond areas covered by current knowledge and capabilities (scanning) (Huber, 1991). The latter type is associated with higher possibilities for identifying path breaking ideas. However, there is also possibility for an unintended learning about environmental changes, which Huber (1991) labels as noticing. Lacking a purposeful character noticing exhibits an alternative approach to identification of changes than the one described as sensing under the dynamic capabilities perspective. Hence, noticing can be linked to ad hoc problem solving mechanism.

In order to spot new possibilities for value appropriation the scope of search should involve not only needs of the current target market, insights into latent demand, but also related and unrelated technology developments, structural developments of industry and markets, behavior of suppliers and competitors (Teece, 2007). Sensed opportunities and threats may refer directly to value appropriation mechanisms (e.g. licensing patented technology in order to capitalize on developed knowledge before competitors invent around the patent, rearrangements due to incidents of sensitive knowledge leakage) or may relate to more broad possibilities for new value creation (e.g. addressing value capture risks and possibilities when identifying a chance for entering a new market). It is important to underline that developed framework assumes that identified changes, events, external shocks should be perceived in terms of threats or opportunities for receiving and retaining value streams already at the time of sensing.

However, it needs to be emphasized that information concerning all those aspects is not always available and even if it is decision-makers may choose not to cope with the change and ignore the data (Helfat et al., 2007). Identified significant information should be further processed and interpreted in order to make a well thought decision on further actions. Besides unused or improperly addressed opportunities and threats the consequences of a misperception may involve also costs related to improper deployment of dynamic capabilities (Zahra et al., 2006). Firms may sense many changes but may choose to respond only to selected subsets. Thus, the necessary and complementary component of this activity cluster concerns a methodical process of organizing, interpreting and filtering gathered information with respect to its strategic relevance.

4.2.2 SEIZING OPPORTUNITIES AND THREATS

Once new opportunities or threats are sensed, a firm needs to address them with an appropriate action pattern. Thus, the main challenges of seizing concern availability of required resources and capabilities, and definition of their combination that most suitably aligns with strategic objectives of a given firm (Teece, 2007).

When approaching to capitalize on the potential of recognized competitive imperfections, a firm may either be in a comfort position of controlling all required resources or suffer gaps of different scale and scope (Alvarez & Barney, 2004; Helfat et al., 2007). In the first case designed response builds on a currently controlled knowledge, physical, financial, human resources and capabilities including possessed isolating mechanisms. Hence, a resource commitment refers to the existing resource base of a firm, e.g. responding by licensing proprietary technology, using own capital to purchase stock of a firm that is undervalued to sell it later on at a higher price. Nevertheless, considering new applications for possessed knowledge and technology a firm needs to recognize and adjust to the new context of deployment, which may affect the efficiency of mechanisms used for protecting and retaining of generated value streams (e.g. Henkel et al., 2013). A good example is a decision of a firm to enter an open source environment with a technology developed and made available as proprietary software so far. It implies a totally different way of capturing value streams as well as a number of technical and legal challenges concerned with the implementation of such decision. Designing such response requires a substantial reconfiguration of possessed resources and capabilities. A comment made by Sun General Counsel Mike Dillon when Sun Microsystems decided to change its product to an open source software aptly illustrates the problem: "Java Standard Edition contains about 6 million lines of code. (…) Our legal team [of 190 lawyers] had to go over it, line by line, and look for all copyrights marks and third-party involvements. Where Sun didn't have the correct licenses, we had to contact the owners, one by one, and determine rights" (Henkel & Baldwin, 2009, pp. 29–30). The complexity of developed technology, underlying knowledge draws attention also to the problem of value dissipation among internal interest groups, i.e. managers and employees, while approaching to seize new opportunity or threat (Mazur, 2011). Designed mechanisms for value protection and capture should be not only externally but also internally oriented. Hence, maneuvering within the borders of own assets does not eliminate the risk and challenges associated with designing the architecture of a particular response.

Nevertheless, drawing on existing resource base and developed portfolio of isolating mechanisms without an inflow of new external knowledge, may lead to "program persistence bias" that hampers more risky, capability-destroying solutions (Teece, 2007, p. 1327). The situation becomes quite different, when a firm needs to gain access to necessary resources and capabilities and to strategize around investment decisions (Teece, 2007). A decision problem of a firm reaches then beyond a selection of new resources (Helfat et al., 2007) and concerns a choice whether to incorporate relevant resources into its structures or to gain a remote access through various contractual arrangements (Alvarez & Barney, 2004). Although both alternatives involve developing complementarity between internally and externally generated resources, differences in governance mechanisms implicate divergence in terms of a scale and scope of necessary investment and consequences for the value appropriation potential.

The extant literature provides a quite broad spectrum of research focused on direct investment as a way of acquiring resources for new business ventures (e.g. Teece, 1986; Peteraf, 1993; Zollo & Winter, 2002; Teece, 2001; Lavie, 2007). The scope of investigated issues ranges from general purpose resources to specialized assets: recruitment of new managers and personnel (e.g. Rindova & Taylor, 2002), intellectual property development (e.g. Jennewein, 2005), additional capital in-sourcing (e.g. Shane, 2003); new technology purchasing and development (e.g. Teece, 2001), whole business acquisitions (e.g. Zollo & Winter, 2002; Helfat et al., 2007). Given that commitment to such investments is time consuming and implies significant irreversibilities, any decision on development or acquisition of resources should be preceded by a thoughtful identification of those that are truly necessary. Then, depending on the specificity of required resources and related isolating mechanisms, as well as on a number and bargaining position of resource providers, type of appropriability regime and the stage in the evolutionary development of a given industry, a firm may decide whether to expand by integrating into complementary assets (e.g. developing proprietary technology and pursuing patents, developing patent portfolio through acquisitions) or acquire resources through contractual arrangements (e.g. using technology provided by partners under licensing agreements). Directing efforts toward accumulation of equity is usually triggered by an evidently unfavorable position against providers of complementary assets together with rather limited possibilities for effective use of currently possessed isolating mechanisms (more on that topic – see Chapter 2). Hierarchical governance is then used to prevent diffusion of proprietary knowledge concerning the structure of a response to opportunities and threats (Alvarez & Barney, 2004). Diffusion of such knowledge among other market players would lead to an increase of the number of competitors aspiring to capture the value to be generated by this knowledge. This competitive pressure forces firms to assembly necessary resources in the shortest possible time.

Nevertheless, a successful acquisition may not bring about an expected idiosyncratic value of acquired resources and capabilities. The potential of new resources and the new context of use may not be sufficiently understandable for managers and employees involved in the resource allocation process. In order to facilitate seizing capabilities, a firm needs to ensure integration of in-sourced knowledge, technology, equipment, human resources with the existing resource base in a complementary way (Teece, 2007; Sirmon et al., 2007). Such integration occurs at different levels of organizational culture, systems, and operations (Zahra & George, 2002). Difficulty of this task increases with the number and complexity of acquired resources. Undoubtedly, business acquisition belongs to the most toughest challenges in this respect (Helfat et al., 2007).

Given that accumulation of equity through direct investments usually requires a longer time span, as well as implies significant irreversibilities and integration challenges, firms reach for alternative solutions enabled by cross-organizational cooperation. A wide spectrum of contractual arrangements enable firms to flexibly extend and enrich the resource base, achieve positive synergy effects, or even absorb knowledge from partners while cooperating (e.g. Inkpen, 1996; Lavie, 2007; Niemczyk et al., 2012; Karpacz, 2014). Nevertheless, formulating a strategic response to identified change on a basis of contractual structures means broadening the range of stakeholders with a legitimate claim to generated value. All firms engaged in an inter-organizational collaborative arrangement participate in the distribution of common and private benefits. The possibility to learn and ultimately acquire knowledge and capabilities of participating partners works in both directions, hence gaining access to necessary resources through inter-organizational collaboration brings in the risk of losing already controlled strategic assets (Najda-Janoszka, 2011a, b). Accordingly, the area of concern involves the problem of asymmetric power balance together with varying effectiveness of isolating mechanisms used for protecting sensitive knowledge and capabilities. It should be expected that the initial composition of isolating mechanisms may turn out inefficient as established cooperation evolve (Teece, 2007; Fischer, 2011). Given that in the context of inter-organizational cooperation social relationships are viewed as a key factor of control and coordination mechanisms, scholars suggest developing personal business relations to reduce the risk of opportunism of business partners (e.g. Alsos et al., 2007; Grudzewski et al., 2008; Madsen, 2010). However, despite the fact that the literature on trust in inter-organizational relationships is impressively broad (Grudzewski et al., 2008), it tends to focus on the links between trust and performance at the network level, narrowing the scope to development and distribution of common benefits. Meanwhile, the role of trust and social networks in the context of knowledge capture by individual partners (private benefits distribution) remains to a large extent underexplored in terms of theoretical as well as empirical research (Inkpen, 1996; Jordan & Lowe, 2004; Kale & Singh, 2007). Nevertheless, a few available studies reveal that relationships based on trust formed at the personal level foster the leakage of critical knowledge (Hamel, 1991; Kale et al., 2000; Mansfield, 1985). It has been emphasized that due to social binding and close cooperation the know-how of the company becomes more transparent, and thus easier to identify and imitate (Jordan & Lowe, 2004). Thus, it supports the argument that the composition and content of used isolating mechanisms need to be continuously reviewed and modified to effectively address changing conditions of business relationships.

4.2.3 RECONFIGURING

Discussion presented in the previous sections confirms that depending on a perception of given selection factors a firm may choose to:
- ignore the signals, or
- notice changes and address them with an ad-hoc problem solving mechanism, or
- sense occurring changes as opportunities or threats and formulate a response based on a current composition of resources and capabilities, or
- approach sensed opportunities or threats by branching current action pattern.

The dynamic capabilities perspective presented in this study refers directly to the latter alternative. It is assumed that in order to maintain fitness with the changing context of performed business activity and escape from unfavorable path dependencies, a firm needs to implement far more reaching reconfiguration of the activity pattern than small scale, incremental adjustments (Helfat et al., 2007). Although a firm's value appropriation model and associated logic for deployment of isolating mechanisms may be sound enough to benefit from current business operations, it may turn out insufficient and ineffective for newly-sensed opportunities and threats. Thus, in order to timely and effectively capitalize on the potential of recognized opportunities and threats a firm may need to break some embedded path dependencies and reconfigure fundamental elements of its value appropriation capabilities and supportive resources.

The design and further implementation of a particular response depends on the nature of perceived opportunities and threats generated by selection effects and may involve different branches of a current value capture capability lifecycle (Helfat & Peteraf, 2003). A firm may decide to gradually reduce deployment or totally resign from using certain isolating mechanisms, which do not fit with changing conditions of the market and technological development (e.g. departing from a protection oriented usage of formal mechanisms toward an informal landscape where value appropriation is enforced by rather a strategy than law). Given the scale of irreversible consequences of such decision it should be preceded by a comprehensive, unbiased evaluation of the potential and inefficiencies of a particular capability. This form of capability branching implies not only learning of new ways of doing things but also unlearning obsolete routines (Eisenhardt & Martin, 2000). This emphasizes the key role of management not only in designing technicalities of the response but also in ensuring necessary engagement and commitment of employees involved in the process of change (Zucchella & Scabini, 2007; Alsos et al., 2007).

Nevertheless, identification of threatening signals from the current market does not have to result in abandoning and a total cessation of certain value appropriation practices, as they may turn out to be still valid and effective however in new geographical or product markets, which a given firm is planning to enter. However, the potential of a capability in a new context of use may not be clear and comprehensible for managers and employees involved in the transfer process. Thus, in order to conduct such transfer and capitalize on an idiosyncratic value of a particular capability, the exact nature of a capability itself needs to be deeply understood and that implies codification of underlying tacit knowledge (Teece, 2001). Deep understanding enables necessary adaptation of transferred capability to a new context. Nevertheless, replicability brings in both, the advantages and risks. As the firm behavior with respect to value capture practices becomes more readable through codified knowledge, a firm becomes more vulnerable to imitation and other harmful practices of current and potential competitors, suppliers, complementors. Moreover, enabling a wider internal audience to decipher underlying logic of existing action patterns increases the risk of opportunistic behavior of internal interest groups (Mazur, 2011). Thus, deciding on redeployment or replication of a given capability a firm needs to address those risks while planning and implementing the action.

Capability branching is also about combining and integrating. A firm may reconfigure the way it captures value by introducing radical improvements to existing practices and by rearranging capabilities deployed in different parts of a firm into new combinations (e.g. broadening the scope of use of already possessed patents not only as formal protection instruments but also for strategic purposes in new projects). However, such approach requires an unbiased and open thinking of top management, middle management and other employees who implement changes into a daily practice. As it was mentioned before changing the action pattern concerned with value appropriation involves alternation in resource allocation processes (framing biases) and in behavior of individuals in organizations (cognitive limitations) (Teece, 2001). Meanwhile, Teece (2007, p. 1335) points out that "enterprises tend to frame new problems in a manner consistent with the enterprise's current knowledge base, assets, and /or established problem-solving heuristics and established business model." Thus, it is argued that in order to prevent biased decisions and to integrate new practices and knowledge across different levels of organizational culture, systems, and operations (Teece, 2007; Sirmon et al., 2007) critical activities of management should be focused on trainings (Zucchella & Scabini, 2007), communication of goals, values, expectations, and continuous motivation (Sprafke & Wilkens, 2014). Such efforts together with decentralization can support greatly "overriding certain dysfunctional features of established decision rules and resource allocation processes" (Teece, 2007, p. 1327) as well as ensuring long term commitment in the face of uncertainty and initial-stage difficulties. However, it needs to be underlined, that all incidents of sensitive knowledge leakage, misuse of intellectual property, dissipation of value to competitors, complementors or suppliers should be monitored and managed in a continuous manner. Circumstances sensed and analyzed while designing an appropriate response may change subtly but meaningfully until a formulated response finally reaches the phase of implementation. Moreover, given that the dynamic capabilities perspective builds on the evolutionary approach and assumes a dynamic nature of social reality, it implies that all new compositions of value capture mechanisms follow a recursive cycle of variation–selection–retention.

5   RESEARCH METHODOLOGY

Categories guiding the analysis of the study are justified theoretically in the previous Chapters 2, 3, and 4. However, a high quality research requires also a clear explanation of methodological choices made. Proper application of scientific procedures enables translating obtained evidence into original contribution to the existing stock of knowledge. Acknowledging the importance of research methodology it is worth recalling the words of Karl Pearson (1900, p. 12), who underlined that "[as] the field of science is unlimited (…) the unity of all sciences consists alone in its methods, not its material." Given that to the best of author's knowledge there is no published analysis approaching value appropriation with the dynamic capabilities framework and facing the fact that multidimensional concept of dynamic capabilities generates considerable challenges for empirical research (Zahra et al., 2006; Pavlou & El Sawy, 2011), ensuring methodological rigour is a prerequisite for a proper accommodation of the complexity of investigated problem. Therefore, the aim of this Chapter is to present not the mere steps adopted in studying research problem, but primarily the logic behind them, remembering that "if (…) work gives a description of phenomena that appeals to his imagination rather than to his reason, then it is bad science" (Pearson, 1900, p. 10). Hence, the Chapter starts by discussing the philosophical underpinnings of the study, since adopted philosophical stance implies far-reaching consequences with regard to the used methodology. After that, the research design of the study is introduced. It embraces the main assumption, objectives of the study, research questions, used research method and description of deployed research procedure. Given the choice of qualitative approach and multi-case design research, the next section presents the criteria used for theoretical sampling. A brief description of resulting set of five case studies is followed by an exhaustive explanation of methods used for gathering data. Recognizing the challenges concerned with generalization from the case study research, the final section provides a thorough description of the research technique used for data analysis.

5.1 PHILOSOPHICAL UNDERPINNINGS

Approaching a new area of scientific exploration with an aim to explain links not addressed before (Gilbert, 2005), requires a thoughtful choice of an appropriate paradigm to ensure a high quality research. The importance of that decision stems from the fact that each paradigm represents a distinct yet cohesive system of ontological, epistemological and methodological elements. Hence, a chosen paradigm guides subsequent decisions on research design and reasoning while analyzing collected data.

Most authors confirm that the field of management is dominated by a positivist paradigm, which assumes one reality, objectively determined and explained through quantitative methodologies (Lincoln & Guba, 2000; Eisenhardt & Graebner, 2007; Sułkowski, 2012). It is quite commonly argued that building knowledge trough deductive reasoning based on testing hypotheses and a pursuit of statistical generalization, is a most suitable, rigorous approach for conducting research that complies with the criteria of reliability and validity (Czakon, 2013). However, given that the selection of a proper paradigm stems from the defined research area and content of formulated research objectives, it was clear that this study is characterized more by expanding existing theories on value appropriation and verification than hypothesis testing and statistical generalizations of known constructs. Along with a qualitative approach inclination, the adopted understanding of key concepts and processes to be observed and verified during the empirical research, revealed a compliance with an assumption of an imperfect apprehension of the reality. In the dynamic capability perspective and value appropriation concept a central role is assign to managers responsible for making strategic decisions (Helfat et al., 2007), thus it suggests a need for acknowledging that the meaning is not necessarily given apriori but also generated by individuals and groups (Lincoln & Guba, 2000; Lisiński, 2011; Sułkowski, 2012). Such approach emphasizes the importance of contextual factors (Piekkari, Welch & Paavilainen, 2009), yet it does not imply a radical relativist perspective (Remenyi et al., 1998; Lincoln & Guba, 2000), as the aim of the study is to provide explanation that exceeds beyond a single, idiosyncratic case. The formulated dynamic capability-based framework of value appropriation builds on the assumption of existence of commonalities across firms and industries (Eisenhardt & Martin, 2000).

Resuming, ontological assumption of this study of a tangible reality concretized by individuals, is compliant with the post-positivist / realist approach (Lincoln & Guba, 2000). Further, recognizing that subjectivist and objectivist approaches are not alternatives but two extremes on the continuum (Remenyi et al., 1998), this study is guided by an intermediate epistemological stance, which proclaims "that knowledge although not absolute, can be accumulated, tested, and either retained or discarded" (Holden & Lynch, 2004, p. 407). Hence, conducted research includes certain features of the objectivist and subjectivist approach (Remenyi et al., 1998; Perry, 1998). Adopted philosophical stance implies certain practical consequences with regard to the used methodology, as the post-positivist approach encourages deploying multiple methods in accordance with a triangulation principle (Denzin, 1970). Therefore, this research builds on a qualitative approach and a case study method due to its widely aproved usefulness in the early stage of scientific problem diagnosis (Czakon, 2013, pp. 92–93), and follows the methodological rigor of a multiple-case design supported by methodological and data sources triangulation. Guided by the chosen paradigm conducted research confirmed a high level of trustworthiness by fulfilling all four criteria of credibility, dependability, transferability and confirmability.

5.2 RESEARCH DESIGN

The author's interest in the value capture process emerged along an extensive study of the literature and research work conducted in previous research projects in the years 2004–2013 under the leadership of professor M. Bednarczyk.[1] Obtained results suggested existence of certain inefficiencies in organizational patterns during studied processes of virtualization and innovation (Bednarczyk, 2006; Najda-Janoszka, 2010; Bednarczyk, 2011; Najda-Janoszka & Bednarczyk, 2014). Collected evidence presented the scope of potential benefits associated with an inter-organizational cooperation determined from the individual-participant perspective. It was confirmed that effective implementation of organizational solutions postulated within the concept of virtual organization is accompanied by improvement of competitiveness of companies employing these solutions (Najda-Janoszka, 2010). Given that there were also firms that implemented the concept but failed in terms of retaining the value generated from cross-organizational ventures, it inspired further areas of inquiry focused on possible reasons of that failure. A confrontation of collected evidence with with the model of innovation value chain for regional tourism developed by Bednarczyk (2014, pp. 56–57) helped to crystallize the research area of interest as it enabled location of the problem within the value appropriation practices. Further research work guided by the logic of competitive gaps (Bednarczyk,

---

[1] Projects financed by the Polish Ministry of Science and Higher Education, and focused on strategic management issues of management system virtualization in small and medium-sized enterprises (1 H02D 065 26), entrepreneurship and competitiveness in the tourism economy based on knowledge (N N115 3730 33), management of regional tourism innovative value chain (N N115 321339).

2006; Bednarczyk, 2011; Najda-Janoszka, 2011) and focused on a broad issue of protection of value generated from innovations (Bednarczyk & Najda-Janoszka, 2014) helped to define the research area of interest. Moreover, the fact that projects concerned tourism industry, very peculiar with regard to the innovation process, imitation practices and efficiency of innovation protection mechanisms (Najda-Janoszka & Kopera, 2014), it strongly enhanced the understanding of the role of contextual conditions while exploring the value capture practices. Resulting publications and conference papers of the author clearly confirm the evolvement of the research concept for this study. Undoubtedly, the feedback received from reviewers, conference participants, research project partners, as well as business practitioners participating in projects, facilitated a revision of the initial problem definition and substantially enhanced the research process by enriching the conceptual picture of the investigated phenomena and strengthening the methodological basis for the study. In result of that broad spectrum of valuable inspiration, the initially defined problem of value capturing was approached with the dynamic capabilities perspective, and has become a part of a broader project conducted by the author and financed by the Polish National Science Centre (Narodowe Centrum Nauki) (2013/11/D/HS4/03965).

According to the logic of the dynamic perspective, the efficiency of the value appropriation process is determined by a firm's ability to build and use specific compositions of isolating mechanisms, and equally by a firm's ability to reconfigure those compositions in response to changes occurring in organizational and environmental contexts. Thus, it is assumed that the value capture should involve both types of organizational capabilities: those focused on ensuring an increase in productivity of existing processes and replication of effective practices, and those driven by organizational learning processes and enabling branching of existing practices. The aim of this study was to enhance understanding of a complex and context-bound process of value appropriation by deploying the dynamic capabilities perspective. There are two integral modules of that aim: (1) the conceptual objective – conceptualization and operationalization of organizational capabilities that enable shaping configurations of value appropriation mechanisms, and (2) the research objective – providing a rich qualitative evidence of a routine-based approach to replication of effective value capture practices and alternation of existing action patterns in response to perceived threats and opportunities. Thus, in an effort to develop a dynamic capability-based framework of value appropriation, three related research questions were formulated:

1. How does a perception of a selection factor affect the way a firm introduces changes into existing practices of value appropriation?
2. Does the pattern branching response to identified opportunities or threats tend to be structured along activity clusters of dynamic capabilities?

3. How do contextual conditions affect the content and implementation of a response?

Providing answer to those questions implicates elaboration of "theoretical links not previously addressed in the literature" (Gilbert, 2005, p. 743). Hence, the contribution to the field of strategic management does not concern statistical generalizations of known constructs but the logic of the developed theoretical framework that expands existing theories on value appropriation. Accordingly, recognizing the challenges of investigating a complex, multifaceted and contextually embedded phenomenon, the problem was addressed with a qualitative approach and a study case method, as "the ultimate goal of the case study [is] to uncover patterns, determine meanings, construct conclusions and build theory" (Patton & Appelbaum, 2003, p. 67). Given that to best of author's knowledge, no studies have yet explored value appropriation practices with reference to dynamic capabilities perspective, a case study research appears as an appropriate vehicle for facilitating in-depth understanding of the problem and developing a refined conceptualization of microfoundations of dynamic capabilities deployed to branch value capture action patterns. It is argued that a case study research provides a fine-grained view from different standpoints, and thus enables gathering rich and versatile data necessary for gaining new knowledge about specific phenomena (Yin, 2014; Eisenhardt & Graebner, 2007; Czakon, 2013). Further, recognizing that the evidence obtained from multiple cases is commonly considered as a more compelling ground for theory building than findings provided by a single case study (Eisenhardt & Graebner, 2007; Yin, 2014, p. 57), the research strategy for this study builds on a multiple-case design. The main intention was to clarify whether emerging findings concerning branching of value capture action patterns are idiosyncratic to the specificity of a single case or can be replicated in several cases leading to framework abstraction (Eisenhart & Graebner, 2007, p. 27). Thus, research was guided not by the uniqueness rationale but by the replication logic (Yin, 2014, p. 57). Although the situational context determines the distinctiveness of every single case, it can also serve as a common denominator for all of examined cases providing specification of certain characteristics for the entire class of objects under study (Karaś, 2014, p. 340).

Case study research designs, single as well as multi-case ones, need to be characterized by methodical rigor to ensure high quality of conducted research (Czakon, 2009). It implies developing a coherent and comprehensive research procedure following that rigor at each stage. A procedure formulated for this study is illustrated in Figure 5.1. The initial stage entails a sound theoretical grounding with respect to two main problem areas of value appropriation process and the dynamic capabilities perspective, followed by formulation of significant research questions not addressed by the extant research. That theoretical foundation provided necessary criteria for selecting appropriate cases as

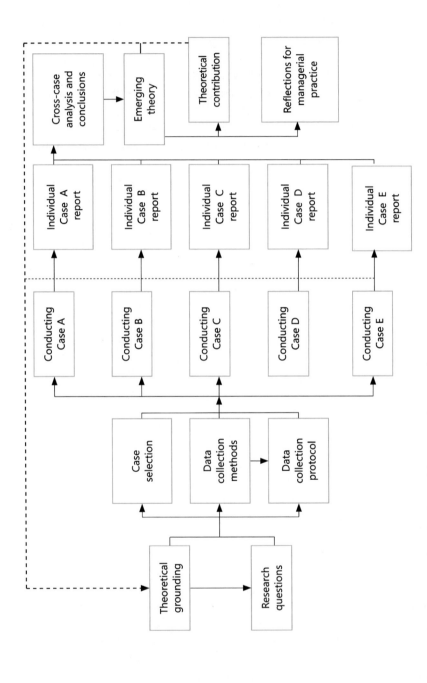

Figure 5.1 Deployed procedure for the multi-case study research

Source: Author's own work based on Eisenhardt (1989, p. 533); Czakon (2013, p. 102); Yin (2014, p. 60).

well as guidelines for choosing data collection methods and developing a data collection protocol used for ensuring reliability of the conducted research. Guided by the replication logic, a selected set of five individual case studies was treated as a series of experiments, each providing evidence in its own right with regard to formulated research questions. Resulting individual case conclusions were considered as subjects to be confirmed or disconfirmed by other cases. During the cross-case analysis the extent of the replication logic was determined providing salient insights for the emerging theory. Recursive confrontation with the extant literature enabled definition of the theoretical contribution of the research and formulation of valuable managerial conclusions.

5.3 CASE SELECTION

Complying with the methodical rigor of a multiple case design, a selection of firms was based on a theoretical sampling (Eisenhardt & Graebner, 2007; Yin, 2014, pp. 57–59). Directed by the theoretical implications of reviewed literature on value appropriation and dynamic capabilities a parsimonious set of five criteria was applied to select suitable cases (Table 5.1).

Table 5.1 Criteria for case selection

Criteria
Intensive use of knowledge and technology in performed business activity
Involvement in cross-organizational value creation process
Minimum 5 years of performance history
Richness and diversity of data
Readily access to key informants

Source: Author's own work.

1. Exhibiting an intensive use of knowledge and technology in performed business activity.

Firms relying heavily on knowledge and technology operate in rather dynamic than stable environments, and thus often face challenges related to discontinuous changes. Dynamic context of business activity generates multiple selection factors, which according to the literature stimulate changes in action patterns of investigated firms. As technology becomes increasingly sophisticated in complexity and its lifespan is shortening quite intensively across industries, rendering obsolete many formal protection mechanisms, firms face an ever more challenging task to ensure a sustainable and effective shield of sensitive knowledge. Thus, there is a robust and sound theoretical justification for selecting firms exhibiting knowledge- and technology-intensive business activity to investigate dynamic capability deployment within the area of value capture practices.

2. Involvement in cross-organizational value creation process.

The extant literature confirms a growing trend of using various interorganizational structures to implement business ventures as it is argued that such structures enable extending the range of performed value chain activities in a relatively flexible manner. Nevertheless, the very nature of inter-organizational arrangements implies coexistence of competition, cooperation and control relations among involved business entities across performed activities and committed resources. Firms enter those arrangements in pursue of certain proportion of common and private benefits, yet a changing context affects the initial structure of expected payoffs and raises additional challenges with regard to management of value appropriation. Hence, choosing to investigate branching of value capture capabilities in such context is strongly supported by the body of knowledge in the field of strategic management.

3. Exhibiting minimum 5 years of performance history.

Organizational capabilities come to existence through a development process. In contrast to ad hoc problem solving mechanism dynamic capabilities require time to achieve a minimum level of functionality. Thus, it is more feasible to observe deployment of dynamic capabilities in established firms with a substantial performance history than in newly founded ventures. Further, a minimum threshold of five years of continuous performance appeared appropriable for firms operating in knowledge- and technology-intensive industries characterized by rapid and discontinuous changes.

4. Providing richness and diversity of data.

Given that dynamic capabilities are deeply embedded in organizational processes it was considered critical for selected firms to yield qualitative richness and diversity of information. Moreover, according to the replication logic of a multiple case design each selected firm should stand on its own merits as unit of analysis, thus should be supported by a broad enough information base.

5. Providing readily access to key informants.

Dynamic capabilities are defined in terms of an organizational capacity, hence, are observable when deployed. It implicates that investigation of dynamic capabilities requires a longer time span, which increases the chances to observe their implementation. Therefore, the contact with key informants should remain readily operable and lasting, i.e. corresponding to the duration of the investigation.

Given that the research area covered very sensitive issues, the risk of non-cooperation by firms was quite high. Therefore, in order to obtain an appropriate set of firms for a cross case analysis, ranging from 4 to 10 (Eisenhardt, 1989, p. 545), the selection process involved re-contacting organizations studied in previous research projects either for participation in the new project or for references to other firms operating in related business areas (knowledge and technology intensive). The initial set consisted of 11 firms (Table 5.2). During a series of short (30 to 45 min) preliminary interviews conducted in October–November of 2012 firms were checked according to formulated criteria. One firm exhibited to short history of performance for identifying dynamic capabilities (Case I). Manager of the firm J informed that the data required for the research are too sensitive to be revealed (Case J). Two other firms proved to be engaged only in purely transactional relations with other market players, as presented performance did not include cross-organizational ventures requiring resource commitment and activity alignment (Case J, Case K). Finally seven firms met the criteria and were selected as objects for further in-depth research.

Table 5.2 Initial sample

Firm	Main business activity	Age	Cross-organizational relationships	Intensity of knowledge and technology use	Meeting defined criteria
Case A	Complex and integrated marketing services	11	Cooperation	High	Yes
Case B	Design and construction of data processing centers	7	Cooperation	High	Yes
Case C	Trade of industrial electronics	27	Cooperation	High	Yes
Case D	Production of suppressors and transformers	24	Cooperation	High	Yes
Case E	Multi-Industry Corporation / Technology solutions for transportation	20/5	Cooperation	High	Yes
Case F	Design and implementation of electrical installations	32	Cooperation	High	Yes
Case G	Construction and installation of wind turbines	8	Cooperation	High	Yes
Case H	Trade of industrial electronics	14	Transaction	High	No
Case I	Complex and integrated marketing services	4	Cooperation	High	No
Case J	Design and implementation of IT systems for logistics	8	Cooperation	High	No
Case K	Design and manufacturing products for intelligent traffic systems (ITS)	11	Transaction	High	No

Source: Author's own work.

Table 5.3 Description of five firms studied

Firm	Main business activity	Number of employees (2014)	Turnover (2014) (PLN in thousands)	Age	Core knowledge area	Intensity of knowledge and technology use	Simultaneously conducted inter-organizational projects (years 2013–2015)
Case A	Complex and integrated marketing services	22	>1 000 PLN	11	Market-related	High	12
Case B	Design and construction of data processing centers	10	~1 000 PLN	7	Technology-related	High	4
Case C	Trade of industrial electronics	34	>10 000 PLN	27	Market-related	High	4
Case D	Production of suppressors and transformers	307	>100 000 PLN	24	Technology-related	High	5
Case E	Multi-Industry Corporation	(1031)	(>1 000 000 PLN)	20	Market/Technology – related	High	Inaccessible
	Technology solutions for transportation	42	~10 000 PLN	5	Market/Technology – related	High	6

Note: 1 EUR = 4,2623 PLN (31-12-2014) Polish National Bank – NBP

Source: Author's own work.

During the first run of in-depth studies, which took place in the time period between January and August of 2013), all seven entities actively participated in research by providing necessary information during interviews. However, in the following stages of the investigation, which involved subsequent interviews, on-site observations and internal documentation review, two of selected firms (Case F, Case G) turn out to be reluctant to reveal more detailed data concerning value appropriation practices. Therefore, the final sample consisted of five cases, which constitutes a manageable number for a reliable and comprehensive analysis (Eisenhardt, 1989). Because of the sensitivity of the collected data, the names of investigated firms were disguised. The final case set is outlined in Table 5.3.

The last Case E needs an additional explanation. This study adopted the organizational level of analysis, and therefore the basic unit of analysis was an individual firm. However, the Case E concerns primarily a division of a large, multi-industry corporation. Since embracing all processes and activities performed by the corporation would be unmanageable for this multi case design study, the investigation was directed toward one division with a substantial decision-making autonomy with regard to budgeting, investment and strategic planning, project management and evaluation. Nevertheless, the individual and cross-case analysis acknowledges the contextual specificity of this case.

5.4 DATA COLLECTION

Given that one of the key characteristics of case study research is that it builds on richness and diversity of information, collection of necessary data followed the logic of triangulation. It is argued that triangulation increases both the reliability of the collected data and the process of gathering it (Czakon, 2013, pp. 105–106), as pointed by Patton (2002, p. 555) "no single method ever adequately solves the problem of rival explanations." In order to reduce a systematic bias in the gathered data and to enhance credibility of the investigation two kinds of triangulation were applied: methodological and data triangulation (Table 5.4).

Table 5.4 Methodological and data triangulation

Methodological triangulation	Data triangulation
Face-to-face interviews	Top managers of selected firms
Direct observations	Project manager of selected firms
Extraction from internal primary sources	Project managers of cooperating partners
Extraction from external secondary sources	Internal documentation
	External records

Source: Author's own work.

Methodological triangulation

Methodological triangulation refers to implementation of different data collection methods. Accordingly in this research data were collected by means of:

- Face-to-face semi-structured interviews. Research involved 11 short (30–45 min) interviews with candidate firms for further investigation and a total of 24 in-depth, two to three hour in-person interviews with highly knowledgeable managers of ultimately selected firms and collaborating partners. Preliminary interviews were conducted in October and November of 2012 (Figure 5.2). In-depth interviews were conducted in two time periods in order to identify changes in the compositions of value appropriation mechanisms and in the contextual conditions in which a given firm operates. The first round of in-depth interviews with seven selected firms took place in the period from January to August in 2013. The second round with five firms (two firms were discarded from the research due to reluctance to provide sensitive but necessary information) occurred between September 2014 and May 2015. Each interview was guided by a semi-structured template entailing open questions concerning broad problems of organizational perception of environmental and organizational changes; definition and changes within the core knowledge area; composition, development and usage of isolating mechanisms; value appropriation challenges during cross-organizational cooperation. Not all informants agreed for recording the interview, thus a lot of effort was put into developing an accurate transcript of all information provided. Each transcript was sent to informants for verification. After approval transcribed interviews were entered into the case study database.
- Direct observations. Over a period of two years (from March of 2013 till May of 2015) a total number of 13 direct observations were conducted. Selected firms provided opportunities for a passive participation in project planning and evaluation meetings, for visiting on-site investments, observing developed product maintenance and servicing. Each observation was followed by a thorough description recorded into the case study database.
- Extraction from internal primary and external secondary sources. In order to control a possible retrospective bias by informants, research involved also a document analysis. A wide variety of internal and external documentation was examined, including financial statements, project documentation, customer and supplier lists, internal memos (a total of 71 documents), as well as press releases, industry statistics and reports. All retrieved, relevant information was recorded into the case study database.

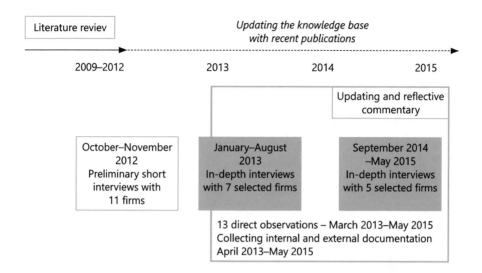

Figure 5.2 Timeline of data collection
Source: Author's own work.

Triangulation of data sources

Data triangulation involves using different sources of information for cross-examining the same phenomenon. Thus, in order to minimize an individual bias resulting from the personal characteristics and perception, informants participating in research represented three distinct groupings – top managers and project managers of selected firms, and project managers of cooperating partners. Informant profile extension revealed some inconsistencies across data sources (in particular between top and project managers of investigated firms). However, instead of weakening the evidence those inconsistencies substantially enhanced understanding of certain observed practices. Further, reaching for a documentation to extract useful information, investigation involved a wide spectrum of internal and external records. Data and related interpretations presented in financial statements were confronted with other internal documents such as project documentation, internal memos etc. Moreover, in order to enhance the understanding of organizational decisions and move beyond the organizational perception of related contextual conditions, investigation also included public documents such as analyst reports, industry press releases.

Due to a large amount of diverse data, which was collected during research, a dedicated software application Atlas.ti. was used to enhance storing, managing and analyzing gathered information. Table 5.5 presents a synthesized version of data sources and methods used.

Table 5.5 Data sources

| Case | Interviews | | | Internal documents | | Direct observations | |
	Informants from the Firm	Informants from cooperating partners	Total	Number	Examples	Number	Examples
Case A	4	1	5	12	Financial statements, customer list, project list, project documentation, internal memos	3	Project planning meeting, developed program maintenance, program servicing
Case B	2	2	4	8	Financial statements, customer list, project documentation	2	Project planning meeting, on-site engineering services
Case C	3	1	4	17	Financial statements, supplier list, project documentation, internal memos	2	Project planning meeting, project evaluation meeting
Case D	4	1	5	16	Financial statements, supplier list, project documentation	2	Project planning meeting, confirming delivery conditions with suppliers
Case E	4	2	6	18	Financial statements, customer list, suppliers list, project list, project documentation, internal memos	4	Project planning meetings, on-site engineering services, evaluation of subcontractors
TOTAL	17	7	24	71	na	13	na

Source: Author's own work.

5.5 DATA ANALYSIS

In this research analytic strategy followed theoretical propositions and reflections (comprehensively presented in the Chapter 4), which formed a point of departure for designing the multiple case research (Yin, 2014). Nevertheless, although the theoretical orientation guided the analysis it does not imply prevalence of a deductive approach (Miles et al., 2014, pp. 237–238). On the one hand, theory-derived propositions were applied to data in order to confirm the appropriateness of introduced conceptual construct. On the other hand, gathered information was simultaneously examined in an inductive manner for emerging understanding of observed relationships and action patterns (Miles & Hubermann, 1994, pp. 431–432). Hence, a conducted analysis exhibited a "continuous interplay" between the two approaches as it involved a sequential iteration between the empirical evidence and theoretical input. However, it needs to be underlined that the aim of the iterative confrontation was not to define new categories but to identify the pattern of value appropriation practices along three activity clusters of dynamic capabilities. In result it can be concluded that the analysis followed a convergent approach, which is consistent with the post-positivist paradigm of this research (Lincoln & Guba, 2000).

The research technique used for data analysis was pattern matching (Yin, 2014, pp. 143–147), which involves an iterative comparison of a theoretically derived pattern described as a dynamic capability-based framework of value capture with an actual pattern in the empirical data. Accordingly with the methodical rigor of a multiple case design, data analysis process focused on pattern matching, consisted of two steps: within-case analysis, and cross-case analysis (Eisenhardt, 1989).

Within-case analysis

Given that the research adopted a multiple case design and a replication logic for the analysis, the extensive narratives of each individual case were broken down to more theory oriented descriptions. Challenged by the spatial constraints and the trade-off between better stories and better theories (Eisenhardt & Graebner, 2007, p. 29) the rich and detailed narratives were compromised in order to convey the emergent theory in a readable and appealing way. Hence, descriptions were organized around identification of core knowledge areas, types and compositions of isolating mechanisms, action patterns of value capturing related to activity clusters of dynamic capabilities, and contextual conditions that generate change impetus and influence the organizational response to selecting factors. Recognizing that dynamic capabilities vary in timing and effects and it is very difficult to separate existence of those capabilities from their effects at a given point in time (Zahra et al., 2006, p. 925), the analyzed evidence concerned a long time span reaching beyond the period of direct observation. Analysis embraced current data obtained through direct observations conducted in several time points (March of 2013–May of 2015) and retrospective and archival data (past performance) collected through interviews and retrieved from documentation. In order to enhance the analysis structured descriptions included also tabular displays and graphical illustrations of gathered data (Eisenhardt, 1989).

Cross-case analysis

Guided by the replication logic the cross-case analysis involved an iterative process of data comparison across cases to elicit certain similarities or differences (analytical generalization) with regard to:
- existing patterns in using isolating mechanisms – the ability to solve problem within the area of value appropriation (operational capability),
- selection factors providing change impetus to existing patterns in using isolating mechanisms,
- the ability to change existing patterns in using isolating mechanisms reflected in actions deployed, which in turn may exhibit (1) ad hoc problem solving approach, or (2) dynamic capabilities approach, i.e. practices identified within activity clusters of sensing, seizing and reconfiguring.

In result of that confrontation, case-specific examples of dynamic capabilities referring to value appropriation were brought to a more abstract level following the theoretical framework presented in Chapter 4. Such procedure was consistent with the fundamental assumption of the dynamic capabilities perspective, that dynamic capabilities are inherently characterized by idiosyncrasies in performative details, yet at certain level of abstraction can also exhibit commonalities across firms (Eisenhardt & Martin, 2000; Zahra et al., 2006; Wang & Ahmed, 2007). In order to provide a more clear picture of the identified pattern, descriptions were enriched with aggregated tabular displays. At that stage of research the deconstructed concept of dynamic capabilities was synthesized allowing for defining the contribution of the study to the field of strategic management and providing an outline for further research paths. The right to follow that procedure was justified by the high quality of conducted research. In pursuit of a trustworthy study author referred to criteria proposed by Lincoln and Guba (1985), Lincoln (1995) as those comply with the post-positivist paradigm and represent a reference set for all subsequently developed propositions for evaluating the goodness of qualitative research.

Table 5.6 Provisions made to meet research quality criteria

Research quality criteria	Means used in the study
Credibility	• Using research methods and techniques for data collecting and analyzing well established in qualitative investigation. • Deploying operational measures for investigated concept drawn from the framework proposed by Teece (2007). • Prolonged engagement between the researcher and informants (from preliminary short-interviews in 2012 till mid-2015). • Including in research sample only those firms with positive attitude toward the study, willing to provide data freely and honestly (firms reluctant to disclose necessary data were discarded from the research). • Triangulation of methods and data sources. • Using feedback offered by academics at presentations during conferences and by key informants, who reviewed interview transcripts and provided commentaries on patterns observed by the researcher. • Relating findings to the existing body of knowledge on value appropriation and the dynamic capabilities perspective.
Transferability	• Providing sufficient contextual information and detailed description of investigated action patterns, which enable comparisons and indicate potential for application of formulated conclusions to other situations. • Adopting the replication logic allowing for identified patterns to be verified at various sites. • Identification of limitations of the study, which affect the transferability of results.
Dependability	• Following case study methodical rigor. • Providing documentation trail (case study protocol, case study database). • Long time span of the study (data gathered at different points in time between years 2012 and 2015). • Triangulation of methods and data sources.
Confirmability	• Developing a record of data collected and providing a chain of evidence. • Reducing the effect of researcher bias by using theoretical frames for interview outlines and reflective commentaries provided by informants.

Source: Author's own work based on Lincoln & Guba (1985); Lincoln (1995).

6 CASE STUDIES

Collected evidence was analyzed by a pattern matching technique, which involves an iterative comparison of a theoretically derived pattern described as a dynamic capability-based framework of value appropriation with an actual pattern in the empirical data. Guided by the replication logic, data analysis process consisted of two steps: within-case analysis, and cross-case analysis, which are presented in the following chapters.

6.1 WITHIN CASE ANALYSIS

Instead of extensive narratives, subsequent chapters present a theory oriented descriptions organized around key issues: profile and outline of the history of the firm; core knowledge area; characteristics of isolating mechanisms; activity clusters of dynamic capabilities; and ad hoc problem solving.

6.1.1 CASE A

Firm A has been on the market for 11 years (founded in 2004) and since its foundation it has specialized in the field of advanced IT based solutions for incentive marketing (motivation programs dedicated to personnel or business partners, not final customers). The company offers development (customer data analysis, mechanics of the program, budget, graphic materials, IT system, a collection of awards, training in the use of created solutions, legal and tax advice) and implementation of complex incentive programs (integration with logistics system, appointing permanent program coordinator, providing IT support, hotline, monitoring activity of the participants, collecting and archiving of data, budget control, tax services, reporting, etc.). The very beginning of that business activity was described as "just a few committed people sharing a common vision that runs the whole project." Start-up period coincided with very favorable market conditions associated with a dynamic economic growth observed in Poland. During the first five years the company experienced a very rapid growth, in terms of the quantity and the value of realized projects. The turnover was systematically increasing around 30 to 45 percent a year. Firm was growing also in terms of its tangible and human assets. Starting with only 4 people on temporary contracts, in 2010 the average employment reached 23 people on permanent contracts. Meanwhile, Firm A moved from a rented office to its own spacious building corresponding to the growing needs of the firm in respect to conducted operations: open space for project managers and co-workers, logistics and storage area, server room, etc. Substantial investments concerned also development and implementation of an advanced IT platform (total value of the investment app. 300 000 PLN), and further a logistics system based on IT platform (total value of the investment app. 200 000 PLN). It needs to be emphasized that for both of those projects Firm A received a financial support from the EU Founds. Since 2010, the company has began to experience the negative effects of the crisis related to the economic downturn and increased competitive pressure – "it is a common observation that in the time of crisis firms turn to cost reduction and it is usually a marketing budget that is being corrected in the first round." Since that year the number of realized projects and their value have decreased substantially. In 2010, for the first time in its performance history, Firm A suffered a loss reaching 25 per cent of its turnover value. The following years have indicated continuance of difficulties in maintaining a positive profit margin: "you can say that the ultimate goal for now is to maintain a stable level of revenues – maintaining the status quo." Nevertheless, undertaken actions have cumulated around staff reduction and tangible asset selling. Despite a small increase in 2012 the turnover has not recovered from the downturn of 2010. Even though Firm A has not suffered a net loss in recent years, a continuing negligible profit on sales (or even loss in 2012) indicate significant internal inefficiencies.

Core knowledge area

The key area of knowledge covers the methodology of creating an incentive program as a complex and integrated business solution. However, "the mechanics of the program is just one of the puzzles in the process of value creation in the company." Firm A is aware of the fact that incentive programs are products widely available in the market, which technical content does not necessarily involve a highly sophisticated know-how. Therefore, the company competes not so much on the technical content but on the way the mechanics of a particular program is integrated with other supporting systems (e.g. logistics system, IT platform for managing the product base). This integration allows for providing a more favorable market offer in terms of time and price. However, as pointed out by the project manager, "the level of experience and knowledge of employees indicate substantial opportunities for increasing the efficiency of the firm, unfortunately, there is a lack of appropriate incentives."

Characteristic of isolating mechanisms

Firm A deploys different kinds of isolating mechanisms, ranging from legal protection instruments as formal contracts with customers, supplier and employees to specific strategic assets and organizational procedures. The most important one refers to the developed proprietary logistic system: "an original, comprehensive solution developed in response to the need to increase efficiency of the Firm and its position among the growing number of competitors." Thus, stand alone proprietary system represents a strategic resource (VRIO) and the way it is deployed in a combination with other systems and program mechanics represents a value appropriation capability. Further, incentive programs provided by Firm A are supported by information systems offered in the SaaS model (Software as a Service). Firm A sells certain functionalities but not the software per se. This model allows for substantial savings on the customer side (subscription fee instead of time and financial costs of hardware and software installation, maintenance, support) but also provides tangible benefits for the Firm A: protection of the intellectual property as customers do not have the access to the source code and executable file; flexible adjustment of payments (charging per transaction, event, type of user) since all customer's data reside on servers own by Firm A. However, surprisingly there is no permanent supervision of implemented systems. The necessary software was created by former employees, who were provided a high degree of freedom in a development process, including no requirements concerning documentation. "The staff responsible for the systems in place is now gone, and new specialists have not received the relevant documentation and are not able to make the necessary changes and adjustments." Thus, in case of any program modification Firm A is forced to ask program authors for necessary services. Drawing conclusions from the problems raised, Firm A is now striving to create as-built documentation, but due to the lack of experience in this respect the results are far from satisfactory (more on that effort in the section – ad hoc problem solving). It can be concluded that Firm A depends on use of IT services over which has quite limited control. Further, recognizing that Firm A is responsible for storing customer's sensitive data, it raises additional challenges, which relate to ensuring data security. Firm A implemented several procedures concerned with protection of confidential information (e.g. appropriate work place arrangements that prevent capturing sensitive information on computer screens by potential customers or other people moving around the office), yet observed incidents of sensitive information leakage (e.g. employment reduction plans, information about customer's internal procedures) suggest substantial inefficiencies in that area.

Activity clusters of dynamic capabilities

During the time of economic prosperity Firm A was engaged in an intentional and systematic search process for opportunities. Top management developed a routinized approach to searching the market for new customers, building broad networks of business relations, scanning the content of solutions provided by close and distant competitors, searching for financial support for firm development. The subsequent lines of actions, which exhibit a response to identified opportunities, confirms the intentionality of performed activities. Sensed opportunities for firm development were addressed with a complex response enabling increase of sophistication of the solutions provided. Firm A developed new strategic resources, deployed them in a complementary way with other resources and thus introduced idiosyncratic combinations enabling value capturing.

When circumstances changed toward more demanding during the economic crisis, the reaction of Firm A followed a different mechanism, namely ad hoc problem solving. Firm A postponed any larger investments and concentrated on maintaining status quo. Signals received from internal and external environments perceived as threats were addressed with ad hoc, spontaneous solutions, which introduced only small scale and in fact temporary changes. In order to keep customers Firm A accepted unfavorable terms of contracts, performed additional tasks not included in contracts and without any additional payments. In search for revenue Firm A decided to engage in a large, difficult project for a customer representing an industry, with which Firm A had no experience: "knowing the size and complexity of the program Firm assigned just one project manager and one IT specialist, no wonder that after 6 months after launching, developed program generates system failures almost every day." During those difficult times the problem of missing system documentation returned with redoubled strength. Nevertheless, instead of a systemic approach based on certain rules and procedures, Firm A decided to solve the problem by shifting responsibility to contracted IT specialist, and "it is the contractor not the Firm that defines the standards and key components of the documentation."

It turned out that facing threats Firm A exhibited a relatively strong routine rigidity, as it maintained existing action patterns even though those practices were not matching the circumstances anymore. A more demanding context revealed certain inefficiencies in organizational behavior that were generated by a limited functionality of operational capabilities of value capture. During the time of prosperity a somehow relaxed attitude toward key issues

Sensing

Searching
- Internal resource base
- current market for new clients
- solutions provided by competitors
- financial support possibilities

Perceived opportunities for broadening value streams and strengthening market position

Triggers for change

Economic prosperity, growing budgets for marketing initiatives, EU funds for small firms, growing competition

Seizing

- Developing own IT platform and system solutions for logistics
- Obtaining financial support from EU funds
- Hiring IT specialists
- Professional trainings for project managers

Reconfiguring

- Integration of new systems (logistics, IT platform) with program mechanics
- Implementing SaaS model for providing information services

Figure 6.1 Activity clusters of Firm A
Source: Author's own work.

Ad hoc problem solving

Perceived threat of weakening market position

Triggers for change

Economic crisis, reduced budgets for marketing initiatives, shrinking market, growing competition, problems with software updating and development

- Introducing procedures for sensitive information protection
- Cost reduction initiatives – staff reduction and hiring new employees, asset selling, renting office space
- Signing contracts after actual commitment of resources
- Accepting additional tasks not included in contracts
- Developing documentation for used programs

Figure 6.2 Ad hoc problem solving in Firm A
Source: Author's own work.

concerning risk assessment, safety provisions of contracts, project knowledge base development, technological security ensuring, was not alarming due to market growth and abundance of opportunities. Discontinuity changes challenged existing action patterns but Firm's A efforts did not address the core problem. Facing threats, Firm A was motivated to commit resources but was unable to change the logic that underlined those investments. Due to the dominance of ad-hoc problem solving approach "each new project is a new venture exploiting selective experiences in a spontaneous and individualized manner." It suggests substantial gaps in the recursive cycle of organizational learning processes, which underlie development of dynamic capabilities.

Resuming, Firm A exhibited certain patterns of actions that could fall into categories of activity clusters of dynamic capabilities. Nevertheless, those activities were performed during favorable circumstances, when Firm A introduced changes in response to perceived opportunities. Facing threats Firm A did not deploy dynamic capabilities to branch existing patterns of actions that mismatch with the new circumstances. Instead it decided to invest resources following spontaneous, ad-hoc responses. Moreover, a deeper insight into organizational practices confirmed significant deficiencies in processes of knowledge accumulation and articulation. It put in question actual functionality of the routinized approach used by Firm A to introduce changes into organizational behavior. Further, it is argued that in order to develop, enhance dynamic capabilities, those capabilities need to be deployed. Meanwhile, activity clusters in Firm A were left unused and unmaintained. Thus, it raises the risk that formerly used capacity may not be ready for activation when market condition change back toward more favorable circumstances.

6.1.2 CASE B[1]

Profile and outline of the history of the firm

Firm B was founded in 2008, thus it has been operating for 7 years. Its domain of business includes engineering services and consultancy in the design and construction of data processing centers (DPC), i.e. buildings or parts thereof, which consist of a server room and areas that support the functionality of the entire center such as separate technical premises with emergency power systems for electrical and electronic equipment (UPS), telecom and technical maintenance rooms, systems for power distribution and cooling. Firm B operates in a specific niche market facing rather limited competition: "other companies implement a very limited range of services just for the server room itself and not the entire DPC." Operating range covers the entire country, although the majority of carried out projects is located in the northern part of Poland. Since its founding till 2011 Firm B was experiencing a robust growth in revenues, number of projects, employment. In 2011 it employed 26 employees and its turnover reached 1 400 000 PLN. In the same year the growth trend collapsed.

---

1   Information concerning Firm B was presented in a separate article: Najda-Janoszka (2015, pp. 424–435).

A strategic partner (general contractor, a large company – Polish branch of a global corporation) did not paid the final crucial tranche of payments for an amount of 250 000 PLN at the final stage of project implementation. It was unexpected shock because firms had a good history of cooperation. In previous years two other projects were carried out successfully: "payments were always settled but in each case there were delays." Held payments caused a very difficult financial situation of the Firm B. Despite the fact that there were other parallel conducted projects Firm B had to reduce employment to only 6 employees. Overall turnover decreased by half, and by 2014 has not yet returned to the level of 2011. As a result of the difficult situation occurred, workers did not received salaries on time. Salaries were paid several months late, but for the full amount, including overtime and additives: "it strengthened relations, trust and mutual support in the Firm." In subsequent years Firm B has turned toward smaller, short-time projects. At the time of investigation Firm B carried out simultaneously four projects. The turnover has stabilized at a satisfactory level of app. 1 000 000 PLN. In 2014 area of business activity was expanded to include hotel services. Rationale for that diversification was to stabilize cash flow in the Firm B: "revenue from hotel services represents a financial buffer, that secures payments for workers and at the same time allows for timely payment of all other obligatory fees." In 2014 those accommodation services generated 1/10 of the total turnover.

Core knowledge area

The key area of expertise of Firm B concerns conceptualization and design of the overall media and building architecture of the data processing centers (DPCs). The high level of expertise sophistication stems from the nature of the DPC. "Those centers contain the most important elements of IT systems of enterprises and institutions, which are responsible for the smooth functioning of the corporate network and a variety of important applications." In addition to the servers and other hardware DPCs also include maintenance facilities, complex power systems, including emergency power supply, air conditioning systems and fire protection systems. "Each new project requires an intelligent integration of a comprehensive concept of the DPC with expert knowledge of professionals of a given industry." For project implementation Firm B engages not only employees but also individual industry experts associated in cooperatives of designers.

Characteristic of isolating mechanisms

To protect its core area of knowledge and the value generated from the projects Firm B adopted a modular process of value creation, where the staff and industry specialists are responsible for specific components of the created system, while the owner of Firm B is the main architect of the designed DPC. The main architect integrates partial solutions into a comprehensive system. The final, complex, integrated design is not accessible to other co-workers. By maintaining architecture level capabilities proprietary Firm B is not challenged by innovations and expertise developed at the level of project modules. Further, Firm B has limited the risk of diffusion of codified knowledge contained in projects by engaging in the implementation of prepared projects. The expertise in the field of design supported by the potential in implementation capablities strengthens the bargaining power of Firm B: *"ordering parties almost always extend the contract for design works with the implementation of prepared projects."*

When considering protection of knowledge it must be noted that Firm B develops "civil" as well as "secret" projects for military units. In the case of sensitive customer data and technical specification of the DPC a special type of collateral applies: "security certificates" held by employees and providing them access to classified information of state secret (Act on Protection of Classified Information[2]). Consequently the risk of information leakage is limited due to the personal liability of employees who have access to the classified data and have the appropriate credentials. In order to receive relevant "security certificates" employees were subjected to a special verification procedure in accordance with the provisions of the Act. It is important to emphasize that a violation of the secrecy clause is associated with a personal criminal liability. Moreover, taking into account the specific area of activity and a broad access to sensitive data, Firm B introduced a complex system of procedures providing a high-level of discretion in action. Implemented approach includes not only signing of contracts that include confidentiality clauses, but "a number of purposeful actions aiming at creating a coherent system of security and a culture of discretion, e.g. employees do not use computers with access to the network, the communication does include emails, data is stored on external disks, employees do not use the WiFi."

Activity clusters of dynamic capabilities

Based on the accumulated knowledge of its founder, Firm B, right from the beginning, was dedicated to development of a sound composition of organizational capabilities enabling value capturing. Implementation of a modular process of designing DCPs is a most evident example illustrating that very thoughtful approach. Through engagement of a diverse group o specialists it has enhanced the process of value creation in terms of quality of the final product and time-cost efficiency of the whole process. Simultaneously the rationale for introducing this modular approach was to protect the most critical are of knowledge, which forms the basis of the competitive advantage of Firm B: "copyright in that case just does not do the job." Nevertheless, facing the problem with unreliable partner it has turned out that the mere modular system of work is not enough to protect value streams. In the first round Firm challenged with that unexpected situation B implemented ad-hoc problem solving mechanism by reducing the number of employees and commencing litigation (Figure 6.3).

---

2   Detailed regulations are described in the Act – Ustawa z dnia 5 sierpnia 2010 r. o ochronie informacji niejawnych (Dz.U. z 2010 Nr 182, poz. 1228).

Figure 6.3 Ad hoc problem solving in Firm B
Source: Author's own work.

Further, after ad hoc initiatives, Firm B decided to introduce a more comprehensive change into existent action patterns. Thus Firm B engaged in a focused and enduring search for new possibilities enabling risk reduction (Figure 6.4). The formulated response entailed a complex set of new procedures, lines of behavior, and assets. Investigated Firm decided to decouple design and implementation services to comply with the new focus on short-term projects associated with a limited resource commitment. It required a thorough reconfiguration of work schedules. Additionally, in order to reduce risk Firm B developed and implemented procedures enabling evaluation of project offers and potential customers before signing the contract. Formulated response included also diversification of value streams. Implementation of that premise involved entering into new business area of hotel services. This investment required a thorough reconfiguration of resources and capabilities.

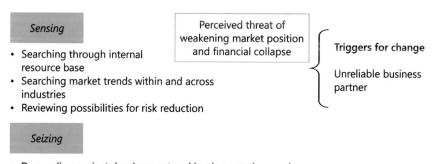

- Decoupling project development and implementation services
- Defining criteria for evaluating project offers
- Developing a system of recommendations
- Developing detailed profiles of investors (customers)

Reconfiguring

- Rearrangement of work schedule according to short-term projects
- Diversification of business activity (using already possessed property)

Figure 6.4 Activity clusters of Firm B – responding to a threat
Source: Author's own work.

Nevertheless, Firm B also sensed opportunities related to market growth for the services provided (Figure 6.5), and introduced a searching activity for new potential customers across industries. Since initiation it has been a continuous and focused search according to the set of formulated criteria related to risk reduction. In order to meet diverse requirements of customers representing different industries (e.g. banking, military, R&D) seizing activity was directed towards a thorough review of those requirements developing networks of industry professionals with a relevant expertise and developing necessary capabilities in the area of sensitive data protection. Implementation of those new initiatives and approaches implied a significant reconfiguration of existent practices. In order to reduce risk and secure own proprietary knowledge, Firm B has decided to engage in both design and implementation of DCP for one customer under condition that those services are to be treated as separately accounted projects.

Sensing

- Searching through internal resource base
- Searching trends on different markets with reference to provided technology

Perceived opportunity for broadening value streams

Triggers for change

Dynamic market growth

Seizing

- Reviewing specific requirements of potential customers
- Developing networks of industry professionals
- Staff trainings in protection of confidential information
- Obtaining security certificates

Reconfiguring

- Engaging in design and implementation of DPC, yet design and implementation are treated as separately accounted projects
- Implementing a coherent system of security and a culture of discretion

Figure 6.5 Activity clusters of Firm B – responding to an opportunity
Source: Author's own work.

Drawing from the experience with unreliable partner, since then, Firm B has proved to be quite cautions although flexible with regard to changes introduced after signing the contract. "We are too small to deny minor changes." However, decision on potential change is always preceded by a calculation of all possible current and future benefits and costs for the Firm B: "sometimes you have to lose in order to win." However, if the partner has a rigid position with regard to settled payments, timeframes and rates, Firm B does opt for any compromise.

6.1.3 CASE C

Profile and outline of the history of the firm

Firm C has been operating for 27 years (founded in 1987). It defines its business domain as sale and servicing of emergency power supply systems (UPS) and power generators. Starting with only one supplier, over the years Firm C has expanded its portfolio to more than twelve global producers of UPS and generators, and introduced its own line of products. In the late 80's and the beginning of 90' of the past century Firm C was a pioneer on the Polish market. Initially, it directed its offer only to banking sector entities. Moreover, the turnover was generated mainly through sales of equipment. The strategic focus on servicing came later, when market circumstances changed to more demanding. As a growing market attracted new entrants, Firm C had to face a competition from new distributors but also from former suppliers that decided to strengthen positions on the market through a forward integration: "firm C entered a new millennium with a loss and difficulties in its main market." In the subsequent years Firm C followed a new strategy focused on broadening the portfolio of suppliers, extending servicing and introducing its own line of products marked with own trademark. This direction proved to be effective as the net profit grew annually by more than 200 percent until 2009. During that year the positive trend collapsed. Firm C recorded a sharp fall in sales (22%) and profits (53%). This situation was caused by the economic crisis that particularly deeply affected the financial sector, sector which purchases accounted for a large part of the revenue of the Firm C. In such difficult period retaining existing customers became a critical task. Unfortunately, Firm C suffered a defeat in this field: "failure of a device installed in one of the branches of the major, long-term customer, and further a negative evaluation of the service provided, resulted in a loss of a significant customer." In following years Firm C recovered the losses and returned on a growth path as it decided to improve management practices through implementation of management quality systems and entered other sectors by providing its services to healthcare, construction and military institutions. It went also through reorganization focused on cost cutting: "after reviewing sales performances we decided to close some regional offices and to change others to service centers." Starting with 2012 Firm C engaged in exploration of foreign markets. First results in the form of profits from export activities were observed in 2014.

Observing current situation in Firm C it can be concluded that firm is usually engaged in relatively long term projects involving equipment ordering and adjusting to specification provided by the customer, equipment installation, maintenance and warranty servicing: "in fact installation and after sale servicing is the main strategic focus of the firm, we service machines purchased in other distribution networks as well." UPS and generators offered by Firm C are sold to a quite broad spectrum of different customers, i.e. financial institutions, hospitals, manufacturing firms with production lines, military units, municipalities for traffic light systems. Thus, ensuring constant and reliable work of installed equipment is the most important issue, since any failure may increase the risk to the safety and health of the population. Around 60 percent of employees are service engineers. Nevertheless, in order to provide fast and always available service backup (24Hotline), which is a must for the type of equipment sold, Firm C also employs external engineers on contracts. Lastly, it is worth mentioning that at the turn of the year 2014, Firm C has developed a preliminary offer that extends the scope of services provided with services concerning broadly defined management and optimization of energy consumption. New solutions offered can be used not only to manage electricity but also water, chemicals, compressed air, gases technological sewage. It is an important element of a new strategic-protection plan, which assumes diversification and extension of the offer by developing activities in new areas not necessarily closely related to emergency power systems.

Core knowledge area

The technical knowledge about the underlying technology of the product sold is a necessity as it enables customization of provided solutions and development of a high quality maintenance and warranty services. A sound technological knowledge base is also a starting point for business activity extension: "we need a fine grained insight into technology advances for our new solutions that go far beyond electricity consumption management." Nevertheless, Firm C is not a producer but a distributor of readymade products, even own product line is produced by other manufacturers. Thus, the core knowledge relates in fact more closely to the market as it concerns current knowledge about market trends, business relations, keeping up to date with the offer of competition: "we need to be always aware of any mistakes made by competitor, any equipment failure on their side, because we must be there at once with better offer." Challenged by a price competition, Firm C puts an emphasis on the quality of the offer and an effort on development of skillful sales force: "the price of UPS depends on two factors, the power of the device and the type of battery. As competitors go only for the power we stress the lasting battery, which is a more costly component but more appealing to customers, such as hospitals, when thoroughly explained." In many cases the key knowledge concerns knowledge of key people, i.e. not general contractors but final customers, system designers as they decide about the type of equipment to be included in a given system: "an early enough contact with designers generally ensures that our devices are included in the project."

Characteristic of isolating mechanisms

Since the strategic fundament of Firm C concerns market related knowledge, possessed isolating mechanisms primarily address the risk of losing that type of knowledge. Sales force is expected to develop and maintain broad networks of business relations, often on a personal level. In order to reduce the risk of losing those contacts with the possible departure of an employee, Firm C implemented complex Customer Relationship Management system. All tasks, contacts, information gathered about the current or potential customer are recorded in the system: "there are no irreplaceable people, all the Firm needs to know is right there in the system." Another group, that have a substantial impact on the value streams generated by Firm C, is represented by service engineers. Some of them are employees and some are external specialists. Given the importance of high quality of installation, maintenance and warranty services for customer retention, Firm C has developed and manages obligatory professional trainings, which take place every year and are obligatory for all internal and external service engineers. Thus, it suggests development of a co-specialized asset, as Firm C invest to expand in the area of complementary services. Further, being an authorized distributor, Firm C has an exclusive access to supplier's product offer, to original spare parts and unique opportunity to provide warranty services. Moreover, while developing own line of products Firm C invested in its own legally protected trademark. Nevertheless, information gathered during interviews suggest that despite all above mentioned instruments and mechanisms, the one that has proved to be most important and most effective is a time based advantage.

Activity clusters of dynamic capabilities

As the business activity area of Firm C concerns sales and servicing, it has put a lot of effort to develop efficient routines for market scanning and searching, which is performed equally intensive by the top management and the sales force (Figure 6.6). Introduced procedures were largely enhanced by the implementation of Customer Relation Management system. It implied significant reconfiguration of existent practices of information gathering and processing, which ultimately reduced Firm's dependence on the market knowledge posessed by individuals. Facing an intensifying competition on the one side and a growing market on the other, Firm C has engaged in a broad scale searching of market trends, technology advances and strategic as well as operational activity of competitors. Formulated response to identified possibilities for effective protection of generated value streams entailed broadening portfolio of suppliers, as Firm C learned that global strategies of producers may not necessarily comply with the interest of local distributors, hence relying on just a few suppliers can turn out to be a rather risky strategy. In order to address the need for strengthening its strategic position, Firm C developed and introduced to the market its own product line, protected by a registered trademark. Subsequent years have confirmed a strategic commitment to development of an individual selling policy independent of strategies executed by transnational suppliers. Firm C has invested heavily in promotion and extension of the offer of devices provided under own trademark. Capitalizing on gathered information concerning advances in complementary technology, Firm C has developed new capabilities necessary for implementing new ventures in the area of building automation, structural cabling, energy consumption management. Thus, it can be concluded that implemented action patterns fall under attempt to establish a strong market position with regard to access to complementary technologies. Further, addressing the threat induced by increasing competition and relating to the risk of diminishing returns, Firm C has reviewed all generated value streams and decided to expand its service activity "were big opportunities for high margins are still hiding."

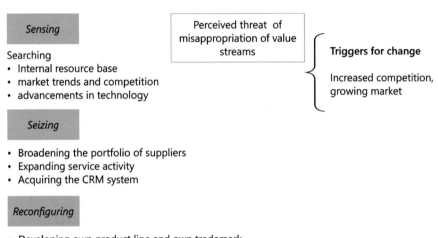

Figure 6.6 Activity clusters of Firm C (1)
Source: Author's own work.

Analysis of financial statements and internal documentation has confirmed a long term commitment to introduced changes and capability branching. Additionally, during interviews informants provided a thorough explanation of the underlying logic of the implemented line of action, which suggests a sound support generated through effective organizational learning processes. Nevertheless, facing a discontinuous change that occurred in 2009, i.e. the economic crisis that strongly and negatively affected the main market served, forced Firm C to again re-examine existent action patterns (Figure 6.7).

Challenged by the perceived threat of weakening its market position Firm C decided to introduce new solutions in attempt to provide better alignment with new environmental circumstances. Implemented changes concerned not only cost-reduction focused reorganization but more importantly a more

Sensing

Scanning and searching
- Internal resource base
- market trends and competition
- advancements in technology
- potential markets across industries

Perceived threat of weakening the market

Triggers for change

Economic crisis

Seizing

- Review and selection of good management practices
- Expanding service activity by engaging external engineers for servicing
- Developing business relations at new foreign markets
- Accessing financial support for export activity (EU funds)

Reconfiguring

- Development and implementation of an integrated training system for all service engineers
- Cost reduction through reorganization
- Improving management practice through implementation of ISO standard
- Entering foreign markets

Figure 6.7 Activity clusters of Firm C (2)
Source: Author's own work.

broadly understood improvement of management practices, replication of existent capabilities into new foreign markets, and a further expansion of service activity guided by a strong emphasis on a high-quality provision. Along with that line of action Firm C applied for financial support in order to enter foreign markets and invested in diversification of its business profile. "We have sensed quite early first symptoms of this financial crisis on our markets and we used the time to come as fast as possible with comprehensive protective solutions. Thanks to that approach we suffered a drop in revenues but not a loss." As pointed by informants, situation of Firm C was not dramatic to reach for drastic, immediate interventions. Thus, instead of ad-hoc problem solving mechanisms Firm C engaged in developing and implementing a more structured response to a sensed threat.

6.1.4 CASE D

Profile and outline of the history of the firm

Firm D was founded 24 years ago. In 1991 it entered the market with production of transformers and inductors for electrical applications in the automotive and railway industries. From the very beginning Firm D put an emphasis on the quality and innovativeness of manufactured products. It invested in own R&D department, whose research work resulted in patented inventions incorporated to production in a short time. "Despite the fact that it was extremely challenging for a small firm to secure its highly innovative solutions against highly interested competitors," Firm D managed to develop its own complex system of procedures and techniques ensuring effective protection of the proprietary technology. By maintaining sensitive knowledge base proprietary, Firm D was able to build a strong position on market served. The high quality of products provided gained recognition not only among domestic customers but also in foreign markets. In 2005 Firm D entered into a cooperation agreement that brought in a big change in the trajectory of its development. Firm D became a prominent supplier of a large German corporation X, a global leader producing photovoltaic systems (i.e. devices that convert solar radiation directly into electricity, without secondary pollution production). Through this cooperation Firm D became present on a totally new, promising market of photovoltaic. "Products offered by the Firm were considered so innovative and competitive, that established cooperation resulted in large orders and enormous growth." The overall turnover increased from app. 13 000 000 PLN in 2004 to over 120 000 000 PLN in 2008. Results are even more impressive when looking on the level of net profits – app. 1 600 000 PLN in 2004 and over 24 000 000 PLN in 2008 (increase in almost 1500%). In subsequent years the growth rate remained high. With revenues reaching 300 000 000 PLN and 400 employees in 2012 Firm D became the largest supplier of the German partner. In 2011 Firm D was sold to the cooperating partner X. In fact a deepening year-on-year cooperation led to a situation in which 98 percent of sales was realized with the main partner, while only 2 percent with other customers. Nevertheless, conditions of the cooperation agreement were favorable for both sides: "Firm has benefited not only through increased sales volumes but also got access to new advanced management practices allowing for substantial cost reduction." Sudden collapse occurred in 2012. Substantial changes in the financing policy of renewable energy in Germany (main market) and the global economic crisis, reduced demand for photovoltaic installations and in turn resulted in the decline of sales of Firm D (37%). This difficult situation was further worsened by the inflow of low-cost solutions from China: "according to industry estimates dumping practices of Chinese producers led to the closure of over 60 factories in EU operating in photovoltaic industry."

As the market collapsed the main partner turned to smaller orders. With the practical absence of other customers, the Firm D reported a quite severe drop in sales and profits. In following years Firm D has adjusted the level of employment for small orders (turnover of 200 000 000 PLN) and introduced comprehensive changes focused on cost reduction, customer and product diversification. At the beginning of 2014 the downward trend has stopped and in subsequent periods volume sales have stabilized at a lower but economically satisfactory level: "even in tough times Firm maintained 20% return on sales." Drawing on recent experiences Firm D has engaged in an intensive search for other customers (participation in trade venues, creating a new sales department) and development of new products, which were not included in the regular offer so far (substantial extension of R&D department). Strong commitment to R&D activity has been additionally supported with funds obtained through the EU Innovative Economy Program. Firm D has received a grant of almost 6 000 000 PLN.

Industry of inductive components is characterized by stable growth yet strong competition (a relatively easy product). Firm D entered photovoltaic industry when the competition was not yet large, and industry itself as well as the market were at an early stage of development. "Currently market is becoming saturated as a growing number of Chinese producers enter the European and American market and we can observe intensification of consolidation processes. Right now we have begun to experience not only technological but also a strong price competition." Thus, it can be concluded that difficult challenges are still in the front of the Firm D.

Core knowledge area

The key, strategic knowledge of Firm D entails most current advances in technology. It refers to solutions used during production and to knowledge about electrical and magnetic materials. "Development of that core knowledge area is supported by a series of tests and studies carried out by the R&D department with a close cooperation with universities in Poland and England." The key department of R&D currently consists of 26 employees, which accounts for app. 10 percent of the total staff. Moreover, quality controllers also account of app. 10 percent of the total workforce. Nevertheless, concerning the core knowledge area it is necessary to emphasize that a great number of solutions developed and implemented by Firm D in products offered are unique and not used yet by the competition. The fact that those solutions are protected by patents confirms the high level of uniqueness and advancement of developed technological knowledge.

Characteristic of isolating mechanisms

Right from the very beginning of business activity a comprehensive approach to knowledge protection has been implemented and systematically improved: "all prototypes were kept in safes, no one was allowed into the building without authorization in a form of a formal document checked by guards 24 hours a day." Currently Firm D uses different complementary formal and informal mechanisms to protect its technology from being copied before the start of serial production. During the whole history of Firm D, there was no incident of confidential information leakage. All key technological innovations are protected by patents. Nevertheless, recognizing limitations of effectiveness of that protection mechanism Firm D has developed and implemented a wide spectrum of techniques and procedures enabling maintaining large areas of unpatentable knowledge proprietary and confidential. The most visible one, yet effective, relates to the final stage of production, when the produced inductor is flooded with resin. This technique prevents spreading of the product into parts and eventual reverse engineering. This tangible method for maintaining secrecy is supported by also legal instruments. "It can be said that a confidentiality clause embraces our entire Firm" – all employees with an access to production technology, production lines, R&D department, etc. are obliged to sign a confidentiality agreement before they actually enter those areas, as well as all partners and suppliers also need to sign agreements with confidentiality clause. Recognizing that usually people are the weakest links, Firm D decided to use encrypted data (e.g. plans, drawings, 3D models) and secured data exchange portals (like FTP) to restrict any third party access. As it was mentioned above R&D is the key department. Hence, in order to reduce the risk of an excessive dependence on an individual expertise Firm D has expanded this department, so that there are at least two employees for each expertise area (department counted 8 people, currently – 26). Moreover, "all meetings end with a note, summary, and the projects are saved in a specific location on the disk where all people dedicated to the project have the access." It is a very important practice enhancing organizational learning processes.

Given that Firm D purchases necessary production materials from app. 80 different domestic and foreign suppliers, the problem of protecting knowledge embedded in manufactured products appears extremely challenging. According to implemented procedures suppliers' design teams should be limited only to truly necessary staff who works on provided encrypted data. Moreover, suppliers receive orders, yet are not informed about the exact usability of the ordered module. By signing a contract supplier agrees to maintain full confidentiality about the ordering: "we conduct control audits and verify the storage of provided documentation, as well as other important issues as for example we check if production lines are covered while visiting." Nevertheless, implemented procedures in some instances collide with the pursue of other strategic goals, such as optimization of costs and time delivery: "it is quite difficult to smoothly change a supplier, since we are not allowed to provide a detailed specification of the ordered material to new candidates."

Activity clusters of dynamic capabilities

Analysis of the practice of Firm D in developing, implementing and managing different isolation mechanisms, enables a conclusion that until 2012 Firm has developed its value appropriation capabilities along a rather stable trajectory. All introduced improvements have not changed the main trajectory, on the contrary, rather reinforced existent action pattern. A substantial change in environmental circumstances that induced further branching of extant lines of actions was noticed already at the end of 2011. Nevertheless, it was 2012 when Firm D has actually perceived those changes in terms of a significant threat of diminishing returns and addressed it with a response involving branching of the extant lines of action (Figure 6.7).

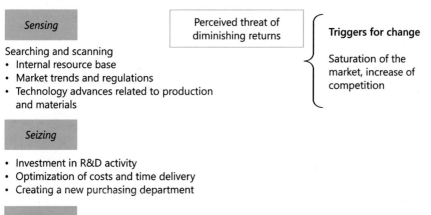

Figure 6.8 Activity clusters of Firm D
Source: Author's own work.

Challenged by negative signals from the market Firm D has engaged in a more intensive scanning and searching process across advances in the main and complementary technologies. In the face of market saturation and emerging aggressive price competition it became clear that optimization of costs and time delivery is a necessary but insufficient mean to maintain a stable market position. Hence, introduced cost reduction initiatives have been somehow restrained by the high quality philosophy, yet supported by associated improvements in management practices: "We need to focus on providing a good product at a good price." Formulated response involved also expansion of R&D (backed up with financial support obtained from EU Innovative Economy Program) to foster innovations based on advancements in complementary technologies, e.g. those concerned with miniaturization. Moreover, simultaneously with strengthening R&D team Firm D has created a new purchasing department "to choose most relevant suppliers and further optimize costs and delivery time." Further, Firm D has departed from the previous practice, according to which project teams included almost exclusively R&D specialists. By introducing new procedures based on the X-team principle, representatives of all departments (R&D, quality, technology, logistics, purchasing) have been provided opportunity to develop the content of the project and influence its assessment. In order to improve project management capabilities staff has undergone a series of trainings on the subject.

Figure 6.9 Ad hoc problem solving in Firm D
Source: Author's own work.

Given that analyzed reconfiguration is a relatively recent process, it is too early for a comprehensive evaluation of the outcomes. Nevertheless, on-site observations suggest that some more changes within the area of value appropriation are to be expected. The increasing time pressure together with cost reduction issues induce ad-hoc decisions, that literally violate the knowledge protection procedures in force: "we have to keep up with the schedule, sometimes there is no time to deal with encryption." Hence, with a growing number of such practices the developed action pattern for sensitive knowledge protection may turn out to be rather virtual.

6.1.5 CASE E

Profile and outline of the history of the firm

Firm E was established in 1991, as the main representative of a Parent Company Y – a global Corporation that has been operating for over 160 years, with current employment of over 350 000 people all over the world and a turnover reaching almost 70 billion EUR. Since its foundation Firm E underwent a number of reorganizations involving new department creation, business acquisitions, spin-offs, etc. Nevertheless, the resulting organizational structure of Firm E always has reflected the structure of the Parent Company Y. This cohesiveness results from the fact, that all strategic decisions of Firm E are always guided by the principles of a global strategy of the Parent Company Y. Hence, analysis, evaluation and selection of most promising markets by Firm E fully complies with the focus of the Parent Company Y on key areas of action a and long-term development, i.e. electrification, automation and digitization. Currently Firm E controls three individual firms providing financial services, comprehensive medical solutions and technological solutions in the areas of energy, automation and control, municipal infrastructure, intelligent building technology, rail transport, aerospace and defense, electronics and semiconductor, industrial machinery and equipment, marine. Moreover, Firm E extends and complements the range of its activities through cooperation with hundreds of local manufacturing enterprises as well as commercial and technical services providers.

The Department chosen for the fine-grained analysis and on-site observation specializes in providing complex products and systems for urban infrastructure and transportation. It was established in 2010 as an answer to sensed opportunities related to promising technology advancement on the one side, and market growth stimulated by the inflow of EU funds on the other. Currently its 42 employees generate a yearly turnover of around 10 000 000 PLN. In just few years since the establishment, the Department has implemented an impressive portfolio of projects in largest cities of Poland. It is worth mentioning that one of those projects is the biggest investment in the history of Firm E – the contract net value is 1.07 billion PLN. Although abundant with opportunities, this business area is also very susceptible to changes in the economic situation. Given that most investors are municipalities, public institutions, economic downturn experienced in years 2010–2013 caused substantial delays and shifts in implementations and thus difficult challenges for the Department to manage unstable value streams.

Core knowledge area

Firm E operates in many different, yet complementary technological areas and develops a wide array of unique solutions that ensure impressive levels of revenues. Developed high edge technologies are dedicated to such diverse business areas as energy, automation and control, municipal infrastructure, intelligent building technology, rail transport, aerospace and defense, electronics and semiconductor, industrial machinery and equipment, marine, pharmaceuticals and medical devices. Nevertheless, "almost all solutions are developed by the Parent Corporation Y that invests annually over 4 billion euro in R&D, while in firm E we are involved mainly in configuration, adaptation and implementation of those solutions." Reviewed financial statements of Firm E confirmed no or negligible expenditures on R&D.

Department of Firm E, which was the main object of a direct observation and a fine grained analysis, generates value streams from an advanced traffic management system for urban traffic control, which entails a proprietary software that "optimizes the switching of urban traffic lights in such a way that traffic moves measurably faster within the existing infrastructure" (internal documentation of Firm E). This technology works with traffic lights controllers, which are also produced by Firm E and thus provides opportunities for building advantages based on the control of access to complementary assets. Due to the complexity of used algorithms, the whole system has been developed for a long time (it is constantly improved and expanded), and in result the end product is recognized as "one of the most effective and reliable systems on the market." Nevertheless, as it was mentioned above, that technological solution, as many others used by Firm E, has been developed by the R&D of the Parent Corporation Y. Thus, given the high level of sophistication of the system, any attempts to expand it with new complementary products requested by customers (e.g. new types of detection cameras, variable message sings) require involvement of the R&D of the Parent Company Y, which is very costly and time consuming: "with a standard implementation everything goes smoothly, when we try to be more flexible toward customer needs, then considered modifications induce costs beyond the project budget." Therefore, in order to strengthen its market position and address the need for flexibility Department has decided to expand its knowledge area into open architecture programming and has engaged in creation of its own R&D team.

Moreover, it is also important to emphasize that "other areas of sensitive knowledge are embedded in procedures of execution, contracting, project quotation, techniques of project management, etc.". The weight of that knowledge should not be underestimated, as it represents accumulated experience allowing to compete effectively for customers. Department has experienced a leakage of that knowledge and its negative consequences – weakening of a position during negotiations, more difficult competition at tenders.

Characteristic of isolating mechanisms

The Parent Company Y submits yearly app. 2000 patent applications. Around half of introduced innovations are protected by patents. Currently patent portfolio embraces over 60 000 patents. In the observed Department of Firm E the main system for urban traffic control rely on a wide spectrum of unique algorithms that are also protected with the use of patents. Access to the system is restricted to people exclusively trained by the Firm E. Any unauthorized attempt to modify the implemented program ends up with the loss of the warranty: "we do control who and how uses the provided solutions." Nevertheless, Firm E and all of its departments recognize the limited functionality of patents as a standalone formal protection mechanism, and therefore Firm E has introduced a coherent action pattern based on an accumulated experience and subsequently developed and implemented procedures (e.g. technical problems are to be solved by more than one person – the dispersion of know-how; e-mails with confidential information should be sent in an encrypted version; rules for providing sensitive information to subcontractors and customers, digital data access procedures, project knowledge bases), technical solutions (e.g. disc drivers of laptops are encrypted; memory-sticks with the ability to encrypt files on it; patent evaluation service that enables optimization of licensing revenues), formal contracting approach (e.g. employment contracts include a clause that all goods produced by an employee are the property of Firm E; very elaborated, comprehensive agreements with business partners, in which a significant part of provisions concerns issues related to intellectual property rights, liability, confidentiality, the right to audit, contractual penalties): "our contracts are so enormous and detailed that many potential cooperators resign when asked to sign the multi-page document." Given that patents and contracts provide protection enforced by law, Firm E has developed a strong legal department to support that enforcement: "the effectiveness of our lawyers is widely known in the market." Further, as Firm E acknowledges that "the biggest risk of data loss is the human factor", it has been organizing regular trainings for its employees on various aspects concerning the problem of know-how protection: e.g. "webinars on what is public, secret, classified; trainings on what you can write about a company on social networking sites; trainings on how to avoid phishing on the Internet, etc.".

Activity clusters of dynamic capabilities

Since its founding Firm E has been following the strategic directions set by the Parent Company Y. It is strongly engaged in scanning and searching processes across markets and industries (Figure 6.10), yet the logic underlying that sensing activity was developed in line with the philosophy of the Parent Company Y and its global product strategy. Hence, introduced responses are idiosyncratic in terms of for example the exact type of businesses being acquired, yet candidates are chosen from most promising long-term development areas defined by the Parent Company Y – electrification, automation and digitization. It can be concluded that performing its sensing activity Firm E capitalizes heavily on sensing performed by R&D of the Parent Company Y. Nevertheless, Firm E has proved to be very efficient in seizing sensed opportunities and in reconfiguring existing resource base together with its capability portfolio. A review of past performance provides an impressive number of reconfiguration initiatives introduced to address environmental changes – almost every year during a more than 20 years of history. A relatively rapid pace and positive final evaluation of conducted reorganization processes, which involved broadly speaking integration of acquired areas of knowledge, complex structural rearrangements, closing whole departments or sections (e.g. department of industrial automation – "it generated losses due to difficulties in estimating costs of engineering for big projects"), confirm a high level of functionality of developed dynamic capabilities. A very illustrative example of a high alertness of Firm E is a recent initiative that concerns adaptation of work arrangements and organizational culture to new generation Z, that is entering the job market.

Figure 6.10 Activity clusters of Firm E – corporate level
Source: Author's own work.

In attempt to take advantage of opportunities related to the technology advances, growing digitalization of economy and social life, as well as enormous EU funds directed toward infrastructure development in Poland, Firm E decided to establish a new Department to provide specialized solutions in the area of municipal infrastructure and transportation. Given that the new Department was established through recombination of existing resources and capabilities, it embraced specialists already employed in Firm E. Thus, the staff was well acquainted with applicable procedures, management practices focused on generating value from a proprietary system developed by R&D of the Parent Company Y. As the Department entered the market in pursuit of high profits, it has soon became clear that lacking the possibility to flexibly extend the system according to various requirements of potential customers, it is going to be very difficult to compete with a growing number of alternative providers. On-going analysis of accumulated project-related knowledge has enabled quite fast recognition of the problematic situation. Due to advances in complementary technologies there is a continuous inflow of new devices on the market, which are not equipped with a functional interface with the system used by the Department. "When the customer asked for an extension of the software to include weight-in-motion system, we had to ask R&D people from the Parent Company Y to deal with the request. As the final price of that extension reached 500 000 PLN the customer just resigned from our services." Carried out on-site observations and a review of project documentation confirmed a number of "costly" incidents related to inability to flexibly expand the usability of the product provided (an example on Figure 6.11).

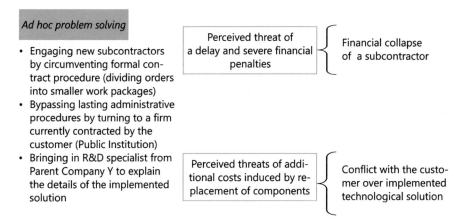

Figure 6.11 Ad hoc problem solving in Firm E – department level
Source: Author's own work.

Challenged by a growing competition offering a more open approach toward system modifications, and a fast pace of complementary technology development, engineering staff and management of the Department have engaged in a systematic scanning and searching for possibilities to enhance strategic position of the unit (Figure 6.12).

Seizing

- Enhancing knowledge base by professional trainings in new technological solutions
- Hiring new specialists
- Defining budget for R&D activity

Reconfiguring

- Reorganization and developing new R&D activity
- Integration of newly acquired knowledge with existing capabilities

Figure 6.12 Activity clusters of Firm E – department level
Source: Author's own work.

Formulated response has entailed investment in development of necessary new areas of expertise by defining the budged for R&D activity, hiring new specialists and providing funds for specialized trainings on open architecture systems for currently employed engineers. It is important to emphasize, that organization of R&D activity has been guided by the principle of four eyes – there are at least two specialists assigned to a certain problem. It enhances the process of finding new, creative solutions as well as provides protection and continuity of the knowledge creation process if a given specialist decides to leave. Undoubtedly, implemented actions have broken existent path of organizational behavior by expanding and recombining value appropriation capabilities.

6.2   CROSS-CASE ANALYSIS

According to the replication logic of a multi-case design, case-specific examples of patterned behavior discussed in previous chapters require a mutual confrontation with each other and the underlying theoretical framework. Therefore, this chapter presents results of that iterative process of data comparison.

Analyzed firms deployed a wide spectrum of value capture mechanisms, as presented on Table 6.1. In all cases firms combined formal and informal protection mechanisms, as well as diverse procedures aiming at cost reduction. According to the data extracted from the archival documentation, on-site observations and interviews, changes in the value appropriation action patterns tend to concentrate within the informal area. While formal instruments grew in numbers, informal ones in diversity. A great part of results obtained through reorganization (aimed at cost reduction) also enhanced and enriched the portfolio of used informal protection mechanisms, e.g. access to complementary assets, time based advantage. The change process was readably enhanced by existing learning processes. In four cases (B, C, D, E) firms exhibited strong engagement in stimulating and nourishing organizational learning – internal and external trainings, various techniques for acquired knowledge sharing (e.g. regular meetings, team work, X-teams, data base), development of project knowledge bases, deployment of four eyes principle, etc. Firm A provided a supportive environment for informal knowledge sharing during first years of operating. Along with the growth of the Firm, used practices proved to be increasingly inefficient, yet Firm has not introduced a comprehensive change in that area. Thus, although Firm A branched value appropriation capability, the functionality of the process remains questionable. When circumstances changed to less favorable, Firm A turn out to be incapable to deploy developed dynamic capability to align its value appropriation action pattern with the altered environment.

Table 6.1 Deployed means for value appropriation

Case	Initial stage	Current state
Case A	• *Formal mechanisms* Lack of proprietary IT solution • *Informal mechanisms* Standard solution • *Cost reduction procedures* No initiatives	• *Formal mechanisms* Intellectual property rights – copyrights • *Informal mechanisms* Complexity of provided solution, access to complementary assets • *Cost reduction procedures* Ad-hoc initiatives concerned with staff reduction, asset selling
Case B	• *Formal mechanisms* Intellectual property rights – copyrights; confidentiality clauses in contracts • *Informal mechanisms* Maintaining architectural knowledge in modular design – internal staff • *Cost reduction procedures* No initiatives	• *Formal mechanisms* Intellectual property rights – copyrights; confidentiality clauses in contracts; security certificates • *Informal mechanisms* Maintaining architectural knowledge in modular design, access to complementary assets, integrated system of knowledge protection procedures • *Cost reduction procedures* Long term commitment to engage external specialists through established network of industry professionals; ad hoc initiative concerned with staff reduction
Case C	• *Formal mechanisms* Formal contracts • *Informal mechanisms* Management procedures for protecting sensitive market--oriented knowledge • *Cost reduction procedures* No initiatives	• *Formal mechanisms* Formal contracts, trademark for own line of products • *Informal mechanisms* Time based advantage, management procedures for protecting sensitive knowledge (CRM), proprietary system of trainings for service engineers, broadening the portfolio of suppliers in order to reduce over-dependency and enhance bargaining power • *Cost reduction procedures* Reorganization along all areas of business activity
Case D	• *Formal mechanisms* Patents, formal contracts, confidentiality clauses in contracts • *Informal mechanisms* Secrecy through management procedures, conventional techniques – storage of documents in safes • *Cost reduction procedures* No initiatives	• *Formal mechanisms* Patents, formal contracts, confidentiality clauses in contracts • *Informal mechanisms* Secrecy through management procedures and technical solutions (e.g. encryption), management procedures for eliminating the risk of an excessive dependency on individual expertise • *Cost reduction procedures* Long term commitment to continuous reorganization in pursuit of cost and time delivery optimization

Case	Initial stage	Current state
Case E (Dept.)	• *Formal mechanisms* Patents, formal contracts, confidentiality clauses in contracts, copyrights • *Informal mechanisms* Managerial procedures for maintaining sensitive knowledge confidential, technical solutions (e.g. encryption), legal services • *Cost reduction procedures* Procedures developed at the central level of Firm E	• *Formal mechanisms* Patents, confidentiality clauses in contracts, developed formal side of contracts, copyrights • *Informal mechanisms* Proprietary knowledge (R&D) providing favorable access to complementary technologies, managerial procedures for internal dispersion of know-how and maintaining sensitive knowledge confidential, technical solutions (e.g. encryption), legal services, trainings on confidentiality • *Cost reduction procedures* Procedures developed at the central level of Firm E

Source: Author's own work.

In order to make a clear distinction between the initial state and the outcomes of dynamic capabilities, Table 6.1 embraces a current portfolio of each analyzed firm as well as initial stage described on the basis of gathered historical and current data. The initial stage refers to a value appropriation activity that "has reached at least a minimum threshold of functionality" (Helfat & Peteraf, 2003, p. 1005) and can be qualified as capability. As mentioned above the observed changes concerned the quantity, diversity and combination of deployed mechanisms.

The next step of the cross case analysis involved data comparison with regard to ability to change existing patterns in using isolating mechanisms reflected in practices identified within activity clusters of sensing, seizing and reconfiguring. Following paragraphs provide a detailed insight into this change process.

Sensing opportunities and threats

Given the assumptions of the theoretical framing presented in the Chapter 4, sensing involves a complex set of interrelated activities of environmental broad scanning, focused searching and making sense of gathered information through filtering. Moreover, since it has been argued that the perception of an event in given circumstances influences the way a firm approaches resource and capability rigidity, the analysis of sensing activity was also focused on indication of whether a particular selection factor was perceived as the domain of loss (threats) or the domain of gain (opportunities).

In all of analyzed cases activation of dynamic capability mechanisms coincides with certain trends and events occurring in business environment of given firms (Table 6.2). Although analyzed firms recognized also internal events, which required a response, a thorough review of undertaken decisions and performed actions, suggests that implemented capability branching mechanisms were environmentally-driven. In all cases it was an external selection factor that served as a lens through which firms detected certain inconsistencies in internal conditions. Performed sensing activities exhibited a conscious linkage between analyzed firms and their environments. Despite the fact that conducted analysis did not revealed any example of internally-driven process of capability branching, the observed pattern of formulation of a structured response to environmental stimuli confirmed theoretical consistency and thus literal replication across cases (Yin, 2014).

Moreover, it was observed that analyzed firms used also an ad-hoc problem solving mechanism to address certain changes occurring in the environment. Interestingly, this way of responding was generally activated when firms decided to address individual, single events perceived as threats. On the contrary, firms were more inclined to deploy structured approach of dynamic capabilities when addressing certain broader sets of events and trends in the environment. Moreover, opportunity recognition was followed rather by a readiness to eventually branch existing capabilities than by acceptance of ad hoc local changes. Further, a deeper insight into undertaken sensing activity enabled a conclusion that in most cases addressing a perceived threat by a thorough scanning and searching process resulted in changing the decision-makers' mind-sets from a threat toward opportunity-oriented.

Comparison of gathered data across all cases enabled a conclusion that a focused search, initiated by an internal gap analysis, prevailed over a broad scanning. It was a less common practice to engage in scanning distant knowledge and capabilities, not directly linked to current problems. Only the largest of analyzed firms (Firm C, Firm D, Firm E), building on the accumulated knowledge and experience, were engaged in a broad, undirected scanning process. Further, all firms were engaged in reviewing collected information in order to figure out implications for subsequent action. Filtering involved certain criteria defined with respect to strategic priorities underlying the whole process. In all cases the bottom line of evaluation referred to volume, stability and/or reliability of generated value streams.

Table 6.2 Sensing opportunities and threats

Case	Selecting factor	Period of emergence	Sensed opportunity/ threat	Focused search	Broad scanning	Filtering
Case A	Economic growth, growing marketing budgets, increasing competition	2005–2008	Opportunity for broadening value streams	Searching internal resource base, new customers, financial support, solutions provided by competitors	–	Accessibility trough networks of personal relationships, cost of financial support, extended functionalities
Case B	Unreliable business partners	2010–2011	Threat of financial collapse and weakening market position → opportunity	Searching, internal resource base, market trends and possibilities for risk reduction	–	Investment requirements, stability of potential value streams
	Dynamic market growth	2013–2015	Opportunity for broadening value streams	Searching, v market trends with a reference to provided technologies	–	Stability and reliability of potential value streams
Case C	Increase of competition, market growth	1995–2008 2012–2015	Threat of misappropriation of value streams → opportunity	Searching internal resource base, market trends, competition, technology advances	–	Investment requirements, volume of potential value streams
	Economic crisis	2009–2010	Threat of weakening market position → opportunity	Searching internal resource base, market trends, competition, technology advances	Scanning foreign markets and advances in complementary technologies	Stability and reliability of potential value streams
Case D	Saturation of the market, increase of competition	2012–2015	Threat of diminishing returns → opportunity	Searching internal resource base, market trends and regulations, technology advances	Scanning advances in production technologies and materials	Investment and time requirements, compatibility with knowledge base, volume and reliability of value streams
Case E	Digitization, convergence of technologies	1991–2015	Opportunities for extending and strengthening value streams	Searching internal resource base, market trends, technology advances across industries	Scanning market trends and advances in close and remote technologies, social changes	Technological synergy, volume of potential value streams
	Sophistication of market demand, growing competition	2011–2015	Threat of diminishing returns, weakening market position → opportunity	Searching internal resource base, market trends, technology advances and competitors' solutions	Scanning technology advances	Stability and reliability of potential value streams

Source: Author's own work.

Seizing opportunities and threats

Activity cluster of seizing concerns formulating a response to identified opportunities and/or threats. All analyzed Firms decided to reach beyond the
current resource base to formulate a proper response (Table 6.3). It is worth
noticing, that a broad sourcing approach was exhibited across all cases. Obtained findings confirm that all firms exhibited an extensive approach toward
resource acquisition (internalization and remote access), which provided
feasible opportunities for extending and enriching possessed knowledge base.
Firms decided to internalize tangible resources (e.g. buildings, equipment)
as well as knowledge assets (recruitment of new staff, trainings for existent
staff). Observed practices concerning remote access to resources confirmed
that inter-organizational cooperation was driven by recognized shortages in
resource portfolio (Case A, Case E) as well as the need to increase the degree
of resource redundancy (Case B, Case C, Case D, Case E). Given that in all
cases remote access involved not only resource commitment but also activity alignement, investigated firms followed certain formal procedures in this
respect. Thus, considering the pattern of observed activities, replicated across
investigated cases, it can be concluded that it fully complies with the theoretical pattern defined as seizing of opportunities and threats. Hence, confirmed
replication allows for an analytical generalization of study findings (Yin, 2014).

Table 6.3 Seizing opportunities and threats

Case	Response based on existing resource base	Response based on resource acquisition	
		Internalization	Remote access (cooperation)
Case A	Engaging currently em-ployed staff into formulating new product offers based on newly developed solutions	Hiring IT specialists and developing proprietary IT platform and system solu-tion for logistics, acquiring new knowledge through professional trainings for project managers	Contracting additional IT specialists
Case B	New procedures and re-configuration of existing resource base	Using property of the owner for a new business activity	Assessing knowledge and information through networks of business rela-tionships
	New procedures for cus-tomer evaluation	Acquiring new knowledge through professional train-ings for project managers, obtaining security certifi-cates	Networks of industry pro-fessionals
Case C	Expanding service activity	Purchase of CRM system	Enlarged portfolio of co-operating suppliers
	Improvement of manage-ment practices	Obtaining financial sup-port from EU funds	Contracting external engi-neers for servicing, devel-oping business relations at foreign markets

Case	Response based on existing resource base	Response based on resource acquisition	
		Internalization	Remote access (cooperation)
Case D	Investing in R&D, creating new department, optimization of resource usage	Hiring R&D specialists	Introducing new manufacturers into developed network of suppliers
Case E	Internal staff trainings	Acquisition of new businesses	Developing networks of business partnerships
	Defining budget for R&D activity	Hiring new specialists, new knowledge through professional trainings for project managers	Cooperation with a provider of a new technological solution

Source: Author's own work.

Reconfiguring

Depending on the nature of perceived opportunities and threats, richness and diversity of available resources and capabilities, implementation of a formulated response may involve different branches of a current value capture capability lifecycle. Firms may decide to cease certain activities (retirement, retrenchment), extend deployment of other capabilities (replicate, redeployment), or reconfigure the content of performed lines of action (renewal, recombination). Obtained results confirm changes of current trajectories of operational capabilities across analyzed firms (Table 6.4). Nevertheless, the cross case analysis provides interesting and valuable insights concerning differences in implemented lines of action. According to the findings reconfiguration of fundamental elements of value appropriation capabitlies and supportive resources most extensively rely on branching practices defined as renewal/recombination. Furthermore, while small firms of Case A and Case B were engaged in recombination and renewal of existent capabilities, large firms of Case C and Case E introduced a whole spectrum of available branches. A broader scale of performed business activities implies a broader scale of possessed capabilities, which can be a subject of possible branching. Moreover, it is not without significance to recall that those large Firms were engaged in a broad, undirected scanning process, which helps to overcome cognitive biases, hence supports the process of unlearning obsolete routines. Firm D as a big entity also introduced more that one of available branches at a time, yet due to fact that almost all sales were realized with one customer (currently – parent company X) there were no alternative markets for replication or redeployment. Additionally, considering the differences in reconfiguration practice it is worth mentioning that those small Firms A and B were also the youngest in the sample. Although certain branches were not observed in several cases, this absence was consistent with the adopted theoretical basis. Thus, considering the last activity cluster, collected evidence provides a sound ground for analytical generalization of study findings (Yin, 2014).

Table 6.4 Reconfiguring

Case	Retirement/Retrenchment	Replication/Redeployment	Renewal/Recombination
Case A	–	–	Integration of new systems with extant technologies and organizational capabilities
Case B	–	–	Diversification of business activity – recombination of extant and new capabilities; value creation process rearrangement, extension and reconfiguration of capabilities along new system and organizational culture of discretion
Case C	Closing regional offices with inefficient performance, changing regional sales offices to service centers	Developing own product line and own trademark, diversification in areas of complementary technology, entering foreign markets	Reconfiguration due to new procedures and philosophy of CRM, implementation of a new training system (across organization and external specialists)
Case D	Reorganization through cost reduction and lean management implementation	–	Reorganization through cost reduction and lean management implementation; management practices improvement and implementation of X-team technique, introducing and integrating new areas of expertise in R&D
Case E	Closing departments and business areas not corresponding to new strategic directions	Expanding into acquired business areas	Integration of newly acquired knowledge with existing capabilities, structural reorganization along new promising business areas

Source: Author's own

6.3 DISCUSSION

Research effort of this study was directed toward the dynamic process of value appropriation through a lens of the dynamic capabilities framework. Collected evidence confirmed that in all cases firms combined formal and informal protection mechanisms, as well as diverse procedures aiming at cost reduction. Observed and analyzed changes concerned the quantity, diversity, and combination of deployed mechanisms. According to the gathered data, changes in the value appropriation action patterns tend to concentrate within the informal area. While formal instruments grew in numbers, informal ones in diversity. Thus, observed action patterns comply with the extant research, that confirms a tendency to use several complementary mechanisms to protect and retain streams of generated value (e.g. Cohen et al., 2000; Hussinger, 2006; Fischer, 2011), a reorientation toward a strategic use of formal protection instruments (e.g. patents – Firm E) and extending informal mechanisms, which are deeply embedded in organizational culture, behavioral paths and knowledge (e.g. Jennewein, 2004; Tether & Massini, 2007; Fischer, 2011). A fine-grained insight into the change of existing patterns in using isolating mechanisms provided comprehensive answers to formulated research questions.

How does a perception of a selection factor affect the way a firm introduces changes into existing practices of value appropriation?

Obtained results support the supposition that **perception of selection factors can have a significant impact on the choice between an ad hoc problem solving mechanism and a structured approach of dynamic capabilities**. While ad hoc initiatives were stimulated by selection factors perceived as threats, dynamic capabilities were deployed to address both opportunities and threats. Moreover, a stronger engagement in sensing activity resulted in a change of a mind-set from threat-oriented to opportunity-oriented. Switching to opportunity driven responses was more evident in Firms, that reached beyond focused search to broad scanning. It enabled those Firms to explore completely new alternatives and to overcome local and cognitive biases (Teece, 2007). While the perception of the initial stimuli was negative, further activity and perception of broader circumstances exhibited an opportunity seeking attitude. Designed and implemented responses tend to address rather those broader circumstances than the exact threatening stimuli. Such observation is in line with the theory claiming that **opportunity-driven responses help overcoming routine rigidity** (Gilbert, 2005). Further, it was evidenced that firms were more inclined to engage in a structured response when challenged by a broader set of stimuli. Dynamic capabilities were implemented to address rather trends than individual incidents. With regard to single events investigated Firms tend to decide either to initiate ad hoc actions or rely on existing capabilities to accommodate noticed signal. This observation is in line with arguments about the cost of developing and implementing dynamic capabilities (Winter, 2003). Obtained findings suggest **a threshold of stimuli for activating a structured response to sensed opportunities and threats**. Hence, it appears as an interesting research problem for further studies.

Does the pattern branching response to identified opportunities or threats tend to be structured along activity clusters of dynamic capabilities?

A cross case analysis confirmed existence of specific action patterns that were replicated across cases and proved compliance with theoretical framing adopted in this study. **A structured response to identified stimuli reflected three activity clusters of dynamic capabilities: sensing, seizing and reconfiguring.** In all analyzed cases the change process was initialized through a particular perception of selection factors and further sensing activities embracing focused search and/or broad scanning. Generally it was an external selection factor that served as a lens through which firms detected certain inconsistencies in internal conditions. It complies with theoretical suppositions that refer to the notion of dynamics in the dynamic capabilities perspective (Eisenhardt & Martin, 2000; Teece, 2007; Helfat et al., 2007). Nevertheless, not all identified stimuli were addressed with dynamic capabilities. An alternative mechanism of ad-hoc problem solving was also deployed (Winter, 2003; Helfat & Peteraf, 2003). Moreover, in all cases the bottom line of response options evaluation referred to volume, stability and/or reliability of generated value streams. Thus, it substantiates the suitability of chosen cases to the problem area of this research. With regard to seizing, observed activities were focused on providing access to required resources and capabilities, and then on defining their optimal combinations that align with strategic objectives of investigated firms (Teece, 2007). According to the findings all firms exhibited a broad sourcing approach, reaching beyond the existent resource base. In essence, drawing on the existent resource base comply with the exploitative logic (March, 1991). In contrast acquisition of new resources and capabilities through various external sources implies shifting toward the explorative logic (March, 1991; Zollo & Winter, 2002). Given that in all investigated cases responses were build on the basis of a combination of the extant internal and new externally acquired resources and capabilities, it suggests implementation of an integrative approach embracing both the exploitative and explorative dimension, which complies with the theoretical grounding of the dynamic capabilities perspective (Teece, 2007). This integrative approach enabled firms to introduce path-braking solutions to sensed stimuli. Collected evidence allowed for identification of all types of capability branching discussed in the literature (Helfat & Peteraf, 2003). Moreover, in accordance to theoretical suppositions, obtained findings confirmed simultaneous implementation of different branches for breaking current trajectories of value appropriation capabilities (Helfat & Peteraf, 2003).

A review of collected data and results of analysis enabled a conclusion that **observed lines of action comply with the formulated dynamic capability-based framework of value appropriation.** Although not all indicators defined for each activity cluster were observed in each case (e.g. broad scanning in sensing cluster, retirement/retrenchment and replication/redeployment in reconfiguration), this absence was consistent with the adopted theoretical basis. Thus, collected evidence exhibited literal and theoretical replication (Yin, 2014). Obtained data also confirmed engagement in learning processes, which enhance development of dynamic capabilities. It was observed that inefficiencies in the area of knowledge accumulation, articulation or deployment resulted in reduced functionality of implemented changes (Case A). Introduced changes concerned the quantity, diversity and combination of formal and informal mechanisms enabling protecting and retaining generated value streams. Thus, the observable direct outcome of dynamic capabilities referred to the operational level capabilities, i.e. resource base. It complies with the logic of the formulated framework, according to which the influence of dynamic capabilities on overall firm's performance is indirect through that operational level.

How do contextual conditions affect the content and implementation of a response?

Observed differences in implementation of sensing and reconfiguring activities enabled identification of certain contextual factors affecting the way analyzed Firms respond to identified stimuli. It was evidenced that although all firms sensed stimuli related to economic crisis, **the perception of that change factor and timing of a response differed depending on the vulnerability of the main business area and market served**. Firm A and Firm C were the ones most early and heavily affected by the crisis. Target market of Firm C was dominated by the banking industry. Firm A developed a much more diversified customer portfolio, yet it were still banks that generated the largest value streams. Although both firms were first to suffer from the crisis, only Firm D decided to branch existing pattern of action and enter new markets. Firm A, which experienced certain major inefficiencies in learning processes, concentrated on maintaining status quo. In other investigated firms responses to economic crisis did not involve sectoral shifts in target markets. In case of Firm B, reorientation toward new sectors was triggered by a financial collapse caused by an unreliable business partner and not the global economic crisis.

Moreover, it was also observed that **conditions for branching value appropriation capabilities are quite specific for firms operating as subsidiaries of larger corporations**. Such dependency of Firm D and Firm E induced important limitations with regard to alternations of existing value appropriation practices (compliance with corporate strategy and specific policies, limitations of decision-making autonomy, internal competitive relations) (Birkinshaw, Hood & Young, 2005). Although, in both cases the parent corporation was geographically distant the internal market kept all actors closely intertwined struggling over power and resources (Birkinshaw et al., 2005). In fact, introduced changes aimed at strengthening bargaining position of investigated Firm D and Firm E not only against market rivals but also within the corporate structure. In order to secure external and internal exploitation of the next-generation technologies Firm D enforced establihing own purchasing department and expansion of existent R&D, while Firm E managed development of own R&D. Observed lines of actions not only comply with the literature on parent-subsidiary relationships (Birkinshaw et al., 2005; Meyer et al., 1992) but also provide new avenues for exploring those relationships from a dynamic perspective.

It is also important to mention that analyzed **action patterns exhibited differences between firms characterized by a larger and smaller resource endowment**. In case of larger Firms the spectrum of sensing and reconfiguration activities was significantly broader than in smaller counterparts. Smaller firms (Firm A, Firm B) relied more heavily on focused search than broad scanning of distant knowledge and capabilities, not directly linked to current problems. Indeed, scanning is a more demanding activity as there are no specific problem benchmarks and a firm needs to firstly develop specific organizational and technical instruments in order to perform such scanning process effectively and efficiently (Huber, 1991). Analogically, comparison of practices belonging to reconfiguration cluster revealed that large firms introduced a whole spectrum of branching options, while small firms concentrated on renewal and recombination of possessed value appropriation capabilities. Undoubtedly, branching opportunities increase with the scale of performed business activity and the number of developed capabilities. Additionally those smaller entities exhibited also a shorter history of performance. This observation brings in the importance of time required for development of dynamic capabilities (Zahra et al., 2006) and the role of recursive cycle of organizational learning, as dynamic capabilities capitalize on accumulated and systematically updated knowledge base (Winter, 2003).

7   CONCLUSIONS

This study aimed to enhance the understanding of a complex and context-
-bound process of value appropriation by deploying the dynamic capabilities
perspective. This aim consisted of two integral modules:
- the conceptual objective – conceptualization and operationalization of
  organizational capabilities that enable shaping configurations of value
  appropriation mechanisms, and
- research objective – providing a rich qualitative evidence of routine-
  based approach to replication of effective value appropriation practices
  and alternation of existing action patterns in response to perceived
  threats and opportunities.

In the light of the theoretical discussion presented in Chapter 2 and 3,
formulated dynamic capability-based framework of value appropriation in
Chapter 4, and findings presented in Chapter 6, it can be stated that these aims
have been achieved. Formulated framework builds on the extant knowledge
presented in the contemporary literature in the field of strategic management
and on a rich evidence obtained during empirical research of this study. A high
quality research based on a multiple case design enabled gathering a highly
informative, rich and diverse collection of features and data, which were necessary to provide reliable answers to key research questions:
1. How does a perception of a selection factor affect the way a firm introduces changes into existing practices of value appropriation?
2. Does the pattern branching response to identified opportunities or
   threats tend to be structured along activity clusters of dynamic capabilities?
3. How do contextual conditions affect the content and implementation
   of a response?

Obtained results provided ample answers to formulated research questions,
and consequently confirmed the line of reasoning underlying the formulated
dynamic capability-based framework of value appropriation. The usefulness

of the insights provided by conducted research refer to the theoretical dimension of the strategic management field as well as to the practical dimension of business performance. Moreover, indicated limitations opens up directions for future research exploration. More detailed description of those contributions is presented in the following chapters.

7.1 THEORETICAL CONTRIBUTION

Given that the conceptual location of the research problem was defined in reference to the field of strategic management (Cyfert et al., 2014), therefore value and usefulness of provided insights are also referred to that field:

1. The first and the foremost, original contribution concerns the formulated dynamic capability-based framework of value appropriation that enables conceptualization and exploration of value capture from a dynamic perspective, beyond a point of transaction. The extant literature lacks a comprehensive, formal proposition for approaching the dynamic nature of a value appropriation action pattern. Incorporating the dynamic capabilities perspective enhanced the understanding that value is not captured instantaneously as it takes time to appropriate extracted value streams, and during that time a conducted action pattern can change through incremental improvements (ad hoc initiatives) or a deep reconfiguration (capability branching).

2. It is also important to emphasize that conducted research filled an important gap concerning a negligible empirical evidence of value capture practices embracing both formal and informal mechanisms. Gathered rich and diverse material can serve as a salient and reliable basis for further studies, as data collection and analysis confirmed a high level of trustworthiness.

3. Not to be underestimated is also a substantial contribution to further development of the dynamic capabilities perspective, which has not yet met the criteria set for evaluating the objectives of a scientific theory (Helfat & Peteraf, 2009). By applying the logic of the dynamic capabilities perspective to the concept of value appropriation, this study addresses the need to move discussion and research beyond the mere relation between dynamic capabilities and performance outcomes, toward other specific managerial problems as well as relate the concept with other streams of the academic literature.

4. Moreover, the input into development of the dynamic capabilities perspective relates also the cohesiveness of introduced understanding of

dynamic capabilities across theoretical and empirical research, that assumes a clear distinction between selection factors, operational capabilities, dynamic capabilities, and outcomes of dynamic capabilities. The extant literature provides a blurred picture of those key categories and in result the whole concept of dynamic capabilities is commonly recognized as incomprehensible and empirically inapproachable (Zahra et al., 2006; Wang & Ahmed, 2007). By decoupling antecedents, outcomes and core action patterns of dynamic capabilities, this study enhances the understanding of the dynamic capabilities perspective and enables further empirical research guided by the presented logic.

5. The dynamic capabilities perspective, as an emerging theory, requires a consolidation of the plethora of proposed explanations across relevant literature (Barreto, 2010). Therefore, the formulated framework draws on the operationalization of dynamic capabilities proposed by Teece (2007) in order to contribute to an emerging consensus on constituent components of dynamic capabilities. Adaptation of the content of action clusters to the value capture activity undoubtedly contribute to the integration of the extant knowledge base on dynamic capabilities into a cohesive, generalizable theoretical construct. Moreover, by introducing operationalization based on a set of three activity clusters, the framework and gathered evidence support the view that although dynamic capabilities exhibit firm-specific idiosyncrasies, there are certain commonalities across firms that allow for developing general frames of the concept (Eisenhardt & Martin, 2000; Barreto, 2010).

6. By conceptualizing dynamic capabilities as one of available alternative mechanisms that enable changes in organizational behavior, study enhances the internal consistency and readiness of the dynamic capabilities construct. Adopted line of reasoning addresses the criticism of vague relation between organizational change and dynamic capabilities, that leads to over-interpretation and identification of all adaptive alternations in organizations as manifestations of dynamic capabilities (Winter, 2003). Formulated framework recognizes that firms can accumulate change through either ad hoc problem solving mechanisms or a patterned way of dynamic capabilities depending on a particular context. The value of that contribution is strengthened by provided empirical evidence confirming a practical use of both mechanisms in the pursuit of change.

7. A case study method is a subject of quite intense methodological disputes. On the one hand it is recognized as a prominent method for theory building (Eisenhart & Graebner, 2007; Czakon, 2013), while on the other hand there is a widespread skepticism about the misplaced precision and a lack of clarity of that theory building process

(Eisenhardt, 1989). In order to address those skeptical arguments the management literature needs case studies that strictly follow methodical rigor and thus meet the criteria of a high quality research. Hence, in this study a lot of effort was put on the development of a proper procedure compliant with methodical rigor of a multiple case design. Exhibiting a high level of trustworthiness, this research contributes to the on-going discussion for a more rigorous use of the case study method and thus to "a renaissance" of that method in the field of strategic management (Czakon, 2013).

7.2 REFLECTIONS FOR MANAGERIAL PRACTICE

Although the main objective of the study concerns theory extension, it is seen also important for the study to provide useful, practical implications for managers challenged with changing circumstances that affect the value appropriation practices in firms they represent. Thus, it is expected that obtained results should generate some propositions for firms aiming to introduce changes in executed action patterns of value appropriation. However, it needs to be underlined that since research involved firms operating in knowledge and technology intensive industries, provided implications pertain only to that specific business context. Qualitative character of conducted research does not allow for statistical generalizations and extrapolation of conclusions to other industries. Nevertheless, there are a few useful insights for firms operating in relatively dynamic environments.

In general technology intensive environments are more turbulent than other business areas. This inherent dynamics is shaped by multidirectional and multisource technology advances, increasing convergence of technology, intensive competition, changes in legal regulations and demand, etc. Hence, firms operating in such industries observe and identify a number of various stimuli (selection factors) that require an organizational response. The main dilemma relates to the choice between ad hoc problem solving mechanism and dynamic capabilities. Drawing on obtained evidence, it is a rare case that a single event initiate a structured response to introduce change in the value capture pattern. Acknowledging the costs associated with dynamic capabilities deployment it appears reasonable to abstain pending a more comprehensive picture of the trend. Nevertheless, allowing in the meantime for spontaneous braking of existing value appropriation procedures may enhance operational flexibility, yet it may inadvertently undermine the underlying logic of value capture policy (e.g. circumventing contract procedures or encryption practices in pursuit of higher time-cost efficiency). Thus, the decision on deployment of a particular change mechanism should be supported not only by a thorough review of environmental circumstances but also by a recognition of existent internal discrepancies between developed procedures and an actual practice. Moreover, the choice becomes even more complicated when realizing that once developed dynamic capability need to be practiced, since reduced utilization of a capability inevitably leads to its degradation.

Further, it is important to acknowledge that functionality of dynamic capabilities depends on efficiency of underlying learning processes. Dynamic capabilities draw from accumulated and systematically updated knowledge. Gaps and drawbacks in a recursive cycle of organizational learning reduce the functionality of developed dynamic capabilities. When performed activities are not analyzed in terms of best practices in regard to value appropriation, managed risks, encountered problems, then an organization does not accumulate new knowledge. Hence, any attempt to develop a salient structural approach to manage change is bounded from the very beginning, as each new project becomes a new venture using only individual, selective experience.

According to the presented framework, dynamic capabilities consist of distinct yet interrelated activity clusters. Given that each cluster entails a complex set of activities and processes, its implementation involves diverse procedural arrangements. Depending on the particular circumstances firms may exhibit various levels of engagement in different types of activities belonging to a given cluster. Nevertheless, such selected commitment should be carefully thought trough, since each of those activities represents a different potential in regard to a formulated response. For example, sensing cluster entails focused search and scanning. The first one, initiated by internal capability gap analysis concentrates on looking for pattern-matching solutions, while the latter reaches beyond areas covered by current knowledge and capabilities. Thus, focused search enables solving current problems and scanning enhances possibilities for identifying path breaking ideas. Analogically, in case of seizing cluster, firms may formulate response on the basis of current resource endowments (exploitative logic) and/or reach for new resources and capabilities through acquisition (explorative logic). While it is possible to design solutions drawing only on existing resource base and developed portfolio of isolating mechanisms, in the long run a lack of inflow of new external knowledge may hamper developing more risky, capability-destroying solutions (Teece, 2007, p. 1327).

Resuming, value appropriation is a continuous process involving complex action patterns focused on value receiving, protecting and retaining. Those patterns may change over time through incremental improvements (ad hoc initiatives) or a deep reconfiguration (dynamic capabilities). Unlike ad hoc mechanisms, dynamic capabilities need to be developed through learning mechanisms and then repetitively deployed in order to maintain satisfactory level of functionality. Therefore, facing threats or opportunities firms may decide to introduce changes in existent action patterns of value capture and turn to a structured approach of dynamic capabilities. However, the mere possession of dynamic capabilities does not necessarily guarantee a satisfactory functionality of introduced reconfiguration. Dynamic capabilities stand for an organizational capacity, a potential for certain outcomes. In order to enhance the outcomes, a firm needs to enhance that potential.

7.3 LIMITATIONS AND DIRECTIONS FOR FURTHER STUDIES

Given the fact that research problem of this study represents a new area of scientific exploration, conducted research by this very reason was not designed to address it through an exhaustive, all embracing approach. Instead it was focused on providing a fine-grained, useful insight into selected important issues related to the dynamic nature of a value appropriation activity. Thus, rather than generating a complete picture, the aim related to developing a sound theoretical and evidence-based ground for further investigation.

Chosen research method supplied a rich and diverse evidence, that enabled achieving formulated research objectives of the study. Nevertheless, although obtained results enabled analytical generalization, a limited number of five cases requires a cautious reflection on contextual conditions and implications of the study. Undoubtedly, limitation of the study refers to formulated criteria for selecting cases. Investigation involved firms operating in knowledge and technology intensive industries. The rationale for choosing such firms was related to the fact, that those industries are affected by rather rapidly changing circumstances, thus provided most suitable environment for investigating dynamic capabilities in a given time period of the study (2012–2015). Nevertheless, the formulated framework and the line of reasoning presented in this work assume that dynamic capabilities can be deployed in also less dynamic environments. Lack of evidence prevents transferring some of the findings to the context of moderate and stable industries. Therefore, despite a readable and logically justified selection of cases, collected evidence and formulated conclusions maintain limited to environments characterized by a higher than average dynamics. Other limitation relates to the timeframe of the study. Although it was a longitudinal study, some of identified and investigated responses were implemented in 2014–2015, thus the study presents description and analysis of the content of introduced changes, but it does not address the issue of effectiveness of implemented reconfigurations.

It is important to underline that limitations discussed above do not reduce the value of the conducted research, formulated dynamic capability-based framework of value appropriation, obtained findings, and conclusions. Those limitations should be treated as a point of departure for subsequent studies. Moreover, the theoretical and empirical input of the study provides interesting avenues for future research. Conducted research evidenced importance of the mind-set of decision makers while addressing environmental signals. Observed change of the mind-set from a threat to opportunity oriented was accompanied with a more complex response, which addressed rather broadly defined circumstances affecting currently deployed appropriation capabilities, than just a single initial threatening stimuli. Therefore, it would be a valuable research direction to explore further the dynamic nature of the value appropriation by locating the inquiry at the level of microfoundations referring to managerial cognition (Helfat & Martin, 2015). This direction of the research effort should provide opportunities for developing the idea of a threshold for a managerial decision concerning activation of dynamic capabilities to alter the trajectory of existing action patterns for value appropriation. Furthermore, formulated framework for investigating value appropriation visibly and cohesively reflects the dynamic nature of the process. It was evidenced that availability, efficacy and deployment of appropriation mechanisms change over time, yet specific conditions of interorganizational collaboration, i.e. coexistence and balance of cooperative, competitive and control relations, may affect the content and the course of such change. Although the inter-organisational networks represent an object of a multithreaded and multi-disciplinary research there is still a lack of a coherent, precise methodology to analyze the dynamics of interdependence of its internal processes. Thus, acknowledging an intense growth of interorganizational business structures on the one side and a paucity of exploration focused on the dynamics of the value distribution in those structures on the other, the formulated dynamic capability-based framework of value appropriation appears as a missing link to a promising area of inquiry.

LIST OF FIGURES

LIST OF TABLES

REFERENCES

Abernathy, W.J. & Utterback, J.M. (1978). "Patterns of industrial innovation." *Technology review*, 80(7), pp. 40‒47.

Adamczak, A. & du Vall, M. (eds.) (2010). *Ochrona własności intelektualnej*. Warszawa: Uniwersytecki Ośrodek Transferu Technologii Uniwersytetu Warszawskiego.

Afuah, A. (2014). *Business Model Innovation: Concepts, Analysis, and Cases*. New York: Routledge.

Enders A., König A., Hungenberg H., Engelbertz T. (2009). "Towards an integrated perspective of strategy: The value-process framework." *Journal of Strategy and Management*, 2(1), pp. 76‒96.

Alchian, A. & Demsetz, H. (1973). "Property Right Paradigm." *Journal of Economic History*, 33(1), pp. 16‒27.

Ali, S., Peters, L.D. & Lettice, F. (2012). "An Organizational Learning Perspective on Conceptualizing Dynamic and Substantive Capabilities." *Journal of Strategic Marketing*, 20(7), pp. 589–607.

Alinaghian, L.S. (2012). *Operationalizing dynamic capabilities: A supply network configuration approach*. Manuscript of paper to be presented at the DRUID Academy 2012, Institute for Manufacturing, Department of Engineering, University of Cambridge.

Alsos, G.A., Borch, O.J., Ljungren, E. & Madsen, E.L. (2008). *Dynamic capabilities –conceptualization and operationalization*. Academy of Management 2008 Annual Meeting, pp. 8–13.

Alvarez, S.A. & Barney, J.B. (2004). "Organizing rent generation and appropriation: toward a theory of the entrepreneurial firm." *Journal of Business Venturing*, 19, pp. 621–635.

Alvarez, S.A. & Barney, J.B. (2007). "Discovery and creation: Alternative theories of entrepreneurial creation." *Strategic Entrepreneurship Journal*, 1(1), pp. 11–26.

Alvarez, S.A., Barney, J.B. & Young, S.L. (2010). "Debates in entrepreneurship: Opportunity formation and implications for the field of entrepreneurship." In: Z.J. Acs & D.B. Audretsch (eds.), *Handbook of Entrepreneurship Research. An Interdisciplinary Survey and Introduction*, Vol. 5. New York: Springer, pp. 23‒45.

Amabile, T.M. (1996). *Creativity in Context: Update to the Social Psychology of Creativity*. Boulder, CO: Westview Press.

Ambrosini, V. & Bowman, C. (2009). "What are dynamic capabilities and are they a useful construct in strategic management?" *International Journal of Management Reviews*, 11(1), pp. 29–49.

Ambrosini, V., Bowman, C. & Collier, N. (2009). "Dynamic capabilities: An exploration of how firms renew their resource base." *British Journal of Management*, 20(1), pp. 9–24.

Amit, R.H.&. Schoemaker, P.J.H. (1993). "Strategic assets and organizational rent." *Strategic Management Journal*, 14(1), pp. 33–46.

Amit, R.H. & Zott, C. (2001). "Value creation in e-business." *Strategic Management Journal*, 22, pp. 493–520.

Anderson, J.C. (1995). "Relationships in business markets: Exchange episodes, value creation, and their empirical assessment." *Journal of the Academy of Marketing Science*, 23(4), pp. 346–350.

Andren, L., Magnusson, M. & Sjolander, S. (2003). "Opportunistic adaptation in start-up companies." *International Journal of Entrepreneurship and Innovation Management*, 3(5–6), pp. 546–562.

Ansoff, I. (1965). *Corporate Strategy*. New York: McGraw Hill.

Ardichvili, A., Cardozo, R. & Ray, S. (2003). "A theory of entrepreneurial opportunity identification and development." *Journal of Business Venturing*, 18(1), pp. 105–123.

Argandoña, A. (2011). *Stakeholder theory and value creation*. Working Paper, WP-922, IESE Business Scholl, University of Navara.

Argyris, C. & Schon, D. (1978). *Organizational Learning*. Reading, MA: Addison-Wesley.

Arundel, A. (2001). "The relative effectiveness of patents and secrecy for appropriation." *Research Policy*, 30, pp. 611–624.

Arundel, A. & Kabla, I. (1998). "What percentage of innovations are patented? Empirical estimates for European firms." *Research Policy*, 27, pp. 127–141.

Ashton, R.H. (2005). "Intellectual capital and value creation: A Review." *Journal of Accounting Literature*, 24, pp. 53–134.

Augier, M. & Teece, D.J. (2008). "Strategy as evolution with design: Dynamic capabilities and the design and evolution of the business enterprise." *Organization Studies*, 29, pp. 1187–1208.

Aumann, R.J. (1985). "What is game theory trying to accomplish? In: K.J. Arrow & S. Honka-pohja (eds.), *Frontiers of Economics*. Oxford: Basil Blackwell, pp. 28–76.

Aumann, R.J. & Maschler, M. (1995). *Repeated Games of Incomplete Information*. Cambridge, MA: MIT Press.

Baden-Fuller, Ch. & Haefliger, S. (2013). "Business models and technological innovation." *Long Range Planning*, 46, pp. 419–426.

Bain, J.S. (1956). *Barriers to New Competition*. Cambridge, MA: Harvard University Press.

Baldwin, C.Y. & Clark, K.B. (2006). *Architectural innovation and dynamic competition: The smaller 'span of control' strategy*. Harvard Business School Working Paper No. 07-014, available at http://www.people.hbs.edu/cbaldwin/ [accessed 12.07.2015].

Banaszyk, P. & Cyfert, S. (2007). *Strategiczna odnowa przedsiębiorstwa*. Warszawa: Difin.

Barney J.B. (1986). "Strategic factor markets: Expectations, luck, and business strategy." *Management Science*, 32, pp. 1231–1241.

Barney J.B. (1991). "Firm resources and sustained competitive advantage." *Journal of Management*, 17(1), pp. 99–120.

Barney, J.B. (1995). "Looking Inside for Competitive Advantage." *Academy of Management Executive*, 9(4), pp. 49–61.

Barreto, I. (2010). "Dynamic capabilities: a review of past research and an agenda for the future." *Journal of Management*, 36(1), pp. 256–280.

Becerra, M. (2008). "A resource-based analysis of the conditions for the emergence of profits." *Journal of Management*, 34, pp. 1110–1126.

Bednarczyk, M. (1996). *Otoczenie i przedsiębiorczość w zarządzaniu strategicznym organizacją gospodarczą*. Kraków: Wydawnictwo Akademii Ekonomicznej w Krakowie.

Bednarczyk, M. (ed.) (2006). *Konkurencyjność małych i średnich przedsiębiorstw na polskim rynku turystycznym*. Kraków: Wydawnictwo Uniwersytetu Jagiellońskiego.

Bednarczyk, M. (ed.) (2011). *Zarządzanie konkurencyjnością biznesu turystycznego w regionach*. Warszawa: CeDeWu.

Bednarczyk, M. (2014). „Model zintegrowanego zarządzania łańcuchem wartości turystyki na poziomie regionu." In: M. Bednarczyk & M. Najda-Janoszka (eds.), *Innowacje w turystyce. Regionalna przestrzeń współpracy w makroregionie południowym*. Warszawa: CeDeWu, pp. 55–65.

Bednarczyk, M. & Najda-Janoszka, M. (eds.) (2014). *Innowacje w turystyce. Regionalna przestrzeń współpracy w makroregionie południowym.* Warszawa: CeDeWu.

Besanko, D., Dranove, D., Shanley, M. & Schaefer, S. (2010). *Economics of Strategy.* New York: John Wiley & Sons Inc.

Birkinshaw, J., Hood, N. & Young, S. (2005). "Subsidiary entrepreneurship, internal and external competitive forces, and subsidiary performance." *International Business Review*, 14, pp. 227–248.

Blind, K., Edler, J., Frietsch, R. & Schmoch, U. (2006). "Motives to patent: Empirical evidence from Germany." *Research Policy*, 35, pp. 655–672.

Blyler, M. & Coff, R. (2003), "Dynamic capabilities, social capital and rent appropriation: Ties that split pies." *Strategic Management Journal*, 24, pp. 677–686.

Bowman, C. & Ambrosini, V. (2000), "Value creation versus value capture: Towards a coherent definition of value in strategy." *British Journal of Management*, 11(1), pp. 1–15.

Bowman, E.H. & Helfat, C.E. (2001). "Does corporate strategy matter?" *Strategic Management Journal*, 22, pp. 1–23.

Bowman, C. & Swart, J. (2007). "Whose human capital? The challenge of value capture when capital is embedded." *Journal of Management Studies*, 44(4), pp. 488–505.

Brandenburger, A. & Nalebuff, B. (1995). "The right game: Using the game theory to shape strategy." *Harvard Business Review*, July–August, pp. 57–71.

Brandenburger, A.M. & Nalebuff, B. (1996). *Co-opetition.* New York: Doubleday.

Brandenburger, A.M. & Stuart, H.W. Jr. (1996), "Value-based Business Strategy." *Journal of Economics & Management Strategy*, 5, pp. 5–24.

Brandenburger, A.M. & Stuart, H.W. Jr. (2007). "Biform Games." *Management Science*, 53(4), pp. 537–549.

Branzei, O. & Vertinsky, I. (2006). "Strategic pathways to product innovation capabilities in SMEs." *Journal of Business Venturing*, 21, pp. 75–105.

Bratnicki, M. (2000). *Kompetencje przedsiębiorstwa. Od określenia kompetencji do zbudowania strategii.* Warszawa: Agencja Wydawnicza Placet.

Bratnicki, M. (2011). „Model przedsiębiorczego rozwoju organizacji: konstrukt i jego wymiary." *Współczesne Zarządzanie*, 3, pp. 34–42.

Bridoux, F. (2004). *A resource-based approach to performance and competition: An overview of the connections between resources and competition.* Belgium Institut et de Gestion: Universite Catholique de Louvain.

Brown, S.L. & Eisenhardt, K.M. (1997). "The art of continuous change: Linking complexity theory and time-paced evolution in relentlessly shifting organizations." *Administrative Science Quarterly*, 42, pp. 1–34.

Burmann, Ch. (2002). *Strategische Flexibilitat und Strategiewechsel als Determinanten des Unternehmenswertes.* Wiesbaden: Springer.

Burt, R.S. (1992). *Structural Holes: The Social Structure of Competition.* Cambridge, MA: Harvard University Press.

Camarinha-Matos, L.M. & Asarmanesh, H. (2006). *Collaborative networks. Value creation in a knowledge society.* Proceedings of PROLAMAT 2006, IFIP International Conference on Knowledge Enterprise – New Challenges, Shanghai, China June 2006, Shanghai: Springer.

Carlton, D. & Perloff, J. (1994). *Modern Industrial Organization.* New York, NY: Harper Collins College Publishers.

Castanias, R.P. & Helfat, C.E. (1991). "Managerial resources and rents." *Journal of Management*, 17(1), pp. 155–171.

Chatain, O. & Zemsky, P. (2011). "Value creation and value capture with frictions." *Strategic Management Journal*, 32(11), pp. 1206–1231.

Caves, R.E. & Porter, M.E. (1977). "From entry barriers to mobility barriers." *Quarterly Journal of Economics*, 91, pp. 241–261.

Chatain, O. (2010). "Value creation, competition, and performance in buyer-supplier relationships." *Strategic Management Journal*, 32, pp. 76–102.

Ceccagnoli, M. & Rothaermel, F.T. (2008). "Appropriating the returns from innovation. Advances in the Study of Entrepreneurship." *Innovation & Economic Growth*, 18, pp. 11–34.

Cepeda, G. & Vera, D. (2007). "Dynamic capabilities and operational capabilities: A knowledge management perspective." *Journal of Business Research*, 60, pp. 426–437.

Chacar, A. & Hesterly, W. (2008). "Institutional settings and rent appropriation by knowledge--based-employees: The case of major league baseball." *Managerial and Decision Economics*, 29(2-3), pp. 117-136.

Chesbrough, H.W. (2003). "The logic of open innovation: managing intellectual property." *California Management Review*, 45(3), pp. 33–58.

Cockburn, I., Henderson, R. & Stern, S. (2000). "Untangling the Origins of Competitive Advantage." *Strategic Management Journal*, 21, pp. 1123–1145.

Coff, R.W. (1999). "When competitive advantage doesn't lead to performance: The resource--based view and stakeholder bargaining power." *Organization Science*, 10(2), pp. 119–131.

Coff, R.W. (2010). "The co-evolution of rent appropriation and capability development." *Strategic Management Journal*, 31(7), pp. 711–733.

Cohen, W.M. & Levinthal, D.A. (1990). "Absorptive capacity: A new perspective on learning and innovation." *Administrative Science Quarterly*, 35(1), pp. 128–152.

Cohen, W.M., Nelson, R.R. & Walsh, J.P. (2000). "Protecting their intellectual assets: Appropriability conditions and why U.S. manufacturing firms patent (or not)." *NBER Working Paper* 7552, Cambridge, MA: National Bureau of Economic Research.

Collis, D.J. (1994). "Research note: How valuable are organizational capabilities?" *Strategic Management Journal*, 15, pp. 143–152.

Collis, D.J. & Montgomery, C.A. (1995). "Competing on resources." *Harvard Business Review* 73(4), pp. 118–128.

Cool, K., Dierickx, I. & Costa, L.A. (2012). "Diseconomies of time compression." *INSEAD Faculty & Research Working Paper* 2012/78/ST

Cordes-Berszin, P. (2013). *Dynamic capabilities. How organizational structures affect knowledge processes*. New York: Palgrave Macmillan.

Cyert, R. & March, J. (1963). *A Behavioral Theory of the Firm*. Englewood Cliffs, NJ: Prentice--Hall.

Cyfert, S. (2012). "Systemowy model organizacji: perspektywa procesów odnowy organizacyjnej." *Prace Naukowe Uniwersytetu Ekonomicznego we Wrocławiu*, (276), pp. 123–129.

Cyfert, S., Dyduch, W., Latusek-Jurczak, D., Niemczyk, J. & Sopińska, A. (2014). „Subdyscypliny w naukach o zarządzaniu – logika wyodrębnienia, identyfikacja modelu koncepcyjnego oraz zawartość tematyczna." *Organizacja i Kierowanie*, (1), pp. 37–49.

Cygler, J. (2009). *Kooperencja przedsiębiorstw*. Warszawa: Oficyna Wydawnicza SGH.

Czakon, W. (2007). *Dynamika więzi międzyorganizacyjnych przedsiębiorstwa*. Katowice: Wydawnictwo Uniwersytetu Ekonomicznego w Katowicach.

Czakon, W. (2009). "Mity o badaniach jakościowych w naukach o zarządzaniu." *Przegląd Organizacji*, 9, pp. 13–18.

Czakon, W. (2010a). "Dynamiczne podejście do zarządzania." *Acta Unviersitatis Lodziensis, Folia Oeconomica*, 234, pp. 3–12.

Czakon, W. (2010b). "Strategia jako reguły zawłaszczania renty ekonomicznej." In: R. Krupski (ed.), *Zarządzanie strategiczne*. Wałbrzych: Wałbrzyska Wyższa Szkoła Zarządzania i Przedsiębiorczości, pp. 137-148.

Czakon, W. (2012). *Sieci w zarządzaniu strategicznym.* Warszawa: Wolters Kluwer.

Czakon, W. (2013). "Zastosowanie studiów przypadku w badaniach nauk o zarządzaniu." In: W. Czakon (ed.), *Podstawy metodologii badań w naukach o zarządzaniu.* Warszawa: Wolters Kluwer, pp. 92–113.

Czakon, W. & Rogalski, M. (2012). "Komplementarność kompetencyjna organizacji a koopetycja na rynku obrotu energią elektryczną." *Prace Naukowe Uniwersytetu Ekonomicznego we Wrocławiu,* 260, pp. 58–68.

Danneels, E. (2011). „Trying to become a different type of company: Dynamic capability at Smith Corona." *Strategic Management Journal,* 32, pp. 1-31.

D'Aveni, R.A. (1994). *Hyper Competition. Managing the Dynamics of Strategic Maneuvering.* New York: The Free Press.

Davidsson, P. (2015). "Entrepreneurial opportunities and the entrepreneurship nexus: A reconceptualization." *Journal of Business Venturing,* 30(5), pp. 674–695.

Denzin, N.K. (1970). *The Research Act in Sociology.* Chicago: Aldine.

DeSouza, K.C. & Vanapalli, G.K. (2005). "Securing knowledge in organizations: Lessons from the defence and intelligence sectors." *International Journal of Information Management,* 3(1), pp. 1–7.

Dierickx I. & Cool, K. (1989). "Asset stock accumulation and sustainability of coopetitive advantage." *Management Science,* 35(12), pp. 1504–1511.

Di Gregorio, D. (2013). "An integrative, multi-level model of value creation and value appropriation." *Journal of Applied Business and Economics,* 15(1), pp. 39–53.

Dosi, G. (1982). "Technological paradigms and technological trajectories. A suggested interpretation of the determinants and directions of technical change." *Research Policy,* 11(3), pp. 147-162.

Dosi, G., Faillo, M. & Marengo, L. (2008). "Organizational capabilities, patterns of knowledge accumulation and governance structures in business firms. An introduction."*Organization Studies,* 29(8-9), pp. 1165-1185.

Dosi, G., Nelson, R.R. & Winter S.G. (2000). "Introduction: The Nature and Dynamics of Organisational Capabilities." In: G. Dosi, R.R. Nelson & S.G. Winter (eds.), *The Nature and Dynamics of Organisational Capabilities.* Oxford: Oxford University Press, pp. 1–22.

Drechsel, J. (2010). *Cooperative Lot Sizing Problems in Supply Chain.* Berlin–Heidelberg: Springer-Verlag.

Drejer, A. (2002). *Strategic Management and Core Competencies: Theory and Application.* Westport: Greenwood Publishing Group, Inc.

Duhamel, F., Reboud, S. & Santi, M. (2014). "Capturing value from innovations: The importance of rent configurations." *Management Decisions,* 52(1), pp. 122–143.

Dutta, S., Narasimhan, O. & Rajiv, S. (2005). „Conceptualizing and measuring capabilities: Methodology and empirical application." *Strategic Management Journal,* 26(3), pp. 277–285.

Dyer J.H. & Singh, H. (1998). "The relational view: Cooperative strategy and sources of interorganizational competitive advantage." *Academy of Management Review,* 23, pp. 660–679.

Dyer, J.H., Singh, H. & Kale, P. (2008). "Splitting the pie: Rent distribution in alliances and networks." *Managerial and Decision Economics,* 29, pp. 137–148.

Eisenhardt, K.M. (1989). "Building theories from case study research." *Academy of Management Review,* 14, pp. 532–550.

Eisehnardt, K.M. & Graebner, M.E. (2007). "Theory building from cases: Opportunities and challenges." *Academy of Management Journal,* 50(1), pp. 25–32.

Eisenhardt, K.M. & Martin, J.A. (2000). "Dynamic capabilities: What are they?" *Strategic Management Journal,* 21, pp. 1105–1121.

Ellegaard, Ch., Geersbro, J. & Medlin, Ch.J. (2009). *Value Appropriation within a Business Network Competitive.* Paper IMP ASIA Conference, 6–10 December, Kuala Lumpur, Malaysia.

Enders, A., König, A., Hungenberg, H. & Engelbertz, T. (2009). "Towards an integrated perspective of strategy, The value-process framework." *Journal of Strategy and Management*, pp. 76–96.

Eriksson, T. (2013) "Methodological issues in dynamic capabilities research – a critical review." *Baltic Journal of Management*, 8(3), pp. 306–332.

Eriksson, T. (2014). "Processes, antecedents and outcomes of dynamic capabilities." *Scandinavian Journal of Management*, 30(1), pp. 65–82.

Fahy, J. (2000). "The resource-based view of the firm: Some stumbling-blocks on the road to under standing sustainable competitive advantage." *Journal of European Industrial Training*, 24(2/3/4), pp. 94–104.

Farag, H. (2009). *Collaborative Value Creation. An Empirical Analysis of the European Biotechnology Industry*. Heidelberg: Physica-Verlag.

Feldman, M.S. & Pentland, B.T. (2003). "Reconptualizing organizational routines as a source of flexibility and change." *Administrative Science Quarterly*, 48, pp. 94–118.

Felin, T., & Foss, N.J. (2009). "Organizational routines and capabilities: Historical drift and a course correction toward microfoundations." *Scandinavian Journal of Management*, 25, pp. 157-167.

Felin, T., Foss N.J., Jeimeriks H. & Madsen, T.L. (2012). "Microfoundations of routines and capabilities: individuals, processes, structure." *Journal of Management Studies*, 49(8), pp. 1351–1374.

Felin, T. & Hesterly, W.S. (2007). "The knowledge-based view, nested heterogeneity, and new value creation: Philosophical considerations on the locus of knowledge." *Academy of Management Review*, 32(1), pp. 195–218.

Fischer, T. (2011). *Managing Value Capture: Empirical Analyses of Managerial Challenges in Capturing Value*. Heidelberg: Gabler Verlag – Springer Fachmedien Wiesbaden GmbH.

Ford, D., Håkansson, H., Snehota, I. & Gadde, L.E. (2011). *Managing Business Relationships*. New York: Wiley & Sons.

Foss, K. & Foss, N.J. (2002). "Creating, capturing, and protecting value: A property rights-based view of competitive strategy." *Working Paper 20002-02*. Department of Industrial Economics and Strategy, Copenhagen Business School, Frederiksberg, Denmark.

Foss, N.J. (1994). "The Theory of the Firm: The Austrians as Precursors and Critics of Contemporary Theory." *Review of Austrian Economics*, 7(1), pp. 31–66.

Foss, N.J. (2005). *Resources, Firms, and Strategies: A Reader in the Resource-based Perspective*. New York: Oxford University Press.

Foss, N.J. & Knudsen, T. (2003). "The resource-based tangle: Towards a sustainable explanation of coopetitive advantage." *Managerial and Decision Economics*, 24, pp. 291–307.

Freeman, R.E. (1984). *Strategic Management: A Stakeholder Approach*. Englewood Cliffs, NJ: Prentice Hall.

Fudenberg, D. & Tirole, J. (1991). *Game Theory*. Cambridge: Massachusetts Institute of Technology.

Galunic, D. & Eisenhardt, K. (2001). "Architectural innovation and modular corporate forms." *Academy of Management Journal*, 44(6), pp. 1229–1249.

Gans, J.S. & Ryall, M.D. (2015). "Value capture theory: A strategic management review." *Rotman School of Management Working Paper*, No. 2549003.

Garcia-Castro, R. & Aguilera, R.V. (2015). „Incremental value creation and appropriation in a world with multiple stakeholders." *Strategic Management Journal*, 36(11), pp. 137–144.

Geroski, P., Gilbert, R.J. & Jacquemin, A. (2001). *Barriers to Entry and Strategic Competition*. Abingdon: Routledge.

Gilbert, R. (1989)."Mobility barriers and the value of incumbency." In: R. Schmalensee & R.D. Willig (eds.), *Handbook of Industrial Organization*. Amsterdam: North-Holland, pp. 475–535.

Gilbert, C.G. (2005). "Unbundling the structure of inertia: Resource versus routine rigidity." *Academy of Management Journal*, 48, pp. 741–763.

Gomes-Casseres, B. (1994). "Group versus group: How alliance networks compete." *Harvard Business Review*, July–August, pp. 62–74.

Grant, R.M. (1991). "The resource-based theory of competitive advantage: Implications for strategy formulation." *California Management Review*, 33(3), pp. 114–135.

Griffith, D.A. & Harvey, M.G. (2001). "A resource perspective of global dynamic capabilities." *Journal of International Business Studies*, 32(3), pp. 597–606.

Grönroos, C. (1997). "Value-driven relational marketing: From products to resources and competencies." *Journal of Marketing Management*, 13(5), pp. 407–419.

Grönroos, C. & Voima, P. (2011). *Making Sense of Value and Value Co-creation in Service Logic*. Helsinki: Hanken School of Economics.

Grossman, S.J. & Oliver D.H. (1986). "The costs and benefits of ownership: A theory of vertical and lateral integration." *Journal of Political Economy*, 94, pp. 691–719.

Grudzewski, W.M., Hejduk, I.K., Sankowska, A. & Wańtuchowicz, M. (2008). *Trust Management in Virtual Work Environments: A Human Factors Perspective*. Boca Raton: CRC Press.

Gulati, R. & Wang, L.O. (2003). "Size of the pie and share of the pie: Implications of network embeddedness and business relatedness for value creation and value appropriation in joint ventures." In: V. Buskens, W. Raub & C. Snijders (eds.), *The Governance of Relations in Markets and Organizations. Research in the Sociology of Organizations*. Amsterdam, Netherlands: JAI, Elsevier Science Ltd., pp. 209–242.

Håkansson, H. & Snehota, I. (1995). *Developing Relationships in Business Networks*. Routledge: London.

Håkansson, H. & Snehota, I. (1989). "No business is an island: The network concept of business strategy." *Scandinavian Journal of Management*, 5(3), pp. 187–200.

Hall, R. (1993). "A framework linking intangible resources and capabilities to sustainable competitive advantage." *Strategic Management Journal*, 14, pp. 607–618.

Hall, B.H. & Ziedonis, R.H. (2001). "The patent paradox revisited: An empirical study of patenting in the US semiconductor industry, 1979-95." *RAND Journal of Economics*, 32(1), pp. 101-128.

Hamel, G. (1991). "Competition for competence and inter-partner learning within international strategic alliances." *Strategic Management Journal*, 12, pp. 83–103.

Hamel, G. & Prahalad, C.K. (1992). "Letter." *Harvard Business Review*, May–June, pp. 164–165.

Hamel, G. & Prahalad, C.K. (1994). *Competing for the Future*. Boston: Harvard Business School Press.

Hansen, F.R. (2008). *The Utility of Strategic Management Knowledge for Strategic Management Practice: The Actors Perspective*. Ann Arbor MI: ProQuest LLC.

Harsanyi, J.C. (1966). "A general theory of rational behavior in game situations." *Econometrica*, 34, pp. 613–634.

Hartman, R.S. (1967). *The Structure of Value: Foundations of Scientific Axiology*. Carbondale and Edwardsville: Southern University Press.

Hawawini, G., Subramanian, V. & Verdin, P. (2003). "Is performance driver by industry-or firm--specific factors? A new look at the evidence." *Strategic Management Journal*, 24(1), pp. 1–16.

Helfat, C.E. (1997). "Know-how and asset complementarity and dynamic capability accumulation: The case of R&D." *Strategic Management Journal*, 18, pp. 339-360.

Helfat, C.E., Finkelstein, S., Mitchell, W., Peteraf, M., Singh, H. & Winter, S.G. (2007). *Dynamic Capabilities: Understanding Strategic Change in Organizations*. Malden, MA: Blackwell Publishing.

Helfat, C.E. & Martin, J.A. (2015). "Dynamic managerial capabilities: Review and assessment of managerial impact on strategic change." *Journal of Management*, 35(4), pp. 1281–1312.

Helfat, C.E. & Peteraf, M.A. (2003). "The dynamic resource-based view: Capabilities lifecycles." *Strategic Management Journal*, 24(10), pp. 997–1010.

Helfat, C.E. & Peteraf, M.A. (2009). "Understanding dynamic capabilities: Progress along a developmental path." *Strategic Organization*, 7(1), pp. 91–102.

Helfat, C.E. & Winter, S.G. (2011). "Untangling dynamic and operational capabilities: Strategy for the (n)ever-changing world." *Strategic Management Journal*, 32, pp. 1243–1250.

Henkel, J. & Baldwin, C.Y. (2009). "Modularity for value appropriation – drawing the boundaries of intellectual property." *Harvard Business School Working Paper 09-097*.

Henkel, J., Baldwin, C. & Shih, W. (2013). "IP modularity: Profiting from innovation by aligning product architecture with intellectual property." *California Management Review*, 55(4), pp. 65–82.

Henkel, J. & Hoffman, A. (2014). *Value capture in hierarchically organized industries*. Paper Presented at the DRUID Society Conference 2014, CBS, Copenhagen, 16–18 June, pp. 1–34.

den Hertog, P., van der Aa, W. & de Jong, M.W. (2010). "Capabilities for managing service innovation: Towards a conceptual framework." *Journal of Service Management*, 21(4), pp. 490–514.

Hodgson, G. (2012). "The mirage of microfoundations." *Journal of Management Studies*, 49, pp. 1389-1394.

Holden, M.T. & Lynch, P. (2004). "Choosing the appropriate methodology: Understanding research philosophy." *The Marketing Review*, 4(4), pp. 397–409.

Hong, J., Kianto, A. & Kylaheiko, K. (2008). "Moving cultures and the creation of new knowledge and dynamic capabilities in emerging markets." *Knowledge and Process Management*, 15(3), p. 196–202.

Howells, J. (2005). *The Management of Innovation and Technology: The Shaping of Technology and Institutions of the Market Economy*. London: Sage Publications.

Huber, G.P. (1991). "Organizational learning: The contributing processes and the literatures." *Organization Science*, 2(1). Special Issue: Organizational Learning Papers in Honor of (and by) James G. March, pp. 88–115.

Hurmelinna-Laukkanen, P. & Puumalainen, K. (2007). "Nature and dynamics of appropriability: Strategies for appropriating returns on innovation." *R&D Management*, 37(2), pp. 95–110.

Hurmelinna-Laukkanen, P. & Ritala, P. (2012). "Appropriability as the driver of internationalization of service-oriented firms." *The Service Industires Journal*, 32(7), pp. 1039–1056.

Hussinger, K. (2006). "Is silence golden? Patents versus secrecy at the firm level." *Economics of Innovation and New Technology*, 15(8), pp. 735–752.

Inkpen, A.C. (1996). "Creating knowledge through collaboration." *California Management Review*, 39(1), pp. 123–140.

Jacobides, M.G. (2005). "Industry change thorugh vertical disintegration: how and why markets emerged in mortgage banking." *Academy of Management Journal*, 48(3), pp. 465–498.

Jacobides, M.G., Knudsen, T. & Augier, M. (2006). "Benefiting from innovation: Value creation, value appropriation and the role of industry architectures." *Research Policy*, 35, pp. 1200–1221.

Jacobson, R.J. (1992). "The 'Austrian' School of Strategy." *Academy of Management Review*, 17(4), pp. 782–807.

Jankowska, B. (2012). *Koopetycja w klastrach kreatywnych. Przyczynek do teorii regulacji w gospodarce rynkowej*. Poznań: Wydawnictwo UEP.

Janssen, M.J., Castaldi, C. & Alexiev, A. (2015). „Dynamic capabilities for service innovation: Conceptualization and measurement." *R&D Management* (in press).

Jap, S.D. (2001). "'Pie Sharing' in Complex Collaboration Contexts." *Journal of Marketing Research*, February, 38(1), pp. 86–99.

Jennewein, K. (2005). *Intellectual Property Management*. Heidelberg: Physica-Verlag.

Jordan, J. & Lowe, J. (2004). "Protecting strategic knowledge: Insights from collaborative agreements in the aerospace sector." *Technology Analysis & Strategic Management*, 16(2), pp. 241–259.

Kahle, L.R. & Valette-Florence, P. (2015). *Marketplace Lifestyles in an Age of Social Media: Theory and Methods*. New York: Routledge.

Kale, P., Singh, H. & Perlmutter, H. (2000). "Learning and protection of proprietary assets in strategic alliances: Building relational capital." *Strategic Management Journal*, 21, pp. 217–237.

Kale, P. & Singh, H. (2007). "Building firm capabilities through learning: The role of the alliance learning process in alliance capability and firm-level alliance success." *Strategic Management Journal*, 28(10), pp. 981–1000.

Kaplan, R.S. & Norton, D.P. (2001). *The Strategy-Focused Organization*. Boston, MA: Harvard Business School Press.

Karaś, M. (2014). "Studium przypadku jako narzędzie badawcze." In: K. Kuciński (ed.), *Naukowe badanie zjawisk gospodarczych*. Warszawa: Wolters Kluwer, pp. 321-342.

Karim, S. (2009). "Business unit reorganization and innovation in new product markets." *Management Science*, 55(7), pp. 1237–1254.

Karpacz, J. (2014). „Organizacyjne rutyny i zdolności – spojrzenie literaturowe." *Marketing i Rynek*, 5, pp. 801–807.

Katkalo, V.S., Pitelis, C.N. & Teece, D.J. (2010). „Introduction: On the nature and scope of dynamic capabilities." *Industrial and Corporate Change*, 19(4), pp. 1175–1186.

Kay, J. (1995). *Foundations of Corporate Success: How Business Strategies Add Value*. Oxford: Oxford University Press.

Kay, N. (2010). "Dynamic capabilities as context: The role of decision, system and structure."*Industrial and Corporate Change*, 19(4), pp.1205–1223.

Khanna, T.R., Gulati, R. & Nohria, N. (1998). "The dynamics of learning alliances: Competition, cooperation, and relative scope." *Strategic Management Journal*, 19, pp. 193–210.

Kim, J. & Mahoney, J.T. (2006). "How property rights economics furthers the resource-based view: Resources, trans action costs and entrepreneurial Discovery." *International Journal of Strategic Change Management*, 1(1–2), pp. 40–52.

Kirzner, I.M. (1973). *Competition and Entrepreneurship*. Chicago: University of Chicago Press.

Kitching, J. & Blackburn, R. (1998). "Intellectual property management in the small and medium enterprises (SME)." *Journal of Small Business & Enterprise Development*, 5(4), pp. 327–335.

Klein, P., Mahoney, J., McGahan, A., & Pitelis, C.N. (2012). "Who is in charge? A property rights perspective on stakeholder governance. SO!" *APBOX Special Issue*, 10(3), pp. 304–315.

Kogut, B. & Zander, U. 1992. "Knowledge of the firm, combinative capacities, and the replication of technology." *Organization Science*, 3(3), pp. 383–397.

Korhonen, S. & Niemelä, J.S. (2005). "A conceptual analysis of capabilities: Identifying and classifying sources of competitive advantage in the wood industry." *Liiketaloudellinen aikakauskirja LTA - Finnish Journal of Business Economics*, 1, pp. 11–47.

Kraaijenbrink, J., Spencer, J.C. & Groen, A.J. (2010). "The resource-based view: A review and assessment of its critiques." *Journal of Management*, 36(1), pp. 349–372.

Krupski, R. (2007). "Elementy koncepcji zarządzania okazją w organizacji." In: Dynamika zarządzania organizacjami. Paradygmaty – Metody – Zastosowania. *Prace Naukowe Akademii Ekonomicznej w Katowicach*, pp. 95–106.

Krupski, R. (2011). "Okazje w zarządzaniu strategicznym przedsiębiorstwa." *Organizacja i Kierowanie*, 4(147), pp. 11–24.

Krupski, R. (2012). "O okazjach raz jeszcze. Trochę teorii i raportu z badań." *Przegląd Organizacji*, 11, pp. 3–5.

Krupski, R. (2014). "Okazje i zagrożenia w strategii przedsiębiorstwa. Model i badania empiryczne." In: M. Pawlak (ed.), *Nowe tendencje w zarządzaniu. Tom V*. Lublin: Wydawnictwo KUL, pp. 55–62.

Krupski, R., Niemczyk, J. & Stańczyk-Hugiet, E. (2009). *Koncepcje strategii organizacji.* Warszawa: PWE.

Kuuluvainen, A. (2012). "How to concretize dynamic capabilities? Theory and examples." *Journal of Strategy and Management,* 5(4), pp. 381–392.

Kuuluvainen, A. (2013). "International growth of a finnish high-tech SME: A dynamic capabilities approach." *Research in Economics and Business: Central and Eastern Europe,* 4(2), pp. 26–40.

Larsson, R. & Finkelstein, S. (1999) "Integrating strategic, organization, and Human Resource. 23 perspectives on mergers and acquisitions: A case survey of synergy realization." *Organization Science,* 10(1), pp. 1–26.

Lavie, D. (2007). "Alliance portfolios and firm performance: A study of value creation and appropriation in the US software industry." *Strategic Management Journal,* 28(12), pp. 1187–1212.

Leiponen, A. & Byma, J. (2009). "If you cannot block, you better run: Small firms, cooperative innovation, and appropriation strategies." *Research Policy,* 38(9), pp. 1478–1488.

Leonard-Barton, D. (1992). "Core capabilities and core rigidities: A paradox in managing new product development." *Strategic Management Journal.* Summer Special Issue, 13, pp. 111–126.

Lepak, D.P., Smith, K.G. & Taylor, M.S. (2007). "Value creation and value capture: A multilevel perspective." *Academy of Management Review,* 32(1), pp. 180–194.

Lewin, P. & Phelan, S.E. (2002). "Rent and resources: A market process perspective." In: N.J. Foss & P.G. Klein (eds.), *Entrepreneurship and the firm: Austrian Perspectives on Economic Organization.* Northampton Cheltenham: Edwar Elgar Publishing Inc., pp. 221–247.

Lewin, A.Y., Weigelt, C.B. & Emery, J.D. (2004). "Adaptation and selection in strategy and change: Perspectives on strategic change in organizations." In: M.S. Poole & A.H. Van de Ven (eds.), *Handbook of Organizational Change and Innovation.* New York: Oxford University Press, pp. 108–160.

Lieberman, M.B. & Balasubramanian, N. (2007). "Measuring value creation and its distribution among stakeholders of the firm." *Working Paper,* UCLA Anderson School of Management.

Lieberman, M.B. & Montgomery, D.B. (1998). "First-mover advantages." *Strategic Management Journal,* 9, pp. 41–58.

Lincoln, Y.S. (1995). "Emerging criteria for quality in qualitative and interpretive research." *Qualitative Inquiry,* 1(3), pp. 275–289.

Lincoln, Y.S. & Guba, E.G. (1985). *Naturalistic Inquiry.* Beverly Hills: Sage Publishing Inc.

Lincoln, Y.S. & Guba, E.G. (2000). "Paradigmatic controversies, contradictions and emerging confluences." In: N.K. Denzin & Y.S. Lincoln (eds.), *Handbook of Qualitative Research,* 2nd ed. California: Sage Publications, pp. 163–188.

Lippman, S.A. & Rumelt, R.P. (1982). "Uncertain imitability: An analysis of interfirm differences in efficiency under competition." *Bell Journal of Economics,* 13, pp. 418–438.

Lisiński M. (2011), "Analiza metodologii nauk o zarządzaniu." In: J. Czekaj, M. Lisiński (eds.), *Rozwój koncepcji i metod zarządzania.* Kraków: Fundacja Uniwersytetu Ekonomicznego w Krakowie.

Ma, H. (2000). "Competitive advantage and firm performance." *Competitiveness Review,* 10(2), pp. 16–32.

Madsen, E.L. (2010). "A dynamic capability framework – generic types of dynamic capabilities and their relationship to entrepreneurship." In: S. Wall, C. Zimmermann, R. Klingebiel & D. Lange (eds.), *Strategic Reconfigurations: Building Dynamic Capabilities in Rapid--Innovation-Based Industries.* Cheltenham: Edward Elgar, pp. 223–240.

Mahoney, J.T. (2012). "Towards a stakeholder theory of strategic management." In: J. Ricart (ed.), *Towards a New Theory of the Firm.* Barcelona: IESE Research Unit.

Mahoney, J.T. & Pandian, J.R. (1992). "The resource-based view within the conversation of strategic management." *Strategic Management Journal,* 13(5), pp. 363–380.

Makadok, R. (2001). "Toward a synthesis of the resource-based and dynamic-capability views of rent creation." *Strategic Management Journal*, 22, pp. 387–401.

Makadok, R. & Coff, R. (2002) "The theory of value and the value of theory: Breaking new ground versus reinventing the wheel." *Academy of Management Review*, 27(1), pp. 10–13.

Mansfield, E. (1985). "How rapidly does new industrial technology leak out?" *The Journal of Industrial Economics*, XXXIV(2), pp. 217–233.

March, J.G. (1991). "Exploration and exploitation in organizational learning." *Organization Science*, 2(1), pp. 71–87.

Markman, G.D., Gianiodis, P.T. & Buchholtz, A.K. (2009). "Factor-market rivalry." *Academy of Management Review*, 34(3), pp. 423–441.

Marr, B. & Roos, G. (2005). "A strategy perspective on intellectual capital." In: B. Marr (ed.), *Perspectives on Intellectual Capital*. Oxford: Elsevier Butterworth-Heinemann, pp. 28–41.

Mazur, K. (2011). *Tworzenie i przywłaszczanie wartości: perspektywa relacji: pracownik – organizacja*. Zielona Góra: Oficyna Wydawnicza Uniwersytetu Zielonogórskiego.

Mazur, K. & Kulczyk, Z. (2013). "Isolating mechanisms as sustainability factors of resource-based competitive advantage." *Management* 2(17), pp. 31–46.

MacDonald, G. & Ryall, M.D. (2004). "How do value creation and competition determine whether a firm appropriates value?" *Management Science*, 50(10), pp. 1319–1333.

McAfee, R.P., Mialon, H.M. & Williams, M. (2004). "What is a barrier to entry?" *American Economic Review*, 94 (2), pp. 461–465.

McGahan, A.M. & Porter, M.E. (1997). "How much does industry matter, really?" *Strategic Management Journal*, 18 (Summer Special Issue), pp. 15–30.

McMullen, J. & Shepherd, D. (2006). "Entrepreneurial action and the role of uncertainty in the theory of the entrepreneur." *Academy of Management Review*, 31(1), pp. 132–152.

Meyer, M., Milgrom, P. & Roberts, J. (1992). "Organizational prospects, influence costs, and ownership changes." *Journal of Economics and Management Strategy*, 1, pp. 9–35.

Miles, L.D. (1961). *Techniques of Value Analysis and Engineering*. New York: McGraw-Hill Book Company.

Miles, M.B. & Huberman, M. (1994). "Data management and analysis methods." In: N.K. Denzin & Y.S. Lincoln (eds.), *Handbook of Qualitative Research*. Thousand Oaks CA: Sage Publications Inc., pp. 428–444.

Miles, M.B., Huberman, M. & Saldana, J. (2014). *Qualitative Data Analysis. A Methods Sourcebook*. Thousand Oaks CA: Sage Publications Inc.

Miller, D. & Shamsie, J. (1996). "The resource-based view of the firm in two environments: The hollywood film studios from 1936 to 1965." *Academy of Management Journal*, 39(3), pp. 519–543.

Mizik, N. & Jacobson, R. (2003). "Trading off between value creation and value appropriation: The financial implications of shifts in strategic emphasis." *Journal of Marketing*, 67, pp. 63–75.

Mol, J.M., Wijnberg, N.M. & Carroll, Ch. (2005). "Value chain envy: Explaining newentry and vertical integration in popularmusic." *Journal of Manage Studies*, 42, pp. 251–276.

Moran, P. & Ghoshal, S. (1997). "Value creation by firms." *Proceedings of the Academy of Management*, pp. 41–45.

Morgan, N.A., Vorhies, D.W. & Mason, C.H. (2009). "Market orientation, marketing capabilities, and firm performance." *Strategic Management Journal*, 30(8), pp. 909–920.

Morgenstern, O. (1963). "Limits to the Uses of Mathematics in Economics." *Mathematics and the Social Sciences*. J. Charlesworth (ed.). A a symposium sponsored by the American Academy of Political and Social Sciences, pp. 12–29. (Reprinted in Schotter, 1976.)

Morris, C.R. & Ferguson, C.H. (1993). "How architecture wins technology Wars." *Harvard Business Review*, March–April, pp. 86–96.

Mowery, D.C., Oxley, J.E. & Silverman, B.S. (1996). "Strategic alliances and interfirm knowledge transfer." *Strategic Management Journal*, Winter Special Issue, 17, pp. 77–92.

Myerson, R.B. (1991). *Game Theory: Analysis of Conflict*. Cambridge: Harvard University Press.

Najda-Janoszka, M. (2011a). "Zatrzymywanie wartości w sieciach kooperacyjnych przedsiębiorstw." *Zeszyty Naukowe Uniwersytetu Ekonomicznego w Poznaniu*, 169, Poznań, pp. 48–62.

Najda-Janoszka, M. (2011b). „Ochrona zasobów niematerialnych w sieciach kooperacyjnych." *Zeszyty Naukowe Uniwersytetu Szczecińskiego Ekonomiczne Problemy Usług*, 650, Szczecin, pp. 427–438.

Najda-Janoszka, M. (2012). "Matching imitative activity of high-tech firms with entrepreneurial orientation." *Journal of Entrepreneurship, Management and Innovation*, 8(1), pp. 52–67.

Najda-Janoszka, M. & Kopera, S. (2014a). "Exploring barriers to innovation in tourism industry – the case of southern region of Poland." *Procedia – Social and Behavioral Sciences*, 110, Elsevier Ltd., pp. 190–201.

Najda-Janoszka, M. (2014b). "Zdolność do współpracy." In: M. Bednarczyk & M. Najda-Janoszka (eds.), *Innowacje w turystyce. Regionalna przestrzeń współpracy w makroregionie południowym*. Warszawa: CeDeWu.

Najda-Janoszka, M. (2015). "Dynamic capabilities: on a developmental path from an approach towards a theory." In: J. Kaczmarek & P. Krzemiński. *Development, Iinnovation and Business Potential in View of Economic Changes*. Cracow: Foundation of Cracow University of Economics, pp. 27–34.

Najda-Janoszka, M. (2015a). "Problem zatrzymywania wartości przez MŚP – studium przypadku działalności podwykonawczej." *Marketing i Rynek*, 9, pp. 424–435.

Najda-Janoszka, M. & Wszendybył-Skulska, E. (2015). *Knowledge leakage in the context of staff outflow – the case of small hotels in Southern Poland*. Conference Proceedings of EIASM 5th International Conference on Tourism Management and Related Issues, Kos, 8–9 October.

Nanda, A. (1996). "Resources, capabilities and competences." In: A. Edmondson & B. Moingeon (eds.), *Organizational Learning and Competitive Advantage*. London: Sage Publications Ltd., pp. 93–120.

Narayandas, D. & Rangan, V.K. (2004), "Building and sustaining buyer–seller relationships in mature industrialmarkets." *Journal of Marketing*, 68 (July), pp. 63–77.

Nelson R. & Winter S.G. (1982). *An Evolutionary Theory of Economic Change*. Cambridge, MA: Belknap Press.

Neuhäusler, P. (2012) "The use of patents and informal appropriation mechanisms: differences between sectors and among companies." *Technovation*, 32, pp. 681–693.

Newbert, S.L. (2007). "Empirical research on the resource-based view of the firm: An assessment and suggestions for future research." *Strategic Management Journal*, 28(2), pp. 121–146.

Newbert, S.L. (2008). "Value, rareness, competitive advantage, and performance: a conceptual--level empirical investigation of the resource-based view of the firm." *Strategic Management Journal*, 29(7), pp. 745–768.

Newell, S. & Edelman, L.F. (2008). "Developing a dynamic project learning and cross-project learning capability: Synthesizing two perspectives." *Information Systems Journal*, 18(6), 567–591.

Niemczyk, J., Stańczyk-Hugiet, E. & Jasiński, B. (2012). *Sieci międzyorganizacyjne. Współczesne wyzwanie dla teorii i praktyki zarządzania*. Warszawa: C.H. Beck.

Niemczyk, J. (2006). "Możliwości strategicznego zarządzania kompetencjami." In: R. Krupski (ed.), *Zarządzanie strategiczne – ujęcie zasobowe. Prace Naukowe Wałbrzyskiej Wyższej Szkoły Zarządzania i Przedsiębiorczości*, Wałbrzych, pp. 119–130.

Nogalski, B. & Bors, K. (2000). „Zarządzanie przez wartość." *Przegląd Organizacji*, 4, pp. 16–21.

O'Hara, P.A. (2001). *Encyclopedia of Political Economy*, vol. 2. New York: Routledge.

Park, R. (1999). *Value Engineering: A Plan for Invention*. Boca Raton FL: St. Lucie Press.

Patton, M.Q. (2002). *Qualitative Research & Evaluation Methods*, 3rd ed. Thousand Oaks, CA: Sage Publications.

Patton, E., & Appelbaum, S.H. (2003). "The case for case studies in management research." *Management Research News*, 26(5), pp. 60-71.

Pavlou, A.P. & El Sawy, O.A. (2011). "Understanding the elusive black box of dynamic capabilities." *Decision Sciences*, 42(1), pp. 239-270.

Pearson, K. (1900). *The Grammar of Science, London: Adam and Charles Black*, https://archive.org/details/grammarofscience00pearuoft [accessed 12.09.2015].

Peleg, B. & Sudhölter, P. (2007). *Introduction to the Theory of Cooperative Games*. Heidelberg: Springer-Verlag.

Penrose, E.T. (1959). *The Theory of the Growth of the Firm*. Wiley: New York. (Reprint: Oxford University Press, 2009.)

Perry, C. (1998), "Processes of a case study methodology for postgraduate research in marketing." *The European Journal of Marketing*, 32(9/10), pp. 785-802.

Peteraf, M., Di Stefano, G. & Verona, G. (2013). "The elephant in the room of dynamic capabilities: bringing two diverging conversation together." *Strategic Management Journal*, 34, pp. 1389-1410.

Peteraf, M.A. (1993). "The cornerstones of competitive advantage: A resource-based view." *Strategic Management Journal*, 14, pp. 179-191.

Peteraf, M. & Barney, J. (2003). Unraveling The Resource-Based Tangle, *Managerial and Decision Economics*, 24, pp. 309-323.

Peteraf, M.A. & Bergen, M.E. (2003). "Scanning dynamic competitive landscapes: A market--based and resource-based framework." *Strategic Management Journal*, 24, pp. 1027-1041.

Pfeffer, J. & Salancik, G.R. (1978). *The External Control of Organizations: A Resource Dependence Perspective*. New York: Harper & Row.

Piekkari, R., Welch, C. & Paavilainen, E. (2009) "The case study as disciplinary convention. Evidence from international business journals". *Organizational Research Methods*, 12(3), pp. 567-589.

Pierce, J.L., Boerner, C.S. & Teece, D.J. (2002). "Dynamic capabilities, competence, and the behavioral theory of the firm." In: M. Augier & J.G. March (eds.), *The Economics of Choice, Change and Organization: Essays in Honor of Richard M. Cyert*. Northampton, USA: Edward Elgar, pp. 81-95.

Piórkowska, K. (2014). "Micro-foundations w teorii zarządzania strategicznego – czy to tylko retoryka?" *Prace Naukowe Wałbrzyskiej Wyższej Szkoły Zarządzania i Przedsiębiorczości*, 2(27), Wałbrzyska Wyższa Szkoła Zarządzania i Przedsiębiorczości, pp. 129-137.

Pitelis, C.N. (2013). „Towards a more 'ethically correct' governance for economic sustainability." *Journal of Business Ethics*, 118(3), pp. 655-665.

Pitelis, Ch. (2009). "The co-evolution of organizational value capture, value creation and sustainable advantage." *Organization Studies*, 30(10), pp. 1115-1139.

Porter, M.E. (1985). *Competitive Advantage*. New York: Free Press.

Porter, M.E. (1990). *The Competitive Advantage of Nations*. New York: Free Press.

Powell, T.C. (1996). "How much does industry matter? An alternative empirical test." *Strategic Management Journal*, 17(4), pp. 323-334.

Prahalad, C.K. & Hamel, G. (1990). "The core competencies of the corporation." *Harvard Business Review*, May–June, pp. 97-148.

Priem, R.L. (2007). "A consumer perspective on value creation." *Academy of Management Review*, 32(1), pp. 219-235.

Priem, R.L. & Butler, J.E. (2001a). "Is the resource-based 'view' a useful perspective for strategic management research?" *Academy of Management Review*, 26, pp. 22-40.

Priem, R.L. & Butler, J.E. (2001b). "Tautology in the resource-based view and the implications of externally determined resource value: Further comment." *Academy of Management Review*, 26, 57-66.

Protogerou, A., Caloghirou, Y. & Lioukas, S. (2012). "Dynamic capabilities and their indirect impact on firm performance." *Industrial and Corporate Change*, 21, pp. 615–647.

Ramirez, R. (1999). "Value co-production: Intellectual origins and implications for practice and research." *Strategic Management Journal*, 20, pp. 49–65.

Reed, R. & DeFillippi, R.J. (1990). "Causal ambiguity, barriers to imitation, and sustainable competitive advantage." *Academy of Management Review*, 15, pp. 88–102.

Remenyi, D., Williams, B., Money, A. & Swartz, E. (1998), *Doing Research in Business and Management. An Introduction to Process and Method*. London: Sage Publications Inc.

Rindova, V. & Taylor, S. (2002). *Dynamic Capabilities as Mcro and Micro Organizational Evolution*. Maryland: University of Maryland, Robert H. Smisths School of Business.

Roberts, N. & Grover, V. (2012). "Investigating firm's customer agility and firm performance: The importance of aligning sense and respond capabilities." *Journal of Management Information Systems*, 65(5), pp. 579–585.

Rokita, J. (2005). *Zarządzanie strategiczne. Tworzenie i utrzymywanie przewagi konkurencyjnej*. Warszawa: PWE.

Romanowska, M. (2002). "Alianse strategiczne w świetle koncepcji zasobowej." In: M. Romanowska & M. Trocki (eds.), *Przedsiębiorstwo partnerskie*. Warszawa: Difin, pp. 163–176.

Rothaermel, F.T. & Deeds, D.L. (2004). "Exploration and exploitation alliances in biotechnology: A system of new product development." *Strategic Management Journal*, 25, pp. 201–221.

Rothaermel, F.T. & Hess, A.M. (2007). "Building dynamic capabilities: Innovation driver by individual, Firm, and network level effects." *Organization Science*, 18(6), pp. 898–921.

Rugman, A.M. & Verbeke, A. (2002). "Edith Penrose's contribution to the resource-based view of strategic management." *Strategic Management Journal*, 23(8), pp. 769–80.

Rumelt, R.P. (1991). "How much does industry matter?" *Strategic Management Journal*, 13(2), pp. 167–185.

Rumelt, R.P. (1984). "Towards a strategic theory of the firm." In: R. Lamb (ed.), *Competitive Strategic Management*. Englewood Cliffs, NJ: Prentice-Hall, pp. 556–570.

Rumelt, R.P. (1987). "Theory, strategy and entrepreneurship." In: D.J. Teece (ed.), *The Competitive Challenge: Strategies for Industrial Innovation and Renewal*. Cambridge, Mass: Ballinger.

Ryall, M. (2013). "The new dynamics of competition." *Harvard Business Review*, June, pp. 80–87.

Sanchez, R., Heene, A. & Thomas, H. (1996). "Towards the theory and practice of competence--based competition." In: R. Sanchez, A. Heene & H. Thomas (eds.), *Dynamics of Competence-based Competition: Theory and Practice in the New Strategic Management*. London: Elsevier, pp. 1–35.

Schienstock, G. (2009). "Knowledge management practices in low-tech and medium-tech industries. Findings from a Finnish business survey." *IAREG Working Paper*, 4(3).

Schilling, M.A. (2000). "Toward a general modular systems theory and its application to inter-firm product modularity." *The Academy of Management Review*, 25(2), pp. 312-334.

Schmalensee, R. (1985). "Do markets differ much?" *American Economic Review*, 75(3), pp. 341–351.

Schmidt J. & Keil, T. (2013). "What makes a resource valuable? Identifying the drivers of firm--idiosyncratic resource value." *Academy of Management Review*, 38(2), pp. 206–228.

Schnaars, S.P. (1994). *Managing Imitation Strategies*. New York: The Free Press.

Schreyögg, G. & Kliesch-Eberl, M. (2007). "How dynamic can organizational capabilities be? Towards a dual-process model of capability mobilization." *Strategic Management Journal*, 28, pp. 913–933.

Schumpeter, J.A. (1934). *Theory of Economic Development*. Harvard University Press: Cambridge, MA. (Reprint: Transaction Publishers, 2012.)

Schumpeter, J.A. (1942). *Capitalism, Socialism, and Democracy*. Harper: New York. (Reprint: Routledge, 2013.)

Shane, S. (2000). "Prior knowledge and the discovery of entrepreneurial opportunities." *Organization Science*, 11(4), pp. 448–469.

Shane, S. (2003). *A General Theory of Entrepreneurship: The Individual-Opportunity Nexus*. Cheltenham, UK, Northampton, MA: Elgar.

Shenkar O. (2010). *Copycats*. Boston: Harvard Business Press.

Short, J.C., Ketchen, D.J., Shook, C.L. & Ireland, R.D. (2010). "The concept of 'opportunity' in entrepreneurship research: Past accomplishments and future challenges." *Journal of Management*, 36(1), pp. 40–65.

Sirmon, D.G., Hitt, M.A. & Ireland, R.D. (2007). "Managing firm resources in dynamic environments to create value: Looking inside the black box." *Academy of Management Review*, 32(1), pp. 273–292.

Sojer, M. (2010). *Reusing Open Source Code. Value Creation and Value Appropriation Perspectives on Knowledge Reuse*. Wiesbaden: Gabler.

Sprafke, N. & Wilkens, U. (2014). *Proposition of an actor-centered measurement instrument for dynamic capabilities research*. Paper accepted for the 23rd Conference of the French Strategic Management Society (AIMS), Rennes, 26–28 May.

Stalk, G., Evans, P. & Shulman, L.E. (1992). "Competing on capabilities: The new rulet of corporate strategy." *Harvard Business Review*, March–April, pp. 57–69.

Stańczyk-Hugiet, E. (2011). "Koopetycja czyli dokąd zmierza konkurencja." *Przegląd Organizacji*, 5, pp. 8–12.

Stańczyk-Hugiet, E. (2015). "Rutyna relacyjna w świetle podejścia ewolucyjnego i relacyjnego." *Marketing i Rynek*, 9, pp. 612–624.

Stadler, C., Helfat, C.E. & Verona, G. (2013). "The impact of dynamic capabilities on resource access and development." *Organization Science*, 24(6), pp. 1782–1804.

Stigler, G.J. (1968). *The organization of industry*. Chicago, IL: University of Chicago Press.

Stuart, H.W. (2001). "Cooperative games and business strategy." In: K. Chatterjee & W.F. Samuelson (eds.), *Game Theory and Business Applications*. Boston: Kluwer Academic Publishers.

Sułkowski, Ł. (2012). *Epistemologia i metodologia zarządzania*. Warszawa: PWE.

Sydow, J., Schreyogg, G. & Koch, J. (2009). "Organizational path dependence: opening the black box." *Academy of Management Review*, 34(4), p. 689–709.

Teece, D.J. (1986). "Profiting from technological innovation: Implications for integration, collaboration, licensing and public policy." *Research Policy*, 15, pp. 285–305.

Teece, D.J. (2001). *Managing Intellectual Capital*. Oxford: Oxford University Press.

Teece, D.J. (2007). "Explicating dynamic capabilities: The nature and microfoundations of (sustainable) enterprise performance." *Strategic Management Journal*, 28(13), pp. 1319–1350.

Teece, D.J., Pisano, G. & Shuen, A. (1997). "Dynamic Capabilities and Strategic Management." *Strategic Management Journal*, 18(7), pp. 509–533.

Tether, B., & Massini, S. (2007). "Services and the innovation infrastructure." *DTI Occasional Paper no. 9 – Innovation in Services*, pp. 135–186.

Thomä, J. & Bizer, K. (2013). "To protect or not to protect?: Modes of appropriability in the small enterprise sector." *Research Policy*, 42(1), pp. 35–49.

Tu, Q., Vonderembse, M.A., Ragu-Nathan, T.S. & Ragu-Nathan, B. (2004). "Measuring modularity-based manufacturing practices and their impact on mass customization capability: A customer-driven perspective." *Decision Sciences*, 35(2), pp. 147–168.

Vargo, S.L. & Lusch, R.F. (2004). "Evolving to a New Dominant Logic for Marketing." *Journal of Marketing*, 68, January, pp. 1–17.

Verona, G. & Ravasi, D. (2003). "Unbundling dynamic capabilities: an exploratory study of continuous product innovation." *Industrial and Corporate Change*, 12(3), pp. 577–606.

von Weizsacker, C.C. (1980). "A welfare analysis of barriers to entry." *Bell Journal of Economics*, 11(2), pp. 399–420.

Wang, C.L. & Ahmed, P.K. (2007). "Dynamic Capabilities: A Review and Research Agenda." *The International Journal of Management Reviews*, 9(1), pp. 31–51.

Wernerfelt, B. (1984). "A resource-based view of the firm." *Strategic Management Journal*, 5(2), pp. 171–180.

Wernerfelt, B. (1995). "The resource-based view of the firm: Ten years after." *Strategic Management Journal*, 16(3), 171–174.

Wernerfelt, B. & Montgomery, C. (1988). "Tobin's q and the importance of focus in firm performance." *American Economic Review*, 78, pp. 246–251.

Whitley, R. (2003). *Institutional frameworks, organizational capabilities and national innovation Systems: Some comments band suggestions.* Paper prepared for the third Loc Nis Workshop "Labour, Organisation and Competence in National Innovation Systems", 22–23 May, Paris.

Williamson, O.E. (1985). *The Economic Institutions of Capitalism.* New York: Free Press.

Williamson, O.E. (1996). *The Mechanisms of Governance.* New York: Oxford University Press.

Williamson, O.E. (1999). "Strategy research: Governance and competence perspectives." *Strategic Management Journal*, 20(12), pp. 1087–1108.

Winter, S.G. (2003). "Understanding Dynamic Capabilities." *Strategic Management Journal*, 24(10), pp. 991–995.

Woodruff, R.B. (1997). "Customer value: The next source for competitive advantage." *Journal of The Academy Marketing Science*, 25(2), p. 139.

Yin, R.K. (2014). *Case Study Research. Design and Methods.* Thousand Oaks: Sage Publications Inc.

Zahra, S.H. (2008). "The virtuous cycle of Discovery and creation of entrepreneurial opportunities." *Strategic Entrepreneurship Journal*, 2, pp. 243–257.

Zahra, S. & George, G. (2002). "Absorptive capacity: A review, reconceptualization and extension." *Academy of Management Review*, 27(2), pp. 213–240.

Zahra, S.A., Sapienza, H.J. & Davidsson, P. (2006). "Entrepreneurship and Dynamic Capabilities: A Review, Model and Research Agenda." *Journal of Management Studies*, 43(4), pp. 917–955.

Zakrzewska-Bielawska, A. (2013). "Zasobowe uwarunkowania koopetycji w przedsiębiorstwach high-tech." *Przegląd Organizacji*, 2, pp. 3–8.

Zhou, K.Z. & Wu, F. (2010), "Technological Capability, Strategic Flexibility, and Product Innovation." *Strategic Management Journal*, 31(5), pp. 547–561.

Zollo, M. & Winter, S.G. (2002). "Deliberate Learning and the Evolution of Dynamic Capabilities." *Organization Science*, 13(3), pp. 339–351.

Zott, C. (2003). "Dynamic capabilities and the emergence of intra industry differential performance: insights from a simulation study." *Strategic Management Journal*, 24(2), pp. 97–125.

Zucchella, A. & Scabini P. (2007). *International Entrepreneurship: Theoretical Foundations and Practices.* Hampshire, UK: Palgrave MacMillan.

TECHNICAL EDITOR
Renata Włodek

PROOFREADER
Agnieszka Toczko-Rak

TYPESETTER
Tomasz Pasteczka

Jagiellonian University Press
Editorial Offices: ul. Michałowskiego 9/2, 31-126 Kraków
Phone: +48 12-663-01-97, Fax: +48 12-631-01-98